Wik, Mining and

Aborigines

PAUL KAUFFMAN and his family lived with the Wik people of Aurukun in 1978. He has a doctorate in history and anthropology from the Australian National University and he has worked for the Commonwealth Government and Aboriginal organisations since 1982. Since November 1996, he has been Associate Professor of Native Title at the University of Canberra. In 1997 he wrote *First Nations: Report on North America* and *Sharing Land and Sea: Report on New Zealand* for the Australian Centre for Regional and Local Government Studies.

Wik, Mining and Aborigines

Paul Kauffman

ALLEN & UNWIN

First published in 1998 by
Allen & Unwin
9 Atchison Street, St Leonards NSW 1590 Australia
Phone: (61 2) 8425 0100
Fax: (61 2) 9906 2218
E-mail: frontdesk@allen-unwin.com.au
Web: http://www.allen-unwin.com.au

National Library of Australia
Cataloguing-in-Publication entry:

    Kauffman, Paul.
    Wik, mining and Aborigines.

    Bibliography.
    Includes index.
    ISBN 1 86448 850 6

    1. Australia. Native Title Act 1993. 2. Australia. High Court. Wik peoples v. State of Queensland and others. 3. Mining leases—Australia. 4. Aborigines, Australian—Land tenure. 5. Land tenure—Law and legislation—Australia. 6. Native title. I. Title.

346.940432

Typeset by Grant Heggie
Printed by Southwood Press Pty Limited, Sydney

10 9 8 7 6 5 4 3 2 1

Foreword
New Possibilities

Dr Lowitja O'Donoghue, AM, CBE

First Chair, Aboriginal and Torres Strait Islander
Commission

Since the High Court's *Mabo* decision in 1992, there has been a tremendous upheaval in relations between Aboriginal and Torres Strait Islander people and companies that wish to carry out mining operations on their land. It is important to understand Australia's long history of dispossession of Indigenous people, to learn from the past and to examine new possibilities for the future.

Aboriginal people have no rights of veto over mining developments in any Australian State, yet major developments can disrupt our lives in significant ways. Legislation does provide some protection of Indigenous rights and interests, and a framework for the diverse arrangements that have been made with Aboriginal and Torres Strait Islander communities. However, the law in this area is becoming increasingly complex, and a number of recent Federal and High Court judgments have grappled with the position of claimants under the *Native Title Act*.

There are complex commercial, economic, environmental and social relationships which set the context for Aboriginal and Torres Strait Islander corporations making agreements of various kinds with mining companies and governments. In many cases monetary or other compensation could never repay the loss of traditional country and waters to Indigenous people. The significance of the present *Native Title Act* is that for the first time in many States, Aboriginal and Torres Strait Islander people have the right to negotiate the terms and conditions on which mining may take place.

This book will assist Aboriginal people and other Australians to be informed about negotiations for mining enterprises on Aboriginal land. It provides a detailed account of modern developments with regard to mining on Indigenous land, which now take account of the three principles of:

- respect for land and seas;
- sustainable development; and
- consultation and negotiation with Indigenous peoples.

It is in the interest of Aboriginal and Torres Strait Islander people and other Australians to understand what these arrangements have been, their legal basis and economic importance. Details of some mining agreements between companies and Aboriginal people have been kept secret in the past at the insistence of the companies involved. Often the most significant facts find their way into newspapers, or are summarised in academic articles. We hope that in future mining companies will see that it is in their own interests to conduct open and transparent negotiations with Aboriginal people. Following the High Court's *Wik* judgment of 1996, which found that native title may co-exist with pastoral leases, reconciliation between Aboriginal and other Australians is no longer an idealistic objective, but a practical necessity.

Contents

Maps

Figures

Tables

Graphs

Acknowledgments

The purpose of writing this book is to provide an understanding of the mining agreements made with Aboriginal people in Australia during the past 30 years, with a view to gaining a perspective on mining and the current native title debate in Australia, and developing better outcomes in the future. This resource book draws on reports, legislation and negotiated agreements. It also considers how various arrangements have come into place, what are the success stories, particularly as far as Aboriginal and Torres Strait Islander people are concerned, and what we as Australians should aim for in a practical way in the future. There is no definitive answer to these questions, but these concerns were present during writing, and the principles which Aboriginal people and some mining companies have identified are explained.

I am particularly indebted to Professor Rolf Gerritsen and Vice-Chancellor Don Aitkin at the University of Canberra. It was their hospitality, and their appointing me to an academic position in the Australian Centre for Regional and Local Government Studies in 1997 and 1998, which provided the environment and support for writing this book. Professor Jon Altman had written a book in 1982 on *Aborigines and Mining Royalties in the Northern Territory* which I found helpful, and he suggested I write a resource book of mining agreements with Aboriginal people over all of Australia up to the present day. My friend and colleague Neil Andrews of the University of Canberra's School of Law made many detailed improvements on early drafts and the glossary. John Iremonger, Christa Munns and Bernadette Foley of Allen & Unwin were positive, helpful and expert editors.

I would like to thank Patrick Dodson, former Chair of the Council for Aboriginal Reconciliation, for permission to reproduce his address to the National Press Club, and Aden Ridgeway, Executive Director of the New South Wales Aboriginal Land Council, for permission to reproduce his address to the Australian Bankers Association. I also thank the following people for their comments: Nathan Hancock; Russell Kelly; Joe Kilby; Rosemary Littlewood; Greg Marks; Vic Sharman; Dr Jakelin Troy; Don Wilkinson and Ruby Zimmermann, of the Aboriginal and Torres Strait Islander Commission (ATSIC); Robert Orr, Attorney-General's Department; Bill Frollan and John Rumble, Department of Employment, Education, Training and Youth Affairs; Professor Ciaran O'Faircheallaigh, Griffith University; Dr Michael Jones, University of Canberra; David Avery, Central

Land Council; Penny Joyce and Lucy Tarrant, Goldfields Land Council; Chips Mackinolty, Jawoyn Association; Alex Rorrison, Kimberley Land Council; Sean Sexton, Mirimbiak Nations Aboriginal Corporation; Simon Blackshield, New South Wales Aboriginal Land Council; Dan O'Dea, Ngaanyatjarra Land Council; Brett Medina, Northern Land Council; Alec Temperley, Cape Flattery Silica Mines (CFSM); Peter Eggleston, Hamersley Iron; Noel Bridge, Normandy Mining Group; Susan Becconsall, Pasminco Ltd; Paul Wand, Rio Tinto Ltd; and Frank Baarda and Adrian Winwood-Smith, Yuendumu Mining Company. A survey of employment was completed by staff at Acacia, Argyle Mining, CFSM, Comalco, ERA, GEMCO, Hamersley Iron, Magellan Petroleum, MIM, Murrin Murrin, Nabalco, North Flinders and Normandy.

Dr John Gardiner-Garden in the Parliament House Library provided references to three mining agreements. Grant Heggie converted the text type into camera ready form.

The Wik peoples of Aurukun, including Francis Yunkaporta and Danny Bowenda, taught my family about Aboriginal life. Isolde Kauffman first edited the book. Any mistakes are my own. The stated and implied views remain my personal responsibility, and do not purport to represent the views of current or previous employers.

Abbreviations

ABR	Aboriginals Benefit Reserve [Northern Territory]
ALC	Anindilyakwa Land Council [Northern Territory]
ALT	Aboriginal Land Trust
ABTF	Aborigines (Benefits from Mining) Trust Fund [1952–1976]
ABTA	Aboriginals Benefit Trust Account [1976–1997]
ATSIC	Aboriginal and Torres Strait Islander Commission
ATSICDC	Aboriginal and Torres Strait Islander Commercial Development Corporation
BHP	Broken Hill Proprietary Company Ltd
CFSM	Cape Flattery Silica Mines
CLC	Central Land Council [Northern Territory]
COMALCO	Commonwealth Aluminium Company Corporation Ltd
CRA	Conzinc Rio-Tinto Australia Ltd
CYLC	Cape York Land Council [Queensland]
CZL	Century Zinc Ltd
DOGIT	Deed of Grant in Trust [Queensland Aboriginal lease]
EIS	Environmental Impact Statement
ERA	Energy Resources of Australia Ltd
GEAT	Groote Eylandt Aboriginal Trust [Northern Territory]
GEMCO	Groote Eylandt Mining Company Ltd
ha	hectares
KLC	Kimberley Land Council [Western Australia]
km	kilometres
NABALCO	North Australian Bauxite and Alumina Company Ltd
NLC	Northern Land Council [Northern Territory]
RTZ	Rio Tinto Zinc Corporation Ltd
sq km	square kilometres
TLC	Tiwi Land Council [Northern Territory]
YBE	Yirrkala Business Enterprises

Glossary of terms

Aboriginal Land Rights (Northern Territory) Act 1976 **(Cth)**
Aboriginals Benefit Reserve (ABR)
The fund into which royalty equivalents are paid, and then distributed, under s. 62, administered by six Commonwealth public servants, a Managing Committee and the Minister for Aboriginal and Torres Strait Islander Affairs.

s. 63 royalty-equivalents
Moneys equivalent to the funds received by the Commonwealth or the Northern Territory from mining royalties are paid to the Aboriginals Benefit Reserve. These moneys fund Aboriginal land councils and also assist all Northern Territory Aboriginal people. They are distributed to land councils, local communities and all Northern Territory Aboriginal people in the following way:

s. 64(1) moneys
Forty per cent of statutory royalties that are paid to four land councils in proportions determined by the Minister for Aboriginal and Torres Strait Islander Affairs.

s. 64(3) moneys
Thirty per cent of statutory royalties that are paid to Aboriginal councils, incorporated groups or communities in areas affected by mining operation.

s. 64(4) grants
Up to 30 per cent of statutory royalties that are distributed by the Minister for Aboriginal Affairs, on the advice of the Aboriginals Benefit Reserve Managing Committee, for the benefit of Aboriginal people residing in the Northern Territory.

s. 64(7) funds
Supplementary funds from the Aboriginals Benefit Reserve paid to land councils when their budgets exceed receipts from s. 64(1) moneys.

Conjunctive and disjunctive agreements
Prior to 1987 amendments, mining companies had to negotiate for both exploration and mining rights on Aboriginal lands in the Northern Territory. Agreements made were said to be 'disjunctive'. Since 1987, a mining company only has to negotiate once. If approval for exploration is given by Aboriginal land owners, they are obliged to also agree to allow mining to proceed. That agreement is said to be 'conjunctive'.

Negotiated royalty
In the Northern Territory, Aboriginal land councils are paid statutory royalty equivalents when mining occurs on Aboriginal land. An additional royalty may be negotiated by a land council for payment to traditional owners of land affected by mining.

Right of veto
Under s. 40(b) and s. 48G the Governor-General, by a proclamation which is disallowable by either House of Parliament, may affirm that mining is in the national interest and may grant a mining interest irrespective of the traditional owners' wishes. This has not been done since 1976 and therefore it is believed that Aboriginal people in the Northern Territory do have an effective 'right of veto' over mining on their lands.

Statutory royalty
Under Australian law, the Crown generally owns minerals. Mining companies must pay a royalty for extracting minerals, which is prescribed by a law of a parliament, that is, a statute. In the Northern Territory, Aboriginal land councils are paid statutory royalty equivalents when mining occurs on Aboriginal land.

Ad valorem
'According to the value.' A method of calculating royalties according to the gross sales value, not according to the profit margin of the mining company, which can be altered by transfer pricing of a company's subsidiaries.

Alienated and unalienated land
Under English and Australian law all title to land derives from the Crown, which is the only body which can own it completely and outright. Alienated land is freehold or perpetual leasehold land which has been vested in another

party. Unalienated land is Crown land in which no person other than the Crown has an estate or interest.

Mabo (1)

The Queensland Parliament passed the *Queensland Coast Islands Declaratory Act 1985*, which sought to extinguish any native land rights claimed to exist in the Murray Islands, with effect from 1879 when the islands were annexed by the Crown to Queensland, and to deny any right to compensation. In 1988 the High Court found the Queensland Act inconsistent with s. 10 of the *Racial Discrimination Act 1975* (Cth).

Mabo (2)

On 3 June 1992 the High Court found that Eddie Mabo and the people of Mer in the Torres Strait had full beneficial ownership of their lands. The common law of Australia now recognises 'native title', which is the term used by the High Court to describe the rights and interests of Aboriginal and Torres Strait Islander peoples in land according to their traditions, laws and customs. They 'are entitled as against the whole world to possession, occupation, use and enjoyment of the lands of the Murray Islands'. Native title is extinguished by legislation or government action such as issuing freehold title to land or a perpetual lease which gives exclusive possession of land.

Native Title Act 1993, s. 223(1)

'Native title' or 'native title rights and interests' means the communal, group or individual rights and interests of the Aboriginal peoples or Torres Strait Islanders in relation to land or waters, where:

(a)   the rights and interests are possessed under the traditional laws acknowledged, and the traditional customs observed, by the Aboriginal peoples or Torres Strait Islanders;

(b)   the Aboriginal peoples or Torres Strait Islanders, by those laws and customs, have a connection with the land and waters; and

(c)   the rights and interests are recognised by the common law of Australia.

Native Title Representative Body

A Native Title Representative Body is a representative Aboriginal/Torres Strait Islander body determined by regulation by the Commonwealth Minister for Aboriginal and Torres Strait Islander Affairs under s. 202 of the *Native Title Act*. Some of them have also been established as statutory land councils.

A Native Title Representative Body's functions are to facilitate the recognition and protection of the native title rights of the Aboriginal people of its region (see Map 1.2). In furtherance of this objective the Native Title Representative Body may:

- facilitate the researching, preparation or making of claims, by individuals or groups of Aboriginal peoples, for determinations of native title or for compensation for acts affecting native title;
- assist in the resolution of disagreements among Aboriginal individuals or groups about the making of native title claims or claims for compensation for acts affecting native title;
- assist Aboriginal individuals or groups, by representing them, or by providing financial or other assistance to enable them to be represented or assisted by other people or organisations, in negotiations and proceedings relating to the doing of acts affecting native title, the provision of compensation in relation to such acts or any other matter relevant to the operation of the *Native Title Act*;
- undertake any other activities and functions relating to the recognition, protection and development of the law in relation to native title.

Right to negotiate
The right to negotiate about the terms and conditions of major developments on land.

***Pitjantjatjara Land Rights Act 1981* (SA) and *Maralinga Tjarutja Land Rights Act 1984* (SA)**
'Traditional owner', in relation to the lands, means an Aboriginal person who in accordance with Aboriginal tradition, has social, economic and spiritual affiliations with, and responsibilities for, the lands or any part of them.

Radical title
'Fundamental' or 'priority' title to land. Under English and Australian law, all land is ultimately owned by the Crown. Radical title is the title the Crown takes as political sovereign. It underlies all titles granted by the Crown. If land has been alienated or given or sold by valid actions of Commonwealth, State and Territory governments, individuals or groups are entitled to full beneficial ownership of that land.

Royalty
A royalty is a periodical payment to the owner of minerals by a party authorised to extract and remove minerals.

Statutory and non-statutory land councils
Some of the land councils in Australia are established by statute, that is, a law of the Commonwealth Parliament (*Aboriginal Land Rights (Northern Territory) Act*), or a State Parliament (*Pitjantjatjara Land Rights Act* and *Maralinga Tjarutja Land Rights Act* in South Australia and *Land Rights Act* in New South Wales). Other land councils are not established by statute but are native title representative bodies established by regulation under the *Native Title Act.*

Terra nullius
'Land belonging to no-one', the view which held that all land belonged to the Crown upon the English settling in Australia in 1788. This view was rejected by *Mabo (2).*

Wik
On 23 December 1996 the High Court found that native title can only be extinguished by legislation or an action by government. The native title rights of the Wik people of Aurukun, in Cape York, North Queensland, persisted as the pastoral leases issued for those lands had not given exclusive possession to the pastoralists. Where native title and pastoral leases are in conflict, the pastoral lease prevails.

Map 1.2 describes the Native Title Representative Bodies. Appendix B provides a list of the Native Title Representative Bodies, both statutory and non-statutory, and their addresses, telephone and fax numbers.

Map 1.1   Locations of current mining developments

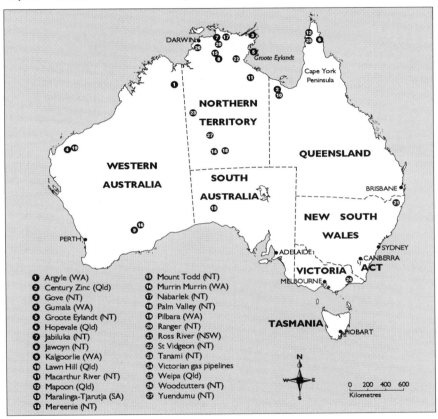

❶ Argyle (WA)	⓯ Mount Todd (NT)
❷ Century Zinc (Qld)	⓰ Murrin Murrin (WA)
❸ Gove (NT)	⓱ Nabarlek (NT)
❹ Gumala (WA)	⓲ Palm Valley (NT)
❺ Groote Eylandt (NT)	⓳ Pilbara (WA)
❻ Hopevale (Qld)	⓴ Ranger (NT)
❼ Jabiluka (NT)	㉑ Ross River (NSW)
❽ Jawoyn (NT)	㉒ St Vidgeon (NT)
❾ Kalgoorlie (WA)	㉓ Tanami (NT)
❿ Lawn Hill (Qld)	㉔ Victorian gas pipelines
⓫ Macarthur River (NT)	㉕ Weipa (Qld)
⓬ Mapoon (Qld)	㉖ Woodcutters (NT)
⓭ Maralinga-Tjarutja (SA)	㉗ Yuendumu (NT)
⓮ Mereenie (NT)	

Map 1.2   Native Title Representative Bodies

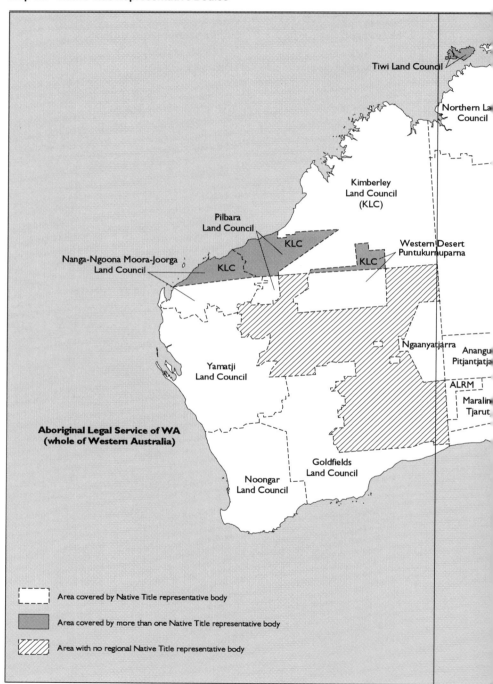

Source: Adapted from ATSIC

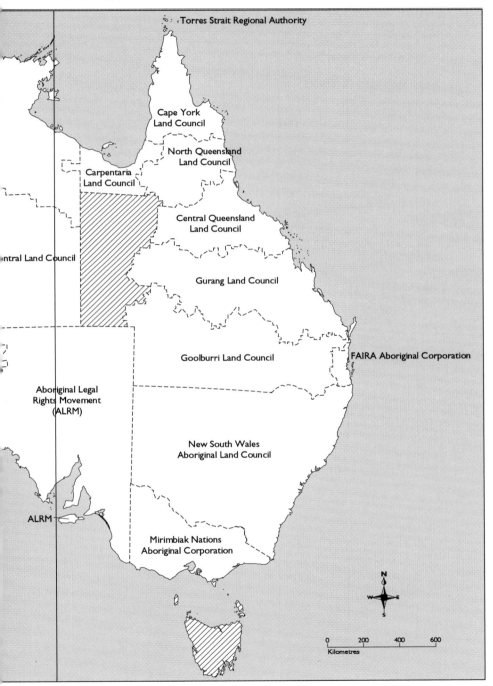

1 Introduction

It is true that the people who are belonging to a particular area are really part of that area and if that area is destroyed they are also destroyed.

Silas Roberts, former Chair of the Northern Land Council[1]

From the earliest times, Aboriginal people have made statements such as this one from Silas Roberts to all those who would listen across the continent. Aboriginal people in many different parts of Australia, speaking different languages, also say, 'the land is my mother'. But what do they mean by such statements? Why is the land so important?

In a 1996 address to the National Press Club, which is reprinted at the end of this book, Patrick Dodson, then Chair of the Council for Aboriginal Reconciliation, explained: 'We Aboriginal people find it hard to think without the land. My grandfather taught me how to think about relationships by showing me places.' Patrick's grandfather also taught him where to fish. In his speech he used salt water and fresh water as a metaphor. He said that their coming together is like the reconciliation process between Indigenous and other Australians. Patrick also spoke of 'the umbilical link of Aboriginal people to the land, just as other Aboriginal people have talked of their country since time immemorial'.

Aden Ridgeway is Executive Director of the New South Wales Aboriginal Land Council, and his address to the Australian Bankers Association is reproduced in full at the end of this book. It is entitled 'Success in business with Aborigines'. He encourages business to become involved with

Aboriginal and Torres Strait Islander people, but stresses that there are some special conditions of which business should be aware.

The first is the recognition that business with an Aboriginal community must take account of the pivotal role of the land. Indigenous people feel a sacred obligation to exercise immense responsibilities for the land, sea and other resources, to use them with care and diligence for the benefit of future generations.

Business, he says, must learn to recognise the links between the land and Aboriginal people and their culture, as well as the moral, political and perhaps legal imperatives to deliver social justice. A further condition is the need to understand the hurt and injustice that Aboriginal people feel at their past treatment and their continuing lack of opportunities.

Thirdly, any mining project should have social benefits for the community—for example, employment, infrastructure, housing and health.

The *Aboriginal Land Rights Act 1983* (NSW) has provided Aboriginal people of that State with a source of funding for economic and social development over fifteen years. He notes that the New South Wales Aboriginal Land Council investment fund has increased its asset base from around $280m in 1994 to $455m in 1998,[2] a performance made possible by constant attention to fiscal monitoring and accountability.

Economic development also requires the development of people to make it work, and Aden Ridgeway believes that there is a tremendous need for training, employment and education. He stresses that business cannot be divorced from other issues. The relationship with the land, sea and other resources is too strong, the background too recent, and the sense of hurt and injustice too personal to permit such isolation.

MINING IN AUSTRALIA

The mining industry in Australia is an important part of an advanced economy, using high technology and benefiting from a stable political regime. The industry currently contributes over $36 billion to Australia's export earnings and represents over 60 per cent of commodity exports. In addition, over $12 billion of Australia's manufactured exports are dependent on mineral production.[3]

Major gold and other mining operations have taken place in Australia for over 140 years. Further large-scale mining operations have been developed in remote areas of Australia since the 1960s. Australia's proven unmined mineral resources have been valued at $145 billion.[4] In 1996/97, as in previous years, coal and gold produced a greater export income for Australia than wool, which is only just ahead of iron ore and alumina. Coal produced $8 billion export income in the year to 30 June 1997, and gold produced $5.4 billion. Iron ore, alumina and aluminium, oil, iron and steel, natural gas, nickel and copper are our major mineral and energy commodities exports, which totalled $36 billion in 1996/97.[5]

Australia is a major world producer of iron, aluminium, lead, zinc and uranium. It is the world's largest exporter of bauxite (aluminium ore) and alumina. It is the world's largest exporter of lead and the second largest exporter of zinc. It is the world's third largest producer of both nickel and gold.[6]

Commercial mining is not necessarily hostile to native title. Following the passage of the *Native Title Act* in 1993, resource developers have often recognised that native title parties are not anti-development. With the incentive of returns from commercial activity on land where native title may be established, Indigenous people have often been pro-development. Aboriginal people increasingly accept development, but want it to occur under certain conditions and wish to share in some of the benefits, such as profits. Through Native Title Representative Bodies they are seeking a profit share or business and development opportunities. Creative forms of joint venturing under a native title regime have already occurred in many areas. There have been projects involving native title stakeholders and tourism, in Cairns, North Queensland. Native title stakeholders have agreed to real-estate development in Broome, Western Australia, and at Crescent Head in northern New South Wales. Native title stakeholders have agreed to exploration, mining and the construction of gas pipelines in every mainland State, and in the Northern Territory (see Map 1.1 and Chapters 6 and 7). The 'right to negotiate' provisions of the *Native Title Act* are less confrontationist than the 'right of veto' or 'right of consent' available under the *Aboriginal Land Rights (Northern Territory) Act*.

There are several arguments why Australian governments and mining companies should make greater rather than lesser provision to Aboriginal landowners when mining on their land. First, Aboriginal people are the original owners of Australia. They have a special economic, social and cultural relationship to their land established since time immemorial. The High Court and the Commonwealth Parliament have recognised their native title rights. Despite prior ownership, Aboriginal people in general have few if any other assets apart from their land. And they are now a cultural minority in their own country. They have poor health, education, employment, housing, and are subject to traumatic changes to their traditional life and culture.

MABO (2)

In 1985 the Queensland Parliament passed the *Queensland Coast Islands Declaratory Act 1985*, which sought to extinguish any native land rights claimed to exist in the Murray Islands, with effect from 1879 when the islands were annexed by the Crown to Queensland, and to deny any right to compensation. The High Court in *Mabo (1)* found the Queensland Act inconsistent with s. 10 of the *Racial Discrimination Act 1975* (Cth). The High Court's rejection of Queensland legislation in 1988 allowed it to decide a most important case in 1992. There are two findings in the historic *Mabo (2)* judgment. First, the Meriam people of Murray Island, because they have maintained their connection with the land since European settlement, are 'entitled as against the whole world to the possession, occupation, use and enjoyment of the lands of Murray Island'.[7] Secondly, native title in the Torres Strait, and throughout the Australian continent, is extinguished by valid acts of Commonwealth, State or Territory governments.

In 1982, Eddie Mabo and four other islanders brought an action in the High Court of Australia. They sought a declaration that, as members of the Meriam people in the Torres Strait, they continued to enjoy rights associated with the traditional occupation and use of Murray Island (Mer) and surrounding islands and reefs. Ten years later, on 3 June 1992, the High Court handed down its judgment in *Mabo (2)*[8] which recognised for the first time the existence of native title in Australia. Prior to that judgment it had been assumed that Australia was unoccupied (*terra nullius*) at the time of European settlement. Australia had always been treated as uninhabited land because a majority of early settlers did not appreciate the complex social and political organisation of Aboriginal and Torres Strait Islander societies. The doctrine of *terra nullius* was still a part of Australian law and had been confirmed by Justice Blackburn in 1971 in the Northern Territory case of *Milirrpum v Nabalco*.[9] In *Mabo (2)*, the Meriam people argued that their land was not unoccupied at the time the Crown acquired sovereignty. They presented evidence that their islands had been continuously inhabited and exclusively possessed by the Meriam people who lived in permanent communities with their own social and political organisation.

A fundamental issue identified by Justice Brennan in *Mabo (2)* was 'whether absolute ownership vested in the Crown'. In 1992 the High Court, in a six to one majority, found that native title exists when Aboriginals and Torres Strait Islanders have maintained a traditional connection to the land. Native title is not extinguished on settlement. It is only extinguished in the

Torres Strait, and throughout the Australian continent, by valid actions of Commonwealth, State and Territory governments.

The Court found that the lands of the Australian continent were not *terra nullius* (land belonging to no-one) at the time of European settlement in 1788.

The Crown gained a form of title (called radical title) to Australian land on settlement. Radical title, in English law, is the title the Crown takes as political sovereign. It underlies all titles granted by the Crown. Radical title did not extinguish native title. After settlement, governments (British, State, Territory and Commonwealth) could extinguish native title by legislation or by granting interests in land, such as freehold and certain leasehold interests. The Court also ruled that the power of States to extinguish native title rights since 1975 was subject to the provisions of the *Racial Discrimination Act 1975* (Cth), which prevents States from passing laws in relation to property rights that discriminate against members of a certain race.

Subject to the provisions of the *Racial Discrimination Act*, a majority of the Court ruled that no compensatory damages were legally payable for the extinguishment of native title prior to 1975. The Court recognised that traditional laws and customs may have 'undergone some change since the Crown acquired sovereignty'.[10] However, changes in tradition would not affect native title so long as they did not 'diminish or extinguish the relationship between a particular tribe or other group and particular land'.[11]

In relation to Murray Island (Mer), which was the subject of the *Mabo (2)* case, the Court ruled that the Meriam people had maintained their connection with the land since European settlement and that their native title rights had not been extinguished by any action of the Crown. Accordingly they were 'entitled as against the whole of the world to the possession, occupation, use and enjoyment of the lands of Murray Island'.

Queensland-based legal academics described the *Mabo (2)* judgment as creating a legal revolution.[12] Other scholars described the judgment as an overdue correction, which brought Australia into line with other modern democracies. For the first time in Australia, the right of some Aboriginal and Torres Strait Islander peoples to occupy and use their land, in accordance with their traditions and customs, had been given recognition and protection by the Australian legal system. However, because the High Court was only called upon to decide on the facts that were before it, many questions remained unanswered. The precise definition of native title rights was unclear, as were the areas of land that could be subject to native title and the Aboriginal groups that continued to hold it. Furthermore, the Court in this case did not determine with exactness which Crown grants were inconsistent with (and therefore extinguished) native title.[13]

THE *NATIVE TITLE ACT 1993*

The *Mabo (2)* case did not rule on mining, but in deciding important questions of Indigenous land ownership for the first time, it provided a new environment for mining companies and Indigenous people in Australia. Commercial mining is not necessarily hostile to native title. There have been significant changes in the relationship between governments, mining companies and Aboriginal and Torres Strait Islander people since 1992, as a result of *Mabo (2)*.[14] *Mabo (2)* recognised for the first time the existence of native title, and *Wik* [15] recognised that native title may continue to exist on pastoral leases, and the *Native Title Act*. The Act sought to clarify the rights of Indigenous people with respect to traditional land, and the responsibilities of those who wish to conduct mining or exploration activities on that land. It validated doubtful interests granted by various Crowns, or Commonwealth, State and Territory governments since the *Racial Discrimination Act 1975* (Cth) came into force.

A key feature of the *Native Title Act,* as passed in 1993 is that registered native title holders and claimants have a right to negotiate with governments. The Commonwealth Parliament enacted the *Native Title Act* in December 1993. The Act clarified issues left unresolved by the High Court, validated otherwise invalid grants by various Crowns since the *Racial Discrimination Act 1975* came into force, and established a process by which native title rights can be determined. Section 223 of the *Native Title Act* defines 'native title' as the rights and interests possessed by Aboriginal and Torres Strait Islander peoples under traditional laws and customs. The definition is quoted in full in the Glossary.

The *Native Title Act* recognises that native title has been extinguished by valid acts of Commonwealth, State and Territory governments over the settled part of the Australian continent, consistent with the findings of the *Mabo (2)* High Court decision of 1992. Where native title has not been extinguished, for example by a valid freehold or perpetual leasehold grant, the Act allows Aboriginal groups to make a native title claim to traditional lands under processes identified in the Act. It allows for the Minister for Aboriginal and Torres Strait Islander Affairs to recognise certain Aboriginal and Torres Strait Islander organisations as Native Title Representative Bodies (see Map 1.2). These bodies negotiate on behalf of Aboriginal groups with interested parties. Their functions are described in full in the Glossary.

The Act also provides for non-native title claimants to provide notice that they are engaging in certain acts on native title land, such as mining. It is envisaged that a mining company would negotiate with Aboriginal parties or their representatives.

The *Native Title Act* provides native title holders with no veto over mineral exploration activity and no royalty rights. In 1993 the Northern Territory Government was refused special leave to appeal in *Pareroultja v Tickner*.[16] In that decision the main principles of the *Mabo (2)* judgment are summarised. The *Native Title Act* does not overrule the *Aboriginal Land Rights (Northern Territory) Act.* A grant of land pursuant to the *Aboriginal Land Rights (Northern Territory) Act,* without the consent of the native title holders, is not unlawful. The Full Federal Court also found that there is almost no inconsistency between native title and the *Aboriginal Land Rights (Northern Territory) Act.* Both the inalienable freehold title of that Act and native title can co-exist so the appellants were not prejudiced. Aboriginal and Torres Strait Islander land owners are provided similar negotiation and appeal rights with respect to exploration as other land owners in Australia, but disagreements may be resolved before the National Native Title Tribunal.

The *Mabo (2)* judgment recognised native title that, in the cases where it has not been extinguished, entitles the Indigenous inhabitants to exercise their native title rights to their traditional lands, in accordance with their laws or customs. As *Mabo (2)* was a case involving Mer, an island in the Torres Strait, it did not elaborate on mining or pastoral rights. The *Native Title Act* outlines procedures which mining companies must follow when mining on Aboriginal land. Registered native title holders and claimants may surrender their native title under an agreement with the Commonwealth, a State or a Territory (s. 21). They have a right to negotiate with governments intending to create, vary or extend mining rights on native title land. They also have a right to negotiate with people such as miners who wish to explore or drill over land where native title has been recognised or claimed (ss. 26–44). Justice French, the inaugural President of the National Native Title Tribunal, has said that it is possible for a mining company to enter into a s. 21 agreement under the *Native Title Act*, obtain a s. 29 coverage, and come up with a right to mine.[17] The disadvantage for the mining company is that such an agreement may only cover some of the potential native title holders. Many companies have therefore relied on the extended procedures of the National Native Title Tribunal to attempt to obtain agreement to mine.

Under the legislation in place in 1998, a government must give two months notice to the public and all relevant parties of its intention to issue or vary mining rights. A government may proceed with the issuing of a mining lease after two months if there are no existing native title holders or registered claimants in the area affected by the action.

If a government refuses to negotiate and its proposed granting of a mining lease can be shown to affect native title, the granting of that lease may be invalid. Negotiations may include entitlement for native title parties to receive payments from miners based on profits, income or production. Validated mining leases do not extinguish native title but suspend native title rights until the mining leases expire.

Native title holders can apply to the National Native Title Tribunal to decide whether the act can be done and if so, under what conditions. The National Native Title Tribunal, or equivalent State or Territory body, cannot impose profit-sharing conditions, although the parties themselves may agree to this.

The *Native Title Act* ensures that registered native title holders and registered native title claimants have a right to negotiate before certain permissible future acts, such as mining, take place on their land. If no agreement is reached, any party to the negotiations may apply to the arbitral body within a period of four months if a mining exploration lease is involved, or a period of six months in other cases.[18] The arbitral body must take all reasonable steps to reach an agreement within a further period of four months if a mining exploration lease is involved, or a period of six months in other cases.[19] There is a heavy emphasis on 'alternative dispute resolution'. Section 38(2) emphasises that the value of minerals cannot be taken into account by an arbitrating body. There are therefore incentives for both owners and miners to settle out of court.

The Act also provides for compensation to native title holders for loss of native title and establishes a National Aboriginal and Torres Strait Islander Land Fund, which will assist Aboriginal and Torres Strait Islander people to buy and manage land in a way that will provide them with economic, environmental, social and cultural benefits.

PROVING NATIVE TITLE

Following the judgment of Justice Brennan in *Mabo (2)*,[20] to establish native title at common law, a claimant group must show, on the balance of probabilities:

- that the claimants are descended from or otherwise related to the group that held native title at the time the British Crown asserted sovereignty;
- non-extinguishment of native title since that time;
- the existence of a coherent group of Aboriginals or Torres Strait Islanders, the membership of which is based on mutual recognition and recognition by persons enjoying traditional authority among the group;

- that the group possesses and acknowledges traditional laws and customs which entitle them to enjoy the land claimed. It is acceptable for the laws and customs to have undergone some change since the Crown acquired sovereignty, provided the general nature of the connection between the Indigenous people and the land remains; and
- that the group continues to practise its traditional laws and customs, as far as possible, and has maintained its connection with the land.

At common law, occupation is the cornerstone of native title rights to exclusive possession of traditional lands or waters: 'Thus traditional title is rooted in physical presence.'[21] Although the *Native Title Act* does not mention that applicants must demonstrate a physical connection with the land, the High Court in a New South Wales case said that native title claimants are required to prove that they have not: '[ceased] to have a requisite *physical* connection with the land.'[22]

The High Court has recognised regional and local differences in the nature of traditional links to the land and in the extent to which various social forces have transformed and in some cases broken those ties.[23]

WHAT RIGHTS ATTACH TO NATIVE TITLE?

There is no guarantee that a determination of native title will result in exclusive possession. A court or tribunal will measure the applicants' native title rights recognisable at common law against the evidence of traditional law and custom. As Justice Brennan observed: 'the nature and incidents of native title must be ascertained as a matter of fact by references to [the particular traditional] laws and customs.'[24]

The New South Wales Aboriginal Land Council and the Cape York Land Council have found that it is preferable to bring together all native title applicants who have a traditional interest in an area. Their intention is to get a court to make more comprehensive findings about the nature and content of native title in a particular area than would be the case if only one person or family made an application.[25] The Dunghutti people successfully employed this strategy when they won the first successful native title compensation claim.

THE DUNGHUTTI'S NATIVE TITLE

The Dunghutti people at Crescent Head, on the northern New South Wales coast, achieved the first native title agreement registered under the *Native*

Title Act. While it does not concern mining, and is a compensation payment for extinguishment of native title, it may be a relevant case study to show how successfully to involve a community in native title negotiations.

The State Government had spent some $1.5m on roads and other facilities in order to develop a housing subdivision over land at Crescent Head. Extensive public works had been carried out. There was a mixture of sold and unsold lots, and a proposed second stage (which was still uncleared land). In July 1994, the New South Wales Minister for Land and Water Conservation lodged a 'non-claimant' application over the subdivision. On 10 August 1994 the non-claimant application was advertised and lodged with the National Native Title Tribunal. On 9 October 1996 an agreement was reached between the Dunghutti people of Crescent Head and the New South Wales Government.

Mary-Lou Buck of the Dunghutti people, with the assistance of the New South Wales Aboriginal Land Council, lodged a positive native title claim. Family trees for about twenty Dunghutti families were constructed, and supported by school records and records of births, deaths and marriages. These family trees were presented as evidence that Aboriginal families, including Mary-Lou's ancestors, had occupied that area prior to the 1840s and continued to reside there after European settlement. This was persuasive in convincing the Court that her ancestors lived on that land prior to white settlement, and of her family's continued association with the land.

Language is an important part of traditional laws and custom, and the Dunghutti language had been preserved. A contemporary Dunghutti dictionary was used to demonstrate that *mandharr* means 'mullet' and *gurul* means 'black', essentially the same words as in the 1887 word list of C. Spencer: *mandara* and *koorool-koorool*. The Dunghutti provided extensive evidence to support their claim that native title may be the equivalent of full beneficial ownership. Over 40 families (5000 people) were involved in the claim, for one-fifth of the 12.4 ha of land that the government had already sold to developers.[26] The Federal Court found that the Dunghutti had native title over this 12.4 ha.

Compensation of $738,000 was paid to the Dunghutti people for nineteen building blocks, covering 5 ha of land that had been built on. Simon Blackshield, a solicitor for the New South Wales Aboriginal Land Council, who was involved in the negotiations, said that the starting point for such claims is 150 per cent of the freehold value of land, because freehold value plus a 50 per cent 'uplift factor' for special attachment to one's land, is appropriate. Instead of a lump sum payment for one of their parcels of land, the Dunghutti accepted a 12 per cent royalty from future sales on 35 other blocks which can now be developed because the Dunghutti have forgone their native title claim over them. There are accordingly benefits to the Dunghutti, by way of compensation, and for the New South Wales Government, which now has clear title and does not have to pay compensation prior to the sale of land.[27]

In some native title cases there are disputes between different native title claimants. This was also the case here. Members of the Burupi clan claimed interests in the land as well, but their position was resolved over time.[28]

The Dunghutti have formed a Prescribed Body Corporate and invested the money received in improving health and education in their community, reviving the local language, building a cultural centre and providing adequate housing. Prior to their native title settlement, some Dunghutti people lived in humpies without water, sewerage or power.[29]

HOPEVALE'S NATIVE TITLE

The *Mabo (2)* High Court judgment of 1992 changed Australia's common law, made Australian legal practice more consistent with other developed countries in their treatment of Indigenous peoples, and changed the way non-Aboriginal society relates to Australia's Indigenous peoples. Legal processes, however, have not resulted in swift native title settlements. The Dunghutti people gained the first native title in mainland Australia in 1996. The following year, native title of the Hopevale Aborigines in North Queensland was recognised.

On 8 December 1997, native title was ratified over 110,000 ha of land at Hopevale, 200 km north of Cairns, North Queensland. Native title now covers land in the parishes of Flattery, Tayeto, Discovery and Haan, and stretches from Lookout Point in the north, 70 km south to Cooktown. Negotiations had commenced in June 1996, and the Queensland Government said that it was a willing partner in the process. Thirteen Aboriginal clans and ten other parties consented to the decision. The ratification consolidated freehold title which Aboriginal people had held to the land since 1986. More than 150 people from Hopevale and Cairns and the Cape York Land Council attended the Federal Court hearing in Cairns. Many wore T-shirts with the words *Guugu Yimithirr Warra*—'Bringing people together' on them.[30]

The mining industry is rapidly coming to terms with native title, not just as a possibility, but as a part of everyday reality. Agreements made under the *Aboriginal Land Rights (Northern Territory) Act* since 1976 have assisted such a change to come about.

2 The *Aboriginal Land Rights (Northern Territory) Act 1976*

Almost 200 years after white settlement, Australia's first Royal Commission into Aboriginal land rights was appointed, and Justice Woodward made the key finding that: 'I believe that to deny Aborigines the right to prevent mining on their land is to deny the reality of their land rights.'[31]

This belated recognition followed generations of political actions by Aboriginal and Torres Strait Islander peoples. For instance in 1963, the Yirrkala people of north-east Arnhem Land brought a petition to the Commonwealth Parliament in Canberra, protesting the mining of their traditional lands for bauxite, which was authorised under Australian law without their permission. The Yirrkala petitions were written in the Yolngu language with an English translation, and presented on bark paintings which are now displayed in Parliament House. The petitions were influential in a land rights campaign which resulted in the appointment of the Woodward Royal Commission into Aboriginal land rights.[32]

The most significant royalty-equivalent benefits to Aboriginal people have flown from the *Aboriginal Land Rights (Northern Territory) Act* (Com), which was the first land rights legislation in Australia. Since statutory land councils were established under that Act, others have been established under the *Aboriginal Land Grant (Jervis Bay Territory) Act 1986* (Com), and State legislation in South Australia and New South Wales. The establishment of statutory land councils means that procedures are now in place for negotiating exploration and mining rights on Aboriginal land.

Under the *Aboriginal Land Rights (Northern Territory) Act*, former Aboriginal reserves in the Northern Territory were transferred to Aboriginal ownership under Commonwealth legislation. This was prior to the Northern Territory being granted self-government in 1978. The *Aboriginal Land Rights (Northern Territory) Act* also provides for a process for the transfer of unalienated Crown land to Aboriginal ownership if traditional ownership can be established to the satisfaction of an Aboriginal Land Commissioner and the Commonwealth Minister (see Map 2.1).

Shortly after coming to office the Labor Prime Minister Gough Whitlam appointed Justice Woodward in February 1973, to inquire into appropriate ways to recognise Aboriginal land rights. Justice Woodward presented his second and final report on Aboriginal land rights in April 1974, after carefully considering submissions by sectional interests including the mining and resources industry. A key issue was providing Aboriginal people with the legal power to prevent mining. The Northern Land Council has outlined the history of the *Aboriginal Land Rights (Northern Territory) Act*:

> The Whitlam government introduced legislation based substantially on Justice Woodward's recommendations. The Bill was before the Parliament when the Government was dismissed in November 1975. The new government of Liberal Prime Minister Malcolm Fraser drafted a new Bill from which many of the advances of the Whitlam Bill were absent. The final Bill removed the needs-based claims and gave to the Northern Territory Legislative Assembly responsibility for 'complementary' legislation covering site protection and access to Aboriginal land. With the advent of the Act, which came into force on 26 January 1977, most of the existing Aboriginal reserves became Aboriginal land, with freehold title held by local Aboriginal Land trusts on behalf of all Aborigines with traditional interests in the land, and a procedure was established for the claiming of unalienated Crown land— that is, land which no one else is using or has an interest in—and Aboriginal-owned pastoral leases.[33]

ABORIGINAL LAND COUNCILS

One of the most significant outcomes of the *Aboriginal Land Rights (Northern Territory) Act* was the establishment of Aboriginal land councils. Under s. 21(3) the Minister for Aboriginal and Torres Strait Islander Affairs may recognise a land council if:

(a)   a substantial majority of residents of a relevant area vote for a land council at an election; and

(b)   the Minister considers that the area concerned is an appropriate area for the operation of a new land council.

The Northern Land Council and the Central Land Council were established under the *Aboriginal Land Rights (Northern Territory) Act* in 1977. The following year the Tiwi Land Council was established to represent separately the interests of Bathurst and Melville Island (Nguiu). The Anindilyakwa Land Council represents the Aboriginal people of Groote Eylandt and Bickerton Islands in the Gulf of Carpentaria east of Arnhem Land, and was established on 1 July 1991 (see Map 4.1). This is the site of a major manganese mine which has operated for some 30 years. Royalty arrangements were in place for Groote Eylandt prior to the *Aboriginal Land Rights (Northern Territory) Act.*

Under s. 35(2) of the *Aboriginal Land Rights (Northern Territory) Act,* moneys paid to a land council under subsection 64(3) shall be paid within six months of their receipt by the land council, to:

(a)   Aboriginal councils in the area affected by a particular mining operation; and
(b)   incorporated Aboriginal communities or groups whose members live in the area affected by the mining operations. It is up to the land council to determine appropriate distributions.

Justice Woodward's concept of an affected community was one within 60 km of a mining operation. Several commentators have suggested that the 'affected community' should be defined by legislation or regulation, to assist decisions on the distribution of mining royalties.[34]

Justice Toohey, subsequently appointed to the High Court, was the first person to hold the position of Aboriginal Land Commissioner. By 1983, fifteen land claim reports had been published, and Justice Toohey reviewed various aspects of the legislation.[35] He discussed the concept of 'traditional Aboriginal owners' as fundamental to the Act, as defined in subsection 3(1). Justice Toohey concluded that the key elements of the definition are that they are local descent groups. Local descent groups may be exogamous (meaning having to marry a person from another group), and patrilineal descent groups (with a common male ancestor), matrilineal (with a common female ancestor), or ambilineal (with a common ancestor who is either male or female). They may include 'managers' (whose mother or father's mother belongs to a clan which owns a site or an estate). Most Aboriginal land commissioners have defined 'traditional Aboriginal owners' flexibly in response to the situation of particular claimants.[36]

A land council may not consent to the grant of a mining interest or construction of a road unless satisfied that the traditional owners of the land in question understand the nature and purpose of the proposed grant or proposed road and, as a group, consent to it.[37] The powers of traditional Aboriginal owners will therefore continue to be important after the conclusion of the land claim process to unalienated Crown land.

Subsequent land rights legislation enacted by State governments has either not attempted to define who the relevant Aboriginal owners are, has used a residency-based definition (New South Wales), or used a broader definition of 'traditional owners' (South Australia).

THE ABORIGINALS BENEFIT RESERVE IN THE NORTHERN TERRITORY

Land returned to Aboriginal ownership in the Northern Territory provided land to Northern Territory Aboriginal people, effective veto rights over mining and arrangements for sharing mining royalties. The Aboriginal land base in the Northern Territory was 549,000 sq km in 1995. New claims could not be lodged after 5 June 1997. However, once all outstanding claims have been determined, Aboriginal land might amount to half of the Northern Territory, or about 650,000 sq km.

The Aborigines (Benefits from Mining) Trust Fund was established in the Northern Territory in 1952. Its successor, the Aboriginals Benefit Trust Account, was established in 1978, and became the Aboriginals Benefit Reserve (ABR) in 1997.[38] It provides for returns from mining on Aboriginal land to be earmarked for the use of Aboriginal people. Thus a double royalty of 2.5 per cent *ad valorem* (based on the value of production) of minerals extracted from Aboriginal land has been levied in the Northern Territory for many years. Royalty-equivalents have provided much greater certainty, for both resource developers and Aboriginal people, than negotiations arbitrated by courts. It has been suggested that the introduction of statutory royalty-equivalents might be a successful innovation in an amended *Native Title Act*.[39]

ROYALTY-EQUIVALENTS

Aboriginal people who own land in the Northern Territory have an effective right of veto over mining, because under the *Aboriginal Land Rights (Northern Territory) Act* an Aboriginal community may refuse mining exploration for a five-year period. The Governor-General may declare that exploration is required in the national interest if both Houses of Parliament have approved a proclamation to that effect. Such a proclamation has not been made since the Act was passed in 1976. It is therefore believed that

Figure 2.1   How royalty-equivalents are paid in the Northern Territory under the
**   *Aboriginal Land Rights (Northern Territory) Act 1976***

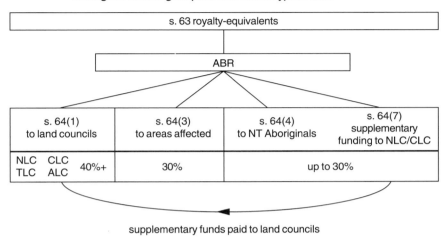

supplementary funds paid to land councils

ABR   Aboriginals Benefit Reserve
ALC   Anindilyakwa Land Council
CLC   Central Land Council
NLC   Northern Land Council
TLC   Tiwi Land Council

Aboriginal people in the Northern Territory do have an effective 'right of veto' over mining on their lands.[40]

The *Aboriginal Land Rights (Northern Territory) Act* provides for statutory royalties to be paid to Aboriginal interests by the Commonwealth Government. In relation to mining projects operating on Aboriginal land, the Commonwealth Government pays the Aboriginals Benefit Reserve an amount equivalent to the royalties paid to the Northern Territory.

The *Aboriginal Land Rights (Northern Territory) Act* refers to payments of compensation for damage or disturbance caused to the land and to the traditional Aboriginal owners of the land. In the assessment of compensation there is specific reference to Aboriginal use of the land and the impact of any disturbance to that use.

Royalty-equivalents under the *Aboriginal Land Rights (Northern Territory) Act* are paid into the Aboriginals Benefit Reserve (ABR). The land councils receive at least 40 per cent, another 30 per cent goes to areas affected by resource development on Aboriginal land, and up to 30 per cent is retained as supplementary funding for land councils, as general grants for Northern Territory Aboriginals and to meet administrative expenses. Traditional owners are therefore guaranteed 30 per cent of royalties (aside

Map 2.1   Aboriginal land in the Northern Territory

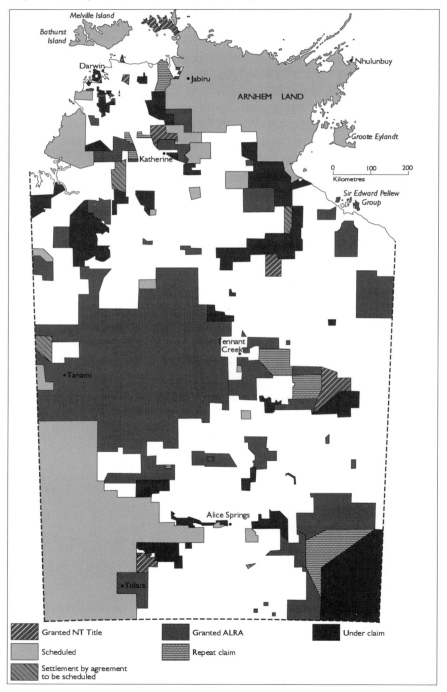

from additional s. 43 and s. 44 agreements). The specific legislative provisions are that ABR disburses the royalty-equivalent monies it receives from the Commonwealth pursuant to s. 64 of the *Aboriginal Land Rights (Northern Territory) Act* in the following way (see Figure 2.1):

- Section 64(1) payments, comprising 40 per cent of royalty-equivalent monies are distributed to Aboriginal land councils in the Northern Territory, in proportion to Aboriginal populations in land council areas. These payments are for land councils' administrative and statutory obligations under the *Aboriginal Land Rights (Northern Territory) Act,* including the making of claims to unalienated Crown land.
- Section 64(3) payments, comprising 30 per cent of royalty-equivalent monies paid by companies into the ABR, are distributed to Aboriginal groups affected by mining operations on Aboriginal land, for example, in the Ranger case they are paid to the Gagudju Association.
- The remaining 30 per cent of royalty-equivalents are used for grant payments to Aborigines throughout the Northern Territory,[41] meeting certain ABR administrative costs,[42] and providing supplements to land councils' administrative budgets.[43]

Income and expenditure for the four Northern Territory land councils, including the Anindilyakwa Land Council which commenced operations on 1 July 1991, are approved by the Minister for Aboriginal and Torres Strait Islander Affairs on the basis of Aboriginal populations in the relevant land council area. Allocations to each of the four Northern Territory land councils in 1996/97 are outlined in Table 2.1.

The allocations to land councils is net of Mining Withholding Tax (5.8 per cent of allocations prior to 1 July 1991, and set at 4 per cent after that date). After payments were made, the accumulated surplus in the ABR reserve amounted to $37.6m at the end of 1996/97.

The administration of the *Aboriginal Land Rights (Northern Territory) Act,* is funded through s. 64(1) and s. 64(7). The cost of funding land councils and prosecuting land claims appears to have decreased during the past five years from $16.2m in 1992/93 to $14.8m in 1996/97. However, $1.9m was paid to the Northern Land Council and $1.9m was paid to the Central Land Council for administrative expenses on 28 June 1996.[44] Combined real administrative expenses for all land councils have in fact ranged between $16m and $18m each year. These expenditures have resulted in Aboriginal people being able to regain title to about half of the Northern Territory's land area (see Map 2.1). During the past five years the distributions to Aboriginal organisations in areas affected by mining (s. 64(3)), combined

Table 2.1   Northern Territory Aboriginal land councils' funding—allocations under
s. 64(1) to meet administrative costs (paid to each land council), 1996/97

Land council	% of total allocation
Northern	22
Central	15
Tiwi	2
Anindilyakwa	1
TOTAL	40

Table 2.2   Northern Territory Aboriginal land councils' expenditure, 1996/97 ($m)

Aboriginal land council	Admin. s. 64(1)	Local payments s. 64(3)	NT grants s. 64(4)	Admin. s. 64(7)
Northern	7.3	4.2	-	0.4
Central	5.0	2.7	-	0.5
Tiwi	0.7	-	-	-
Anindilyakwa	0.3	3.1	-	-
TOTAL $	13.3	10.0	3.8	0.9

Source: ABR annual report 1996/97

with payment of grants to all Northern Territory Aboriginal people (s. 64(4)) have decreased slightly. They were $15.3m in 1992/93 and $14.3m in 1996/97 (see Table 2.3 and Graph 2.1).

Under statute, a minimum of 40 per cent of ABR income is allocated to administrative and statutory obligations under the *Aboriginal Land Rights (Northern Territory) Act*. During the past five years, these costs have ranged between 50 and 60 per cent of total ABR income. Remaining funds have been allocated to communities affected by mining, and for the benefit of all Northern Territory Aboriginal people. In broad terms, total operational expenditure and distributions of royalty-equivalent moneys amounted to $29.1m in 1996/97, for the total benefit of some 46,000 Aboriginal people who live in the Northern Territory. This represents a nominal potential benefit of approximately $630 per person each year. However, about half of this money is never distributed, because it has to be spent on administering land owned and on presenting claims to the Aboriginal Land Commissioner to regain traditional lands.

Because most payments are pooled and paid to regional land councils and local community associations, there is greater scope for royalty-equivalents to have a significant positive and political effect. This can come about in two ways: first, regional land councils such as the Northern and Central Land Councils are required to claim unalienated Crown land where

Table 2.3 and Graph 2.1   Northern Territory Aboriginal land councils' statutory costs and distributions 1991–97 ($m)

Year 19–	($m) s. 64(1)(7)	($m) s. 64(3)(4)
91/92	17.8	15.5
92/93	16.2	15.3
93/94	16.5	10.2
94/95	17.2	10.9
95/96	19.2	11.5
96/97	14.2	13.8

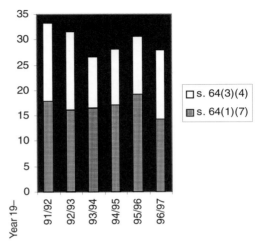

Source: ABR Annual Reports

traditional ownership can be established, and the land councils have the experience and political skills to influence government policy and be effective advocates for their constituencies. Secondly, local community organisations can garnish small individual royalty amounts to purchase substantial assets. Often communities choose to purchase local businesses where they can see and monitor the effects of their investment. Per capita available annual funding is modest. There is an incentive for Northern Territory Aboriginals to allocate more rather than less of their funds to land council operational expenses, to attempt to gain by legal and political means the equality which they have not been able to gain to date by economic development.

With respect to s. 64(3) payments to local communities affected by mining operations, funds are more significant per capita if a community is very narrowly defined. For instance, discretion in the allocation of royalty monies means that before 1988 Nabarlek uranium moneys paid to Kunwinjku went to more than 1200 members, after 1988 they went to some 100 members of the Nabarlek Traditional Owners Association (see Chapter 5). In addition to statutory royalties and royalty payments, agreements have covered a spectrum of commercial arrangements including equity interests, provision of services, employment and training schemes and social and environmental monitoring. Funds have a greater positive effect over a longer period if a significant amount of funds received, for example half their income, is wisely invested for the medium term. This has been achieved in some of the case studies described below.

CONJUNCTIVE VERSUS DISJUNCTIVE AGREEMENTS

In June 1987, Part IV of the *Aboriginal Land Rights (Northern Territory) Act* was amended. The key change in the amended legislation is that Aboriginal consent is now required before an exploration licence can be granted in respect of Aboriginal land, rather than after exploration has been undertaken. Where consent is not given, the Governor-General may declare that exploration is required for the national interest if both Houses of Parliament have approved a proclamation to that effect. Such a proclamation has not been made since the Act was passed in 1976. Once Aboriginal people have given their consent to exploration, the general rule since 1987 has been that Aboriginal consent to further mining is not required. All agreements entered into since 1987 are 'conjunctive'. Terms and conditions for exploration and other mining interests must be agreed by the land council, or determined by a mining commissioner. Statutory time limits govern the conduct of negotiations.[45] Under the amended *Aboriginal Land Rights (Northern Territory) Act 1976* Aboriginal land councils negotiate the terms and conditions of mining on Aboriginal land at the same time as they permit exploration on their land.

In March 1992, the Northern Territory Supreme Court held in the Stockdale decision that disjunctive agreements, where separate permission must be granted for both exploration and mining, were not permitted under the *Aboriginal Land Rights (Northern Territory) Act.* From the point of view of Aboriginal landowners, the disjunctive agreements which existed before the 1987 amendment to the Act may be preferable, because they provide greater negotiation leverage at the mining stage. From the miners' perspective, conjunctive agreements are preferable because once successful exploration has been financed, it is unsatisfactory for mining approval not to be granted. Aboriginal people have learnt to work with these changed arrangements.[46]

A NEO-COLONIAL POLITICAL ECONOMY?

Although the land councils at first glance might appear to be well-resourced, one has to view their funding in the context of the total political economy of the Northern Territory, and the power relations between Indigenous people of the Territory and non-Aboriginal people.

For instance, the *Aboriginal Land Rights (Northern Territory) Act* is 'An Act providing for the granting of Traditional Aboriginal Land in the Northern Territory for the benefit of Aboriginals, and for other purposes'.

The Act has been successful in returning traditional Aboriginal lands. As at 30 June 1997, Aboriginal people had gained inalienable freehold title to 545,707 sq km, or about 41 per cent of the Northern Territory's land area.[47] Some 260,290 sq km (19.33 per cent of the Northern Territory) was returned by way of legislated scheduled grant and 9857 sq km (0.73 per cent of the Northern Territory) by way of agreement reached with the Northern Territory Government. Some 275,560 sq km (21 per cent of the Northern Territory's land area) has been returned to date by way of land granted under the *Aboriginal Land Rights (Northern Territory) Act*, after a land claims process (see Figure 2.2). The land claims process has been in place since 1976, and claims currently lodged will take a further eight years or more to be heard. However, the process has imposed a high cost in financial and human resources for the two large mainland land councils, the Northern Land Council and the Central Land Council, which have scope for claiming unalienated Crown land.

As previously stated, it is likely that about half of the Northern Territory's land area will eventually be returned to Aboriginal ownership. The land claims process has been protracted and expensive; to a substantial degree this is due to claims opposed by the Northern Territory Government. The land claims process differs from legislative provisions in South Australia (1966, 1981 and in 1984), New South Wales (1983), New Zealand and North America, where land rights have generally been effected by way of land grants authorised by a specific parliamentary Act.

The special cost of the land claims process has also imposed additional financial burdens on the Northern Territory Government, but it appears to have been reimbursed for these expenses by way of Commonwealth Grants Commission subsidies.

Payments to the Aboriginals Benefit Reserve have totalled $387m since 1978, or $28m per annum on average during the past five years (see

Table 2.4 and Figure 2.2   Land returned to Aboriginal ownership in the Northern Territory (sq km)

By grant	260,290
By claims	275,560
Agreement	9,857

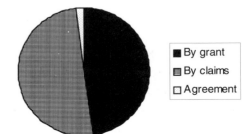

■ By grant
▦ By claims
□ Agreement

Table 5.8). The *Aboriginal Land Rights (Northern Territory) Act* has directly and indirectly assisted Northern Territory Aboriginal people, who comprise 25 per cent of the Territory's Census population.

There has been a long-running debate in the research literature on whether Aboriginals Benefit Reserve moneys are private moneys, or public moneys for Aboriginal basic services, such as education, health, transport, and social and cultural advancement. The Northern Territory Government receives about six times the per capita subsidy received by the State Governments of New South Wales and Victoria from the Commonwealth Grants Commission for all citizens in those States and Territories. The per capita subsidy rate is calculated on the basis of nineteen 'disability' factors identified for the Northern Territory's Aboriginal population.[48] It is critically important that funds are allocated fairly, and are seen to be allocated fairly.

A $290m DISCREPANCY?

The Northern Territory Government's budget is in the order of $1.5 billion per annum. The Northern Territory Treasury's estimate of the Aboriginal component of that budget is $536.3m per annum (36 per cent of its budget), with the largest components being health ($115m) and education ($106.5m). Another significant component is 'other purposes', which includes the cost of opposing Aboriginal claims for traditional lands registered by land councils under the *Aboriginal Land Rights (Northern Territory) Act.* The Northern Territory Government's suggestion that 36 per cent of its budget *should* be spent on Aboriginal people is reasonable, given that most of the 46,277 Aboriginal residents of the Northern Territory live in remote and rural areas. The costs of providing services in such areas are expensive. The fact that Aboriginal health, education, housing and essential services needs are huge has been well documented.[49] However, the Northern Territory Treasury has not revealed the assumptions it has used to conclude that Aboriginal people do *in fact* account for 36 per cent of the Northern Territory Government's budget.

Moreover, a North Australia Research Unit study has found that its best estimates are that only 16.4 per cent of the Northern Territory Government's budget of $1.5 billion can be described as being spent on Aboriginal purposes, which is $246m. This is $290m less than the Northern Territory Treasury's estimate.[50] If that were so, it is likely there would be continuing poor health, education, essential services and housing for Northern Territory Aboriginal people.

Northern Territory Aboriginal leaders have criticised the unfair distributions of Commonwealth Grants Commission funds, and this question is of pressing concern.[51] Without a transparent and fair funding allocation, Commonwealth grants to the Northern Territory may provide limited net benefits for Aboriginal people.

It should also be noted that 72 per cent of the Northern Territory's 1996 non-Indigenous population were not living in the Northern Territory in 1991.[52] They were visiting the Northern Territory for a variety of reasons, including a desire to obtain employment. The Northern Territory is largely dependent on a special level of subsidy determined by the Commonwealth Grants Commission.[53] Many non-Indigenous people come to the Northern Territory to get work, but this is in large measure made possible by the generous level of Commonwealth Government subsidy, even though the subsidy was meant to be directed at increasing the number of services and raising the living standards of Aboriginal people. The subsidies support general government services and infrastructure, which in turn support the Northern Territory economy. It is important that Aboriginal people receive a fair share of these benefits, and the available evidence suggests that they do not.

It may be that the Commonwealth Government is unwittingly subsidising a system of 'internal-colonialism' in the Northern Territory. 'Colonialism' is the policy of 'exploitation of backward or weak peoples'.[54] It refers to a metropolitan power exercising political control over an undeveloped economy and appropriating what is produced in these lands. Mineral wealth extracted from Aboriginal lands in the Northern Territory is significant, over $10 billion in gross revenue during the past twenty years. However, unlike New Zealand, Canada and the United States, there is no constitutional recognition of Aboriginal and Torres Strait Islander people in Australia. The *Northern Territory (Self Government) Act 1978* provides no protection or special status for traditional land owners or Aboriginal people. Their political power and scope for education, training, competing in labour markets and self-government is limited by the largely transitory non-Aboriginal majority population.

Large subsidies are being sent north to the Northern Territory Government, but the subsidies do not appear to be reaching Aboriginal people. Education, health and other government services planned on behalf of Aboriginal people need a greater degree of Aboriginal input and control in order to make them effective. Current government services have long been a source of complaint among Northern Territory Aboriginal people. The Director of the Central Land Council, Tracker Tilmouth, wrote that Aboriginal communities in Central Australia 'subsist in Third World conditions without their fair share of government resources'. He also stated that Northern Territory Health Services figures show primary health care expenditure in Aboriginal communities in Central Australia is $650 per capita compared with $1200 per capita in urban centres.[55] A Federal Court judge has criticised the amount spent by the Northern Territory Government on opposing land claims, and drawn attention to 'the appalling Third World conditions under which so many Aboriginal people live'.[56] ATSIC's 1993 National Aboriginal and Torres Strait Islander Needs Survey revealed that the Northern Territory had the highest housing need, and made up 32 per cent of national need.[57]

Occasionally there are glimmers of hope from people who no longer wield political power. For instance Ian Tuxworth, who was Chief Minister of the Northern Territory during the 1980s, proposed in 1997 that Aborigines should have reserved for them one Senate and two House of Representatives seats per State. He also called for a percentage of State and Federal funds to go to the Aboriginal and Torres Strait Islander Commission:

> Years of combat have yielded nothing and it's time for a mature approach that recognises the High Court's Mabo and Wik decisions…We have got to go beyond negotiation and give Aboriginal people a place in the system. The Northern Territory has spent about $400m on fighting land claims. Some States like Western Australia and Queensland have spent more. We would have been better giving this money to Aborigines.[58]

By contrast, the public understanding shown by the present Northern Territory Government of the purposes of the *Aboriginal Land Rights (Northern Territory) Act* leaves much to be desired. The Chief Minister of the Northern Territory, the Hon Shane Stone QC, ignores the fact that the modified and limited *Aboriginal Land Rights (Northern Territory) Act* was introduced by the Federal Liberal–National Party Government of Malcolm Fraser. In his December 1997 address on the Review of the *Aboriginal Land Rights Act* to the Northern Territory Parliament, the Chief Minister said: 'For the ALP, the *Land Rights Act* was some sort of icon never to be tampered with. Never mind that Aboriginal Territorians might be constrained within a system that amounts to an anthropological zoo.'[59]

CONCLUSION

In summary, the *Aboriginal Land Rights (Northern Territory) Act* has delivered substantial land ownership and royalty-equivalent payments for residents of areas affected by mining and for Northern Territory Aboriginal people. Even though mining royalty-equivalents paid to Aboriginal people in the Northern Territory, under Commonwealth legislation, far exceed any State government's effort, their positive effect is diminished by the 'Third World' poverty of Aboriginal people. Commonwealth Grants Commission funding to the Northern Territory Government is set at a high level because of Aboriginal disability, but Aboriginal people and academic studies maintain that the funding that is provided is not equitably distributed. Aborigines lack appropriate government and essential services, particularly in the Northern Territory and remote Australia. Unlike New Zealand, Canada and the United States, Indigenous people in Australia have no constitutional recognition.

Northern Territory land councils and some royalty associations have over twenty years experience of negotiating with major international mining companies. Northern Territory land councils believe that the *Aboriginal Land Rights (Northern Territory) Act* provides a model for the interaction of Aboriginal owners and third parties which is substantially more efficient and certain than the processes under the *Native Title Act*. Miners have found that the accommodation of land owners' interests under the *Aboriginal Land Rights (Northern Territory) Act* is justified and accords with majority Australian opinion.[60]

However, outside the Northern Territory common law native title rights and the *Native Title Act* have radically changed the potential situation for Aboriginal people in Australia, particularly if they have access to pastoral lease land and unalienated Crown land (see Map 8.1). It is therefore useful, after surveying current State legislation and Aboriginal land tenure, to examine some 30 mining agreements which have been developed with Aboriginal people in Australia during the past 30 years. An important question is whether such agreements have redressed the inequalities which Aboriginal people face in Australia. Prior to the *Native Title Act,* agreements with Aboriginal people only occurred in the Northern Territory, under the *Aboriginal Land Rights (Northern Territory) Act.*

3 State legislation

In New South Wales, Victoria and Tasmania, intensive settlement of the land by Europeans and a long history of assimilation have resulted in only tiny proportions of the land mass in those States remaining in Aboriginal ownership. Aboriginal freehold, leasehold and reserve land either does not exist, or is insignificant in area in Victoria, Tasmania and the Australian Capital Territory. Elsewhere in Australia, these three categories cover large areas of land. Aboriginal freehold covers a large part of the Northern Territory and South Australia. Aboriginal leasehold and reserve land covers a significant area of Western Australia. Aboriginal people also have tenure to significant areas of land in Queensland. Aboriginal freehold, leasehold and reserve land is owned where land is least intensively settled and not suitable for agriculture. In the Northern Territory, Aboriginal people comprise a quarter of the total population, and about half of the total number of residents who have lived in the Territory for more than five years. At present 40 per cent of the Northern Territory's land area is Aboriginal freehold. Aboriginal and Torres Strait Islander land is shown in Map 8.1 in Chapter 8.

NEW SOUTH WALES

Aboriginal rights to land in New South Wales are primarily dealt with by the *Aboriginal Land Rights Act 1983* (NSW). The *Aboriginal Land Rights Act* also creates a land claim process whereby land may be transferred to local New South Wales Aboriginal land councils to be held in trust. The New South Wales Office of Aboriginal Affairs Annual Report 1993/94 stated that since the introduction of the *Aboriginal Land Rights Act 1983,* 780 land claims have been granted to Aboriginal land councils in New South

Wales. This land has a total area of 54 sq km and an estimated value of $104m. By 1995, 400 sq km of freehold and 1100 sq km of leasehold land were held by Aboriginal land councils in New South Wales.

All New South Wales Aboriginal land councils have been funded by 7.5 per cent of State land taxes paid to the New South Wales Aboriginal Land Council for a period of seventeen years from 1981 to 1998. The council receives an allocation from the consolidated fund equal to 7.5 per cent of all land tax paid in New South Wales. For the year ended 30 September 1993, this allocation amounted to $57.5m. The Act states that one-half of this allocation is to be paid directly into a Statutory Investment Fund, which, with interest and other gains, must be reinvested. In 1998 there was a balance of some $455m in the fund. From 31 December 1998 this annual allocation will cease. The Act envisages that amounts previously credited to the statutory fund will be sufficient to sustain the council's operations after that date.

Aboriginal land covers a relatively modest percentage of the State's land area, at 1500 sq km, or 0.2 per cent of the State's land mass (see Table 3.1 and Graph 3.1). Aboriginal land councils in New South Wales do have some significant mineral rights over their land. The *Mining Act 1992* (NSW) provides for the payment of royalties for publicly and privately owned minerals. With respect to Aboriginal land, in 1973 a grant was made under that Act conferring ownership of minerals on or below the land to the NSW Aboriginal Lands Trust, excluding gold, silver, petroleum and coal. Miners are prevented from exploring or exploiting minerals on Aboriginal land and consent is required before mining operations can commence.

VICTORIA

Victorian Aborigines now comprise 0.5 per cent of the State's population and own 0.01 per cent of the land mass, principally comprised of three former reserves in remote areas of the State. In 1970, under the *Aboriginal Lands Act 1970* (Vic), the Victorian Government transferred ownership of two small former Aboriginal reserves to Aboriginal ownership. They were Lake Tyers in Gippsland, eastern Victoria, and Framlingham near Warrnambool, in western Victoria. The total area involved was some 20 sq km. In 1982, the Framlingham community received the title to the adjoining Framlingham forest area. Lake Condah, a former reserve between Portland and Warrnambool, was transferred by an Act of the Commonwealth Parliament in 1987 to the Kerrup-Jmara Elders Aboriginal Corporation. This latter area is of some 15 sq km. Some community organisations own modest office space. Aboriginal groups own no other significant land holdings.[61]

Although land granted to Aboriginal people by statute in Victoria is small in area, legislation does provide some protection with respect to mining. In relation to royalties, the relevant local Aboriginal corporation may negotiate a reasonable payment for mining operations which disturb the lifestyle, culture and traditions of the traditional owners.[62] Payments for exploration licences cannot exceed those which would have been payable as compensation under the relevant mining legislation.

QUEENSLAND

Indigenous people make up 3 per cent of the State's population. Some 2.4 per cent, or 42,200 sq km of the State's land mass is designated Aboriginal or Torres Strait Islander land.

Deeds of Grant in Trust (DOGIT) were introduced for the Aurukun and Mornington Island Aboriginal reserves in 1978. They were extended to other former reserves in Queensland under existing legislation relating to land. Amendments to the *Land Act 1962* and the subsequent *Aboriginal and Torres Strait Islander (Land Holding) Act 1985* (Qld), provided for the grant of freehold estates to the relevant Aboriginal council. In addition to Aurukun and Mornington Island, some fourteen former reserves were transferred to Deeds of Grant in Trust in 1985.

In 1991, the Queensland Parliament passed new legislation relating to Aboriginal rights to former reserve land in Queensland. The *Aboriginal Land Act 1991* and the *Torres Strait Islander Land Act 1991* created a land claim process for the grant of land to Aboriginal land trusts. Under the Acts, 'claimable land' includes 'transferable lands', which may be comprised of DOGIT land, existing Aboriginal reserves and some public reserves.

Under the *Aboriginal Land Act 1991,* a scale of partial royalty-equivalents based on the total royalties payable to the Queensland Government are paid in equal proportions to the relevant trustees and to the Queensland Government for the benefit of Aboriginal people in Queensland.[63]

The Hopevale community negotiated an agreement in this new legislative context with Cape Flattery Silica Mine, a subsidiary of the Japanese company Mitsubishi Ltd. This is discussed in Chapter 5. More recently, as discussed in Chapter 1, the Queensland Government recognised the Hopevale people's native title to 110 sq km of land that they previously owned under a DOGIT lease.

SOUTH AUSTRALIA

Aboriginal freehold land in South Australia now amounts to 19 per cent of the total area of the State or 189,000 sq km. Agriculturally it is the poorest land, but recently some mineral exploration has been undertaken.

No land claim process was created in South Australia but during the 1980s a statutory scheme was enacted which created Aboriginal land. The *Pitjantjatjara Land Rights Act 1981* (SA) vested title to certain lands in the people known as Anangu Pitjantjatjara. The *Maralinga-Tjarutja Land Rights Act 1984* (SA) vested title to the Maralinga lands in the people acknowledged as the traditional owners of those lands. Under the *Pitjantjatjara Land Rights Act 1981*, 102,630 sq km of land was granted to the body corporate Anangu Pitjantjatjara. A further 76,420 sq km of former Maralinga lands were transferred to Pitjantjatjara ownership under the *Maralinga-Tjarutja Land Rights Act 1984*. In April 1991 a further 3600 sq km, which included the historical mission of Ooldea, was transferred to Aboriginal people.[64]

The traditional land rights in the *Pitjantjatjara Land Rights Act 1981* (SA) are broadly defined. The legislation specifies that traditional owners, in relation to the land described, have 'in accordance with Aboriginal tradition, social, economic and spiritual affiliations with, and responsibilities for, the lands or any part of them'.

The *Pitjantjatjara Land Rights Act 1981* (SA), like the *Maralinga-Tjarutja Land Rights Act 1984* (SA), provides that a payment of compensation for mining be 'reasonably proportionated to the disturbance to the lands, the Pitjantjatjara people and their way of life'. There is provision for a special royalty regime in relation to the Pitjantjatjara lands under which one-third of any statutory royalties relating to mining or petroleum activities on the lands shall be paid to Anangu Pitjantjatjara, and a further one-third is applied beneficially for Aboriginal people throughout the State. Additional compensation may also be negotiated.

WESTERN AUSTRALIA

About 12 per cent, or 325,500 sq km, of Western Australia's large land area, is Aboriginal reserve or Aboriginal leasehold. Western Australian Government Aboriginal reserve and Aboriginal leasehold land is indicated in Map 8.1. In 1997, 202,028 sq km was 'Reserves Vested in the Aboriginal Lands Trust'. 'Pastoral leases held by the Aboriginal Lands Trust' amounted to 10,993 sq km and 94 sq km was 'Freehold land leased by Aboriginal communities'.[65] Data compiled by the Australian Land Information Group (Auslig) in 1995, with reference to the Western Australian Department of Lands Administration, records that 199,400 sq km is Aboriginal reserve land and 126,000 sq km is Aboriginal leasehold. This latter category presumably includes lands purchased or leased by Aboriginal organisations with the assistance of funds provided by successive Commonwealth Governments.

The Aboriginal Land Trust is responsible for the control and management of Aboriginal Land Trust land, and its members are appointed by the State Minister for Aboriginal Affairs. A review of Western Australia's Aboriginal Lands Trust, chaired by former Senator Neville Bonner AO, recommended in 1996 that the land held by the Aboriginal Lands Trust be transferred to Aboriginal people over the following six years.[66]

Under the *Aboriginal Affairs Planning Authority Act 1972* (WA), Crown land reserved for the use or benefit of Aboriginal people was vested in the Aboriginal Land Trust. Under the *Mining Act 1978* (WA), the Minister for Mines has full discretion over mining. Aboriginal interests have no mineral rights but can receive a partial royalty for mining on Aboriginal reserves. Royalties paid to the trust to date for mining on Aboriginal reserve land are not significant. Funds must be expended on land related matters.[67]

TASMANIA

The *Aboriginal Lands Act 1995* (Tas) was passed on 6 December 1995. The Act transferred approximately 3.8 sq km (0.06 per cent of the State's area) to Aboriginal people. Aboriginal Tasmanians now hold freehold title to twelve sites, including Oyster Cove and Risdon Cove near Hobart, the Kutkina and Ballawinne Caves in the south-west, and Great Dog, Mount Chappell and Babel Islands in Bass Strait. Rates are not payable on the land unless there is commercial activity on it. All minerals on the land will also be transferred, to a depth of 50 metres, and belong to an Aboriginal land council. This includes gold and silver, but excludes oil, helium or any atomic substances.[68]

LAND TENURE IN AUSTRALIA

Following the *Mabo (2)* and *Wik* judgments, Aboriginal land is no longer confined to the 1095 sq km specifically designated Aboriginal land, or 13 per cent of Australia's total land mass of 7682 sq km. An area just as

Table 3.1 Land tenure in Australia ('000 sq km)

Category	NSW	QLD	SA	WA	NT	TOTAL
Aboriginal freehold	0.4	20.5	189.0	0.0	516.8	726.7
Aboriginal leasehold	1.1	18.9	0.6	126.1	19.2	165.9
Aboriginal reserve	0.0	2.8	0.0	199.4	0.0	202.2
TOTAL all land	801.6	1727.2	984.0	2525.5	1346.2	7682.3

Sources: Australia Land Tenure, Auslig, Canberra 1993 and Auslig land tenure data bases 1995

Table 3.2 Indigenous population and land, by State and Territory

State	Population	% of pop. Indigenous	% of land Aboriginal
NSW	101,485	1.6	0.2
VIC	21,474	0.5	0.0
QLD	95,516	2.8	2.4
SA	20,442	1.5	19.3
WA	50,791	2.8	12.1
TAS	13,873	2.5	0.0
NT	46,277	25.1	40.0
ACT	2,898	0.8	0.0
AUSTRALIA	352,970	1.97	13.5

Source: 1996 Census (there is averaging in each State, so the total is inexact)

large again, of vacant Crown land totalling 961 sq km, and other Crown land totalling 81 sq km Australia wide, is potentially subject to native title claim, and comprises 13.5 per cent of Australia's land mass. Australia's private lands comprise 4820 sq km of Australia's land mass, but only 1585 sq km of these lands are freehold. It is significant that 3235 sq km or 42 per cent of Australia's total land area is Crown lease, mostly in Queensland (940 sq km), Western Australia (900 sq km), Northern Territory (675 sq km) and South Australia (418 sq km).

Map 8.1 in Chapter 8 illustrates the mainly freehold land of eastern and the south-west corner of Australia, the Aboriginal freehold land of Central Australia and Arnhem Land, and the vacant Crown and leasehold land in the vast marginal areas which separate remote and settled Australia. A large proportion of Aboriginal and Torres Strait Islander people continue to live in the Aboriginal freehold land and the vacant Crown and leasehold land. They have native title rights and interests in land according to their traditions, laws and customs. These native title rights may continue to co-exist over the vast pastoral leases issued by colonial governments last century.

As Dr Lowitja O'Donoghue has noted in the Foreword to this book, 'following the High Court's *Wik* judgment of 1996, which found that native

Graph 3.1   Indigenous population by State and Territory

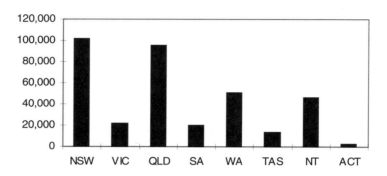

Indigenous population

title may co-exist with pastoral leases, reconciliation between Aboriginal and other Australians is no longer an idealistic objective, but a practical necessity'. The agreements that have been made concerning mining on Aboriginal land during the past 30 years are of various quality, but are the best Australian models we have for making agreements in the future.

4 Mining agreements prior to the *Aboriginal Land Rights (Northern Territory) Act*

Mining agreements between companies and Aboriginal bodies are often complex. They may involve contract law, as well as constitutional law, administrative law and property law, to impose restrictions on the right to mine and the terms and conditions of agreements. An additional challenge is that two cultures are involved. There are different priorities, goals and expectations.

In the Northern Territory, as elsewhere in Australia, Aboriginal rights to possession, occupation, use and enjoyment of the land were first contested, then following pacification, ignored, from the time the English and Europeans first settled on those lands during the nineteenth century.[69] However, an important development occurred after the Second World War. In 1952, the Commonwealth Government made some provision for mining royalties to be paid to Aboriginal residents of Aboriginal reserves in the Northern Territory. It established the Aborigines (Benefits from Mining) Trust Fund (ABTF), which received royalty-equivalent payments for the benefit of Aborigines as a concession for mining on Aboriginal reserve land. The ABTF provided for returns from mining on Aboriginal land to be earmarked for the use of Aboriginal people, irrespective of the absence of statutory or common law recognition of Aboriginal land ownership at that time. A double royalty of 2.5 per cent, based on production of minerals extracted from Aboriginal land was instituted. There were probably several factors that caused the Commonwealth Government to make this provision at this time. Australian servicemen, including influential and active academics such as Bill Stanner and Donald Thompson, had served in north Australia during the war, and wanted to further Aboriginal interests and to acknowledge the assistance Aboriginal people had provided to war operations in north Australia. There was a worldwide trend to decolonisation, which in many

Map 4.1   Mining sites around the Gulf of Carpentaria

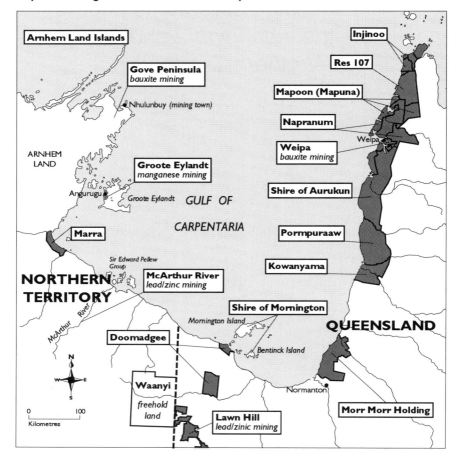

former colonies resulted in self-government. Paul Hasluck had an interest in foreign affairs, and was Minister of Territories in 1951. He convened the First Native Welfare Conference in Canberra, and he had the capacity to effect change. Despite these provisions mining on Aboriginal reserves did not occur for some time, and the first payment from the Trust Fund occurred in 1968.[70] The ABTF became the Aboriginals Benefit Trust Account (ABTA) in 1976 and the Aboriginals Benefit Reserve (ABR) in 1997.

Comalco at Weipa in North Queensland, Nabalco at Gove and GEMCO at Groote Eylandt, both in Arnhem Land in the Northern Territory, commenced prior to the *Aboriginal Land Rights (Northern Territory) Act.* Only at Groote Eylandt were significant royalties paid to Aboriginal people, and this was because the Church Missionary Society had taken out an exploration licence on their behalf. GEMCO has also employed a greater percentage of Aboriginal workers than the other mines, and currently 36 workers (9 per cent of the workforce) are Aboriginal people.

It is reasonable that Aboriginal land-holders should also benefit from mining on their land. It is important that extra care is taken to ensure that financial and other compensation is adequate. If possible, both the local Aboriginal people and the mining company should be fully informed and enter into an arrangement that benefits Aboriginal people. The ideal arrangement is when these agreements lead to long-term benefits such as business, training and employment opportunities, as has occurred in New Zealand and North America. This has been achieved at one of the world's largest coal mines, operated jointly by the Navajo Native American Indians and BHP at Farmington, New Mexico, in the United States. The Navajo–BHP mine commenced operation about the same time as GEMCO. Some 800 employees (80 per cent of the workforce, including management) are local Navajo people.[71] Prior to the *Aboriginal Land Rights (Northern Territory) Act,* Aboriginal people had no power to make agreements. Consequently mining had unhelpful and sometimes devastating effects on their communities.

NAPRANUM (WEIPA SOUTH) AND AURUKUN AND COMALCO LTD, 1957 (QUEENSLAND)

The land along the Gulf of Carpentaria, in the Northern Territory and Queensland, is a source of great mineral wealth (see Map 4.1). There is bauxite in the north, manganese on Groote Eylandt, and lead and zinc deposits along the southern base. The large-scale mining developments in these areas during the past 30 years have had a substantial impact on the environment and the lives of Aboriginal people in both Queensland and the Northern Territory. For example in 1963, in a notorious case on the eastern shore of the Gulf, the people of the settlement of Mapoon north of Weipa were summarily removed by government officials, and their homes were destroyed.[72]

COMALCO'S POSITION

The Queensland Parliament passed the *Commonwealth Aluminium Corporation Pty Ltd Agreement Act 1957* (Qld), which granted Comalco mining rights over lands near Weipa for an initial period of 84 years from

Summary of mining company and Aboriginal community relations

Location of mine	Western Cape York, North Queensland
Mining town	Weipa
Name of company	Comalco Ltd
Current parent company	Rio Tinto Ltd
Signatories	Queensland Government and Comalco
Date of agreement	1957
Type of project	Weipa bauxite mine, western Cape York
Description	Comalco was formed in 1965 to extract bauxite from western Cape York. During the first twenty years, up to 20% of the workforce was Indigenous. By 1998 there were 30 Indigenous employees in a workforce of 510 people. In addition, Napranum Aboriginal Corporation employed 10 Indigenous people. Total annual sales revenue of $1.5 billion. Produces 21% of Australia's aluminium products.
Royalties: statutory	$13.8m in 1996 paid to Queensland Government
negotiated	Nil Aboriginal royalties
(to area affected)	-
Royalty association	-
Scope of agreement	No agreement. Community lodged unsuccessful legal challenge in High Court (*Wik* 1996).
Aboriginal/total employment	30 out of 510.
Outcomes	Weipa Aborigines Society 1973.
	Napranum Aboriginal Corporation 1993.
	Approximate membership 200 adults. Of the Corporation's annual income of $1m, 28% is from Comalco. Comalco staff are also seconded to NAC.
Evaluation/studies	Roberts 1978, Rowley 1972, see Martin 1996.
Native Title Representative Body	Cape York Land Council.

1957 (see Map 4.1). Comalco developed a major bauxite mine near the Aboriginal settlement of Weipa South (Napranum) on Cape York Peninsula in Queensland during the following years. Through the agreement with the Queensland Government in 1957, Comalco was granted a mining lease over nearly 5880 sq km of land along the west coast of Cape York, and built a port and processing plant at Weipa. However, although the land was mostly Aboriginal reserve, Aboriginal people were not offered any share in ownership or decision making. The Queensland Government of that era decided that all royalties should be paid to the State Government. The Wik people of Aurukun took action in the High Court to claim that the Queensland Government had breached a fiduciary duty towards them in passing the *Commonwealth Aluminium Corporation Pty Ltd Agreement Act 1957* (Qld), but this case was lost in *Wik*.[73] Comalco has paid all royalties to the Queensland Government in accordance with Queensland law. In 1996, these amounted to $13.8m.[74]

After representations by the community and supporters, and negotiations between the community council and the company, Comalco paid $300,000 towards the cost of 62 new houses, and established the Weipa Aborigines Society in 1973. It has continued to provide modest support, particularly directed towards training and employment, to the society and its successor since that time.

Comalco is an integrated aluminium company, two-thirds owned by Rio Tinto Ltd. It produces 21 per cent of Australia's bauxite, 8 per cent of its alumina and 17 per cent of its primary aluminium.[75] Comalco's after-tax operating profit dropped from $265m in 1995 to $33m in 1996, leading to new cost-cutting measures and the shedding of a further 500 jobs.[76] In 1998, Comalco had a sales revenue of $1.9 billion and an after-tax profit of $220m.[77] It is likely that Aboriginal people will continue to be affected by tight economy measures, driven by a need for the company to maximise its return on capital.

ABORIGINAL EMPLOYMENT

By 1965, Comalco employed 65 local Aboriginal people in its mining operations. Since that time, some 6 to 20 per cent of Comalco's workforce has been Aboriginal, and after public pressure was applied in 1969, Aboriginal workers at Weipa received the bonuses, paid holidays, board and lodging which other workers received.[78] Comalco employed significant numbers of Napranum people during the 1980s in its mining activities. In 1990, Comalco's total workforce, including Australian, New Zealand and American workers, was 9039 people. By 1996 this had dropped to 4586, after United States, and downstream Australian and New Zealand businesses were sold. The decrease in the number of Aboriginal people employed by Comalco at Weipa must be understood in the context of the downsizing of the workforce which occurred through the contracting out of company employees generally, and the effects of the recession of the early 1990s. Following that recession and the decrease in the numbers of total Comalco employees, no Napranum residents were employed at Weipa in 1994.[79] In 1998, Comalco reported that it directly employed 510 people at Weipa, and estimated that 30 of them were Indigenous.[80]

NAPRANUM ABORIGINAL CORPORATION

Comalco's bauxite and kaolin mine at Weipa is near the Napranum Aboriginal community (see Map 4.1). Comalco's Annual Report states:

> The company's aim is to foster good relations with local communities and to gain long-term Aboriginal support for its goal...In 1995, Comalco handed over funding the infrastructure of the Weipa Aborigines Society to a new Aboriginal-directed body, the Napranum Aboriginal Corporation. As part of Comalco's aim of town normal-isation, local elections were held in Weipa to form membership of the town's Citizen Advisory Committee. The Committee is an interim step in the town's transition to local government control.[81]

The Napranum Aboriginal Corporation developed from the Weipa Aborigines Society, which was established in 1973. It is an example of a public benevolent organisation established to assist an Aboriginal community near a major mining development, when no royalties are paid to Aboriginal people. Only 21 per cent of Napranum Aboriginal Corporation's income is from ATSIC or other government sources, 28 per cent is from corporate grants and subsidies, believed to be from Comalco, and the remainder from sales, contract and other revenues. Comalco also supports the NAC by seconding staff to the NAC.

The Napranum Aboriginal Corporation was formed in May 1993 to assume the operations of the Weipa Aborigines Society, with the goal of Aboriginalisation of the organisation. The objectives of the corporation are to provide services, support, training and advice for the association's members, to promote traditional values, skills and interests, and to provide a forum for social, political and cultural interests. Membership is open to adult residents of Napranum and Weipa, and currently numbers over 200. The Governing Committee's Articles of Association also address the situation where Napranum residents have migrated from elsewhere, including Mapoon and the Torres Strait. The Governing Committee comprises:

- up to five members nominated as Traditional Elders by the 'tribal peoples' of Napranum and Weipa areas;
- two members of the Napranum Community Council appointed by that body;
- five other members of the association, elected at each annual general meeting.

The corporation conducts five major programs: the Napranum Preschool, the Nanum Wungthin Training Centre, finance and administration, cultural programs, and business development. The training centre has developed over the last 24 years. It has an excellent reputation and has been successful in trade training. It provides courses and training in mechanics, carpentry, joinery, office and clerical work. The cultural program assists cultural activities, focusing on traditional lands, including arts and crafts, language and community history. The business development section operates a unit that manufactures concrete-blocks, a sand washing business, a small sawmill and other work. The Napranum Aboriginal Corporation had assets of $708,000 at 30 June 1995 and a cash income for the year of $1m, including 22 per cent from sales and contract revenue. It employed ten Indigenous people in 1998.[82]

GOVE AND NABALCO LTD, 1968 (NORTHERN TERRITORY)

Summary of mining company and Aboriginal community relations	
Location of mine	Gove, Arnhem Land, Northern Territory
Mining town	Nhulunbuy
Name of company	Nabalco Ltd
Current parent company	Alusuisse-Lonza (51%), CSR (30%), AMP Society
Signatories	Commonwealth and Nabalco Ltd
Date of agreement	1968
Type of project	Nabalco bauxite mine at Gove
Description	Nabalco was formed in 1964 to mine bauxite and aluminium ore at Gove. Total annual sales revenue of $400m. Mining will continue to 2030.
Royalties: statutory	(currently) $1.50 per ton and 10% of sales.
negotiated	-
(to area affected)	-
Royalty association	Gumaitj Association, Dhanbul Association and other clan groups. Total approximate membership 1200 adults.
Scope of agreement	Local royalties paid to major clans. Since 1989, 85% of total amounts to Gumatj and Rirratjingu, the traditional owners of land mined.
Aboriginal/total employment	Twenty out of 740.
Outcomes	$2.6m per annum paid in royalty-equivalents to local land councils. Between 40 and 80 Aboriginal people employed with Yirrkala Business Enterprises. Some contract employment with Dhanbul Association.
Evaluation/studies	See Martin 1995.
Statutory land council	Northern Land Council.

Nabalco Ltd was formed in 1964 by Swiss and Australian firms to develop bauxite-aluminium ore at Gove near Nhulunbuy in north-east Arnhem Land (see Map 4.2). The Swiss Company, Alusuisse-Lonza (51 per cent), CSR Ltd and the AMP Society jointly own Nabalco Ltd. Nabalco entered into an agreement for the mining of bauxite and aluminium ore with the Commonwealth Government. Following the convention of paying royalties for mining on Aboriginal reserves in the Northern Territory, Nabalco agreed to a modest royalty payment. In February 1968 the company signed an agreement with the Federal Government under which it was granted a 42-year mineral lease over 20,000 ha, with the right of renewal for a further 42 years. Nabalco Ltd did not provide significant employment to Aboriginal people. In 1971, only 30 of 2700 employees were Aboriginal.[83] The mining royalties paid to Aboriginal people at Gove were also not large.

THE NABALCO AGREEMENT

The original Nabalco agreement dates to 1968 and was exceedingly modest. However, political and cultural protests in the wake of *Mabo (2)* have brought about a new royalty regime, which increased the amount of royalties paid by some 400 per cent, backdated to 1993.

The terms of the original agreement were set out in the *Mining (Gove Peninsula Nabalco Agreement) Ordinance 1968.* The maximum royalty payable to the Aboriginal Benefits Trust Fund, and distributed to land councils and to the Dhanbul and Gumaitj royalty associations, was 40c per tonne on treated bauxite (alumina) and 50c per ton on export bauxite. Mining began in 1973 and produced 4.5m tonnes of crushed ore annually. Under the agreement, royalties of $1m were paid into the Aborigines (Benefits from Mining) Trust Fund, and 10 per cent of them were paid to the local Yirrkala community. The distribution of royalties is illustrated in Figure 4.1. The Yirrkala people fought an unsuccessful court action in the Northern Territory Supreme Court for compensation for the aluminium mining at Gove. In that case Justice Blackburn ruled in 1971 that communal Aboriginal title to land was not a concept recognised in Australian law.[84] Nevertheless, the mine and subsequent political actions and legal action which they facilitated were important for raising land rights as a national political issue.

It was not until 1981, eight years after mining began, that agreement was reached on the rate per tonne actually being fixed at the maximum rate of 40c for treated bauxite and 50c for export bauxite. A lump sum payment of $2.78m, deemed on the basis of the Attorney-General's advice to be a royalty (as opposed to an ex gratia payment) was paid for the period 1 January 1979 to 31 March 1981 (two years, three months). This was the difference between the old and the new royalty rates. Leaders of the twelve clans in the region, at a meeting on 1 June 1979, decided that future royalty payments should be divided equally between the Yirrkala Dhanbul Association and the Gumaitj Association. The Northern Land Council subsequently ratified this decision. The division principally benefits the Rirratjingu and the Gumaitj clans. The rationale for the division is that the Nabalco project and the town of Nhulunbuy are located on the estates of these two clans.[85] In 1981/82, royalties paid by Gove Aluminium to the Aboriginals Benefit Trust Account were $1.7m per annum and estimated to increase to $2.2m per annum by 1992. In fact $2.5m was paid in royalty-equivalent payments for bauxite mining in 1991/92. Production planned was at a rate of 2m tonnes of export bauxite (at 50c per tonne) and 3m tonnes of treated bauxite (at 40c per tonne). For most of the time since 1979, the two relevant royalty bodies have been the Yirrkala Dhanbul Community Association and the Gumaitj Association. ABR royalty-equivalent income was in the order of $2.4m a year from 1983 to 1993. It has averaged $9.3m since 1993, under a new royalty regime, backdated to have effect from 1 January 1993.

Under the new royalty regime, royalties are calculated as the maximum of the following three elements:

- a minimum of $1.50 per tonne of exported bauxite and $0.75 per tonne of domestic bauxite;
- 10 per cent of sales of bauxite at market rates; and
- 10 per cent of the rolling average of sales at market rates for the previous five years.

Between 1978 and 1997, $71m was paid to the ABR for royalty-equivalents for bauxite mining.

INCREASED RECOGNITION

The Yirrkala land owners of north-eastern Arnhem Land have consistently protested against the mine. In August 1963 they presented a petition to Parliament, in Yolngu with English translation. The petition states in part: 'the people of the area fear that their needs and interests will be completely ignored as they have been in the past.'

Table 4.1 and Graph 4.1   Payments to the Aboriginals Benefit Reserve for bauxite

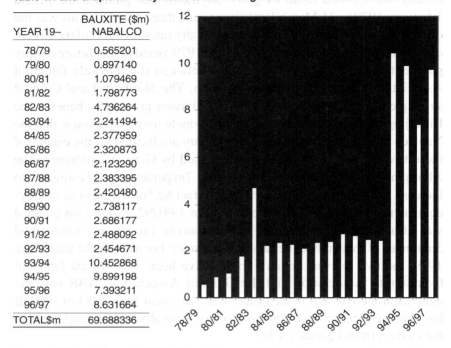

YEAR 19–	BAUXITE ($m) NABALCO
78/79	0.565201
79/80	0.897140
80/81	1.079469
81/82	1.798773
82/83	4.736264
83/84	2.241494
84/85	2.377959
85/86	2.320873
86/87	2.123290
87/88	2.383395
88/89	2.420480
89/90	2.738117
90/91	2.686177
91/92	2.488092
92/93	2.454671
93/94	10.452868
94/95	9.899198
95/96	7.393211
96/97	8.631664
TOTAL$m	69.688336

Source: ABR annual reports 1978–96, and *Hansard*, 25 November 1997

It is noteworthy that Aboriginal paintings, dances, music and modern cultural forms such as films and novels have flourished during the 1980s and 1990s, when Indigenous cultures in Australia and elsewhere around the world are most under threat from immense economic and cultural change. Special poignancy is given to the lack of an agreement for bauxite mining at Gove acceptable to local Aboriginal people by a song composed and performed by Manduwuy Yunupingu. A headmaster and founder of the rock band *Yothu Yindi* (literally meaning 'child/mother'), Manduwuy is a traditional owner of land mined for bauxite. He composed the hit song 'Treaty', about native title, land rights and reconciliation.

In 1995, when 'Treaty' was heading the hit parade, the Northern Land Council commenced a campaign to have Nabalco renegotiate an agreement with traditional owners. The mine site comprises an area of 36,000 ha excised from Arnhem Land, yet traditional owners were excluded from any direct agreement with the company during its first 30 years of operation. Galarrwuy Yunupingu, the Northern Land Council Chair, and brother of Mandawuy, said:

The campaign began in July 1995, when Mandawuy Yunupingu distributed information to European journalists about Nabalco's actions, when Yothu Yindi toured Europe. Nabalco is living in the past if it thinks it can continue to make record profits while it pays the lowest royalties of any mining company in the country.

We are talking about other aspects as well, including environmental safeguards, protection of sacred sites and more business opportunities for Aboriginal people. Traditional owners have no say whatsoever over the operation of the mine and have been continually excluded from an agreement despite repeated calls over the past thirty years.[86]

These protests were successful in increasing the amount of royalties paid by about 400 per cent. An increased royalty rate was backdated to 1993. Since 1993, total bauxite royalty-equivalent payments have averaged $9.1m per

Figure 4.1   Distribution of Nabalco Ltd royalties under the *Aboriginal Land Rights (Northern Territory) Act 1976*

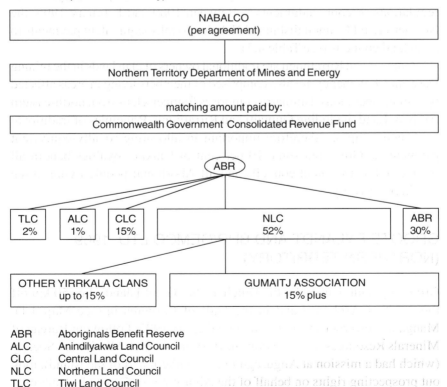

ABR	Aboriginals Benefit Reserve
ALC	Anindilyakwa Land Council
CLC	Central Land Council
NLC	Northern Land Council
TLC	Tiwi Land Council

Table 4.2   Nabalco Ltd payments to local land councils at Gove, 1989–1995

Land councils	$
Gumaitj	5,752,430
Rirratjingu	1,321,820
Laynhapuy	798,230
Dhan/Laynha	192,000
Dhimarru	300,000
Other clans	60,000
TOTAL	8,424,480

Source: Martin 1995: 69

annum. Of this amount, local land councils receive on average $2.7m each year. Nevertheless, the anthropologist David Martin has reported that the system for allocating mining royalties in the Gove area remains a contentious one. The *Aboriginal Land Rights (Northern Territory) Act*, s. 35(2) provides that royalty monies are to be directed to traditional owners or members living in affected areas. Land councils have been left to develop their own interpretations of these terms, as they are not elaborated upon in legislation, regulations or court judgments.[87] Between 1989 and February 1995, the Northern Land Council disbursed Nabalco royalty-equivalent payments to local land councils (see Table 4.2).

Gumaitj and Rirratjingu are traditional owners of clan lands in the mining lease, and Laynhapuy are also comprised of members living in areas affected by mining operations. Dhimarru comprises fourteen clans from north-eastern Arnhem Land, including Gumaitj and Rirratjingu. Principles of traditional land ownership are therefore important in allocating royalty-equivalent payments at Gove, but some 70 per cent of bauxite royalties benefit all Northern Territory land councils and all Aboriginal people living in the Northern Territory.

GROOTE EYLANDT AND BHP/GEMCO LTD, 1969 (NORTHERN TERRITORY)

Groote Eylandt, named by the Dutch as the 'Great Island', lies 50 km off the coast of Arnhem Land in the Gulf of Carpentaria (see Map 4.1). Manganiferous rocks were discovered there in 1907. Following Bureau of Minerals Resources investigations in 1961, the Church Missionary Society (which had a mission at Angurugu in the southern part of the island), took out prospecting rights on behalf of the Aborigines of Groote Eylandt over

Summary of mining company and Aboriginal community relations	
Location of mine	Groote Eylandt, Arnhem Land
Mining town	Alyangula
Name of company	GEMCO Ltd
Current parent company	BHP Ltd
Signatories	Commonwealth of Australia and GEMCO Ltd
Date of agreement	1965
Type of project	GEMCO manganese mine, Groote Eylandt
Description	GEMCO was formed in 1965 to extract manganese, and since 1970, it employed 20 to 55 Indigenous men each year. Royalties have been paid since 1969 because the mission took out a mining lease. $216m sales revenue in 1995/96.
Royalties:　statutory	Approximately 18% of profits
**　　　　　　negotiated**	1.25%
**　　　　　　(to area affected)**	2%
Royalty association	GEAT (Groote Eylandt Aboriginal Trust). Approximate membership: 1200 adults.
Scope of agreement	Royalties and encouragement of Aboriginal employment. Royalties only spent on charitable, clan and community purposes.
Aboriginal/total employment	Out of 385 GEMCO employees, 36 are Aboriginal. There are also 19 Aboriginal employees in 5 organisations which undertake GEMCO work.
Outcomes	Since 1991, significant (notionally $5600 per capita annually) in royalty-equivalents are paid to 88 extended families on Groote Eylandt. High level of investment income.
Evaluation/studies	Kauffman 1978, Turnbull 1980.
Statutory land council	Anindilyakwa Land Council.

an area of approximately 530 sq km (see Map 4.2). Agreements were subsequently entered into between the Groote Eylandt Mining Company (GEMCO, a subsidiary of BHP), and the Commonwealth of Australia under the *Northern Territory Mining Ordinance 1953*. In 1969, the Church Missionary Society decided to establish the Groote Eylandt Aboriginal Trust to receive royalties and other income, and the trust was incorporated in 1969. The beneficiaries were the major clan groups which comprised all Anindilyakwa people living on Groote Eylandt and Bickerton Island.

Since 1978, manganese has provided the ABR with almost one-third of its total income, making it the second most lucrative mineral after uranium (see Table 5.8).

EMPLOYMENT

Although the record has varied over the years, GEMCO has been one of the more significant employers of Aboriginal people at Australian mines. During the 1970s, BHP noted that Groote Eylandt was the only place in Australia where significant numbers of Aboriginal workers were employed in a mining operation. Between 1973 and 1977, some 150 Aboriginal men were employed by the company, and 120 of them were from Groote Eylandt. Between 1966 and 1977 there were 24 to 54 Aboriginal men employed by the company at any one time. Wages from mining made up some 30 per cent of the income of Aboriginal people of Angurugu, a settlement close to the mining operation. Other employment accounted for 30 per cent. Pensions and benefits comprised the other 30 per cent of income. Average per capita income was $1100 per annum, but this was increased by some 50 per cent by mining royalties.

Map 4.2   Mining on Groote Eylandt

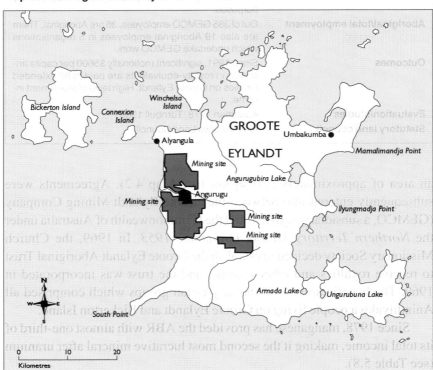

Source: ALC

Royalty-equivalent income was significant, because average Aboriginal income was so much lower than other Australians.[88]

Since 1970, GEMCO has employed 20 to 55 Indigenous people each year. In 1997, 25 of 388 employees were Aboriginal people, and some 36 Aboriginal people were directly employed by GEMCO in 1998. In addition the following five organisations employed a total of nineteen Aboriginal people in five organisations which have undertaken contract work for GEMCO. They are the Angurugu Community Government Council and the Anindilykawa Land Council, which have hired out rangers, and three other businesses.[89] The company has found that a lack of school qualifications limits employment of Indigenous people in mining, but Aboriginal people after the age of 22 have a tremendous capacity to learn. GEMCO is providing Aboriginal people with one day a week training in numeracy and literacy skills, and targeting adult education principles of on-the-job training. In

Figure 4.2   Distribution of GEMCO Ltd royalties under the *Aboriginal Land Rights (Northern Territory) Act 1976*

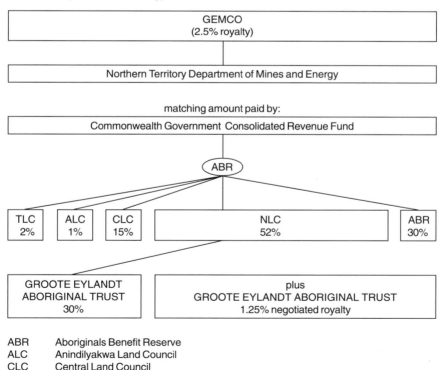

ABR	Aboriginals Benefit Reserve
ALC	Anindilyakwa Land Council
CLC	Central Land Council
NLC	Northern Land Council
TLC	Tiwi Land Council

Table 4.3 and Graph 4.2   Payments to the Aboriginals Benefit Reserve for manganese

YEAR 19–	MANGANESE GEMCO ($m)
78/79	0.570619
79/80	1.186932
80/81	1.183675
81/82	1.102482
82/83	1.189368
83/84	1.281043
84/85	1.835654
85/86	2.335442
86/87	1.963876
87/88	1.841183
88/89	1.894181
89/90	17.833539
90/91	13.907701
91/92	22.217281
92/93	7.156991
93/94	10.376888
94/95	7.950697
95/96	9.868193
96/97	10.791372
TOTAL $m	116.487117

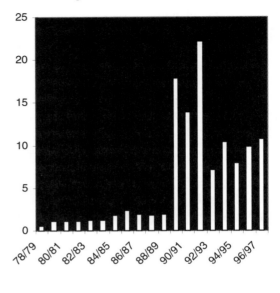

Source: ABR annual reports 1978–96, and *Hansard*, 25 November 1997

1998 GEMCO employed 36 Aboriginal people (or 9 per cent of the workforce) and nineteen other Aboriginal people were employed by organisations such as Angurugu Community Council and Henry Walker, which in turn were subcontracted by GEMCO for various tasks.[90]

ROYALTIES

As a result of the early mining agreement, 2.5 per cent of the gross value of manganese produced after deducting certain expenditures for treatment and cartage were to be paid for the benefit of Groote Eylandt Aboriginal people. GEMCO pays 2.5 per cent of the value of gross production as a statutory royalty to the Northern Territory Department of Mines and Energy. The Commonwealth Government then pays a matching amount to the ABR (see Figure 4.2). By 1978, the Groote Eylandt Aboriginal Trust (GEAT) had a net income of $719,106 a year, and net assets of $3,283,029. Between 1978 and 1982 the amount paid averaged $1.2m per annum, approximately equivalent to $1000 per person each year during this period, although these amounts are paid to extended family groups. Under the *Mineral Royalty Act 1982* (NT) royalties amount to approximately 18 per cent of profits, and are described in a formula outlined in Appendix A.

Thirty per cent of the Northern Land Council's payment is transferred to GEAT under s. 35(2) of the *Aboriginal Land Rights (Northern Territory) Act*. GEAT receives the negotiated royalty of 1.25 per cent *ad valorem* directly from GEMCO. This sum was $600,000 in 1983. Because the GEMCO agreement predates the land rights legislation, the negotiated royalty is not paid via the NLC as it would be under a s. 43 or s. 44 agreement. The effective royalty that GEAT has received is 1.25 per cent negotiated royalty plus 30 per cent of the statutory royalties paid to the Aboriginals Benefit Reserve (ABR). Total royalty-equivalents are approximately 18 per cent of profits under the *Mineral Royalty Act 1982* (NT), (see Appendix A). GEAT had an annual royalty income of some $0.95m in 1983, but has averaged over $7m per year since 1994.

The major increase in royalties occurred in 1989/90. This appears to have come about for two reasons. First, s. 63 of the *Aboriginal Land Rights (Northern Territory) Act* was amended in February 1990. The amendment required GEMCO to pay royalties for mining leases on Groote Eylandt which were granted under the *Mineral Royalty Act 1982* (NT), in addition to those leases which had been issued under the *Mining Act 1939*. Royalties were paid from 1987 onwards. Secondly, audits of GEMCO royalty returns conducted by the Department of Minerals and Energy resulted in additional amounts being paid to the Aboriginals Benefit Trust Account (now known as the ABR).[91]

Almost $120m has been paid to the ABR for manganese royalty-equivalents between 1979 and 1997 (see Table 5.8). Manganese and uranium ($144m) have provided two-thirds of the ABR's income during this period. ABR manganese royalties increased almost tenfold, to $17.8m in 1989/90. They remained high for the following two years and they have averaged some $10m per annum since 1992/93 (see Graph 4.4). The variations in payments during the past six years are recorded in Table 4.4. Total negotiated and statutory payments amounted to $9.5m in 1996/97. Notionally this was equivalent to $5600 per person, for an island population of 1700 people. The Northern Territory Supreme Court heard disputes about royalty payments between members of the communities on Groote Eylandt in 1995, and the outcome is discussed below.

The following data are from the reports of the Anindilyakwa Land Council (ALC). The ALC is the Statutory Land Council for the Groote

Table 4.4 and Graph 4.3   GEAT royalty receipts 1991–1997 ($m)

Year 19–	s. 64(1)	s. 64(3)	s. 64(7)	negotiated	total($m)
91/92	0.4	7.3	0.0	12.2	19.9
92/93	0.2	2.1	0.2	3.5	6.0
93/94	0.3	3.0	0.3	5.0	8.6
94/95	0.3	2.4	0.3	3.7	6.7
95/96	0.3	2.9	0.0	4.7	7.9
96/97	0.3	3.1	0.0	6.1	9.5

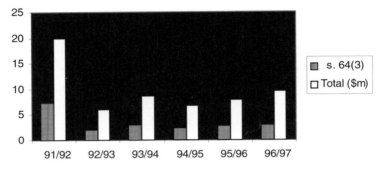

Source: Anindilyakwa Land Council annual reports 1991–97

Table 4.5 and Graph 4.4   Anindilyakwa royalty trust account 1991–97 ($m)

Year 19–	Receipts	Payments to GEAT	Payments to Amangarra	Surplus
91/92	7.3	7.4	0.0	0.0
92/93	2.1	2.1	0.0	0.0
93/94	3.0	1.8	0.0	1.2
94/95	2.4	0.6	2.9	1.2
95/96	2.9	0.7	2.2	0.0
96/97	3.2	0.0	3.2	0.0

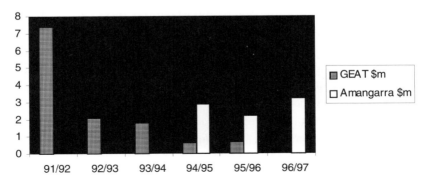

Source: Anindilyakwa Land Council annual reports 1991–97

Eylandt area and was established in July 1991. Anindilyakwa is the name of the language of the people of Groote Eylandt and Bickerton Island. The Council Chair has been Jambana Lalara since inception and it has eighteen members.

Most of the s. 64(3) payments to GEAT are now spent each year. Between 1993 and 1996, two-thirds of royalty receipts were paid to the Amangarra Aboriginal Corporation while the purposes of GEAT were litigated in the Northern Territory Supreme Court by parties on Groote Eylandt.

PURPOSES TO WHICH GEAT FUNDS MAY BE APPLIED

Initially the Church Missionary Society paid royalty payments from GEMCO to an unincorporated association known as the Groote Eylandt Trust. On 28 August 1969, the Groote Eylandt Aboriginal Trust Inc was incorporated and received all royalty payments on behalf of the trust. Clan groups listed in clause 3 of the Trust Deed of 7 March 1989 included all Anindilyakwa-speaking clans resident on Groote Eylandt and Bickerton Island who enjoyed native title rights.

During the 1970s, funds in the GEAT account were spent on community facilities such as community halls, shopping centres, education, housing and community vehicles and boats, and a substantial reserve was maintained. During the 1980s, funds were also spent on broader cultural activities, such as cultural ceremonies.

During the 1980s, a Darwin-based firm of chartered accountants determined GEAT's investment policy. In 1981/82, GEAT's non-fixed assets were held in short-term deposits (46 per cent). They were also in Commonwealth inscribed stock (28 per cent), shares in public companies (4 per cent), housing and other loans to members of GEAT (3 per cent), interest dividends and royalties receivable (11 per cent), and a loan to the Darwin Christian School Association (9 per cent). There was no investment in real estate, land or enterprises.[92] However, given that GEAT is a charitable trust and is susceptible to the risks as well as the benefits of operating businesses, this investment policy has proved sound.

In 1995, there was a dispute over the manner in which royalty payments could be disbursed. Six plaintiffs, including Jambana Lalara, Andy Mamarika and Andrew Wurramarra, took nine defendants from the Umbakumba, Angurugu and Bickerton Island communities to court. On 20 March 1996, Chief Justice Martin of the Northern Territory Supreme Court made findings concerning the GEAT Trust. He found that the Trust Deed had effect from 1965, and that there were 88 family groups that belong to the thirteen clans identified in the Trust Deed. The trust is essentially a charitable organisation. Its funds must only be spent on the education, benefit, welfare, comfort and general advancement in life of eligible Aboriginal persons. The trust funds could be used for:

- the relief of poverty;
- advancement of education;
- advancement of religion;
- other beneficial purposes, such as relief of the disabled, the aged, and advancement of Aboriginal culture.

Funds cannot be used for the benefit of a particular Aboriginal person or persons, which is not beneficial to the community. Chief Justice Martin elaborated on this finding by stating that GEAT funds could be used for medical, funeral and church purposes. They could be used for old-aged pensioner and handicapped purposes and for homeland grants, including the purchase of vehicles to move from the centres to outstations. They could also be used for education purposes, such as adult education and for sport and recreation. They could be used for Anindilyakwa Land Council purposes, including environmental and sea management courses, for the payment of power and water authority charges and for festivals and ceremonies, including the chartering of aircraft to fly people to cultural festivals, and for the purposes of the treatment of substance abuse. However, Chief Justice Martin found that trust funds could not be used for the making of loans to individuals, unless the funds advanced were adequately protected and were at commercial rates of interest.[93]

ENVIRONMENTAL CONCERNS

The settlement of Angurugu is in the middle of mining leases. Environmental issues and protection of the land are of major local concern. For instance, the Chair of the Anindilyakwa Land Council, Jambana Lalara, in his 1994 annual report said:

> Negotiations for the areas on Groote Eylandt known as the Eastern Leases continued, these were given to GEMCO by the Commonwealth Government in the 1960s before Land Rights and at a time when the Traditional Owners were ignorant to the underlying implications of mining on their land. The Eastern Leases contain two major river systems which are considered delicate areas to disturb.

The Groote Eylandt people are extremely disturbed by BHP's attitude to their land and the environmental aspects of mining. Everyone is concerned about environmental issues and GEMCO seem very slow in agreeing to intensive environmental studies. It is important that GEMCO is always aware of, and takes into full consideration, the ties of the land to its people.[94]

In 1997, Jambana Lalara reported that GEMCO was now 'listening to the wishes of the people, and are now taking a more positive approach to the subject of rehabilitation'. On the other hand, the people were concerned about the introduction and spread of exotic weeds introduced by GEMCO for rehabilitation. 'Large open cut mines encroach on the community, unhealthy levels of black dust are constantly in the air. Throughout the night, noise from mining equipment can be heard as GEMCO works their 24 hour shift, while daytime blasting is a common element of life at Angurugu.'[95] Lalara also reported that life with mining seems to have brought the problems of alcohol, drugs, gambling and petrol sniffing.

CONCLUSION

In summary, there has been significant employment of local Aboriginal people in the mining operation, compared to elsewhere in Australia.

The Groote Eylandt Aboriginal Trust has a long history of receiving significant royalties from mining. Royalty-equivalent income, particularly since 1991, has provided substantial income to Aboriginal peoples. Distribution of royalty monies has always been made to a charitable trust, and has always been distributed through clan membership on a community basis for the benefit of the total population of Groote Eylandt and nearby Bickerton Island.

The largest community of 900 people lives at Angurugu settlement which is encircled by a 24-hour mining operation. It is not surprising, therefore, that much of these funds are spent on developing outstations and outlying communities, and commuting to the seas and the lands of Groote Eylandt where the environment has not been damaged. The Anindilyakwa Land Council's annual reports since 1991 record the people's brave attempts to manage massive social and economic changes.

5 Mining agreements during the *Aboriginal Land Rights (Northern Territory) Act* era

Under the *Aboriginal Land Rights (Northern Territory) Act* (Cth), control of mining development on Aboriginal land has been conferred on the traditional owners. Aboriginal people have a 'right of veto' over mineral exploration, and miners are required to negotiate with and pay royalties to Aboriginal landowners. As discussed in Chapters 2 and 3, statutory land councils have been established under the *Aboriginal Land Rights (Northern Territory) Act* (Cth), the *Pitjantjatjara Land Rights Act 1981* (SA), and the *Aboriginal Land Rights Act 1983* (NSW). When statutory land councils have been established, there are procedures in place for negotiating exploration and mining rights on Aboriginal lands.

The most evolved arrangements for negotiating mining agreements have developed under the *Aboriginal Land Rights (Northern Territory) Act*. The Act requires that in all dealings with Aboriginal land, including mineral exploration and development, land councils must act with the consent of the traditional Aboriginal owners. They may also grant lesser interests in land, according to the conditions set out in the *Aboriginal Land Rights (Northern Territory) Act*. Since 1976 there have been many agreements made over the exploration and mining of Aboriginal lands in the Northern Territory. The Northern Territory land councils have negotiated all agreements made since 1976. The Northern Land Council, the Central Land Council and some mining companies, have gained a great deal of expertise in negotiating and making agreements with Aboriginal people.

The *Aboriginal Land Rights (Northern Territory) Act* ensures greater certainty for resource developers than if negotiations had to be arbitrated by courts. Because mining takes place, governments collect taxes. Mining increases economic activity and creates further wealth. For these reasons it has been suggested that the introduction of statutory royalty-equivalents might be a successful innovation in an amended *Native Title Act*.[96] To date this suggestion, surprisingly, has received no support.

RANGER AND ERA LTD, 1978 (NORTHERN TERRITORY)

Summary of mining company and Aboriginal community relations	
Location of mine	Ranger, western Arnhem Land, Northern Territory
Mining town	Jabiru
Name of company	ERA Ltd
Current parent company	North Ltd
Signatories	Commonwealth Government, Northern Land Council and ERA Ltd.
Date of agreement	1978
Type of project	Ranger uranium mine, western Arnhem Land
Description	Uranium mining was recommended in 1977 subject to strict environmental controls and Aboriginal ownership of Kakadu National Park. $74m profit from $230m sales revenue in 1996/97.
Royalties: statutory	4.25%
negotiated	1.75%
(to area affected)	1.275%
Royalty associations	(a) Gagudju Association. Approximate membership 300 adults.
	(b) Since July 1995, Gundjehmi Association (25 adults).
Scope of agreement	Royalties, environmental protection and monitoring, employment, training and liaison.
Aboriginal/total employment	Nineteen out of 245.
Outcomes	Since 1994, some $4.1m per annum paid in royalty-equivalents to local land councils. Local royalties used to make geared investments in major local tourist facilities.
Evaluation/studies	Levitus 1991, Lewis 1996, Altman 1996, Dodson 1997.
Statutory land council	Northern Land Council

One of Australia's largest and most controversial mining projects involves uranium in western Arnhem Land. It has also resulted in the largest financial payments to Aboriginal people from mining. The Alligator Rivers area in the Top End of the Northern Territory has proven to be a major uranium province of world importance (see Map 5.1). Jabiluka/Ranger North is an area 10 km long and 2 km wide between the East and South Alligator Rivers, which has been excised from Kakadu National Park. It is in the territory of the Gagudju people. The area contains over a third of Australia's known uranium reserves. The Ranger mine site is 22 km south of Jabiluka and

Nabarlek is 50 km north-east. Ranger is a major world producer of uranium, which commenced production in 1980 and will continue to mine until at least 2009. Nabarlek contained 10,000 tonnes of uranium oxide that has now been mined. Ranger contains some 80,000 tonnes of uranium oxide, Jabiluka some 180,000 tonnes and Koongarra some 13,000 tonnes (see Map 5.2).[97]

The Ranger Uranium Company was formed by the Peko Mines Ltd and the Electrolytic Zinc (EZ) Company of Australasia after they discovered high-grade uranium ore bodies in 1970. Peko and EZ signed the 'Lodge Agreement' with the Commonwealth on 30 October 1974, under which the Commonwealth was to keep title to uranium mined from the Ranger deposits. In July 1975, a Commission of Inquiry chaired by Justice R.W. Fox was established, and his reports of October 1976 and May 1977 recommended that mining should proceed subject to environmental safeguards, and the granting to Aboriginal people, and the leasing back to government, of the Kakadu National Park.

Map 5.1   Uranium deposits in Australia

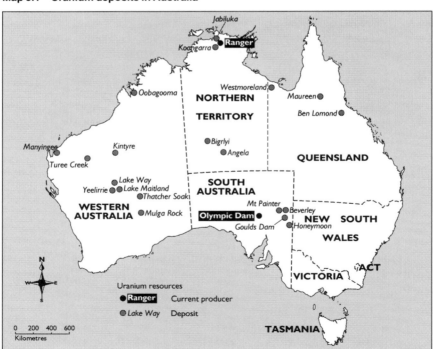

Source: Bureau of Resource Sciences

Map 5.2   Kakadu National Park, Ranger and Jawoyn land

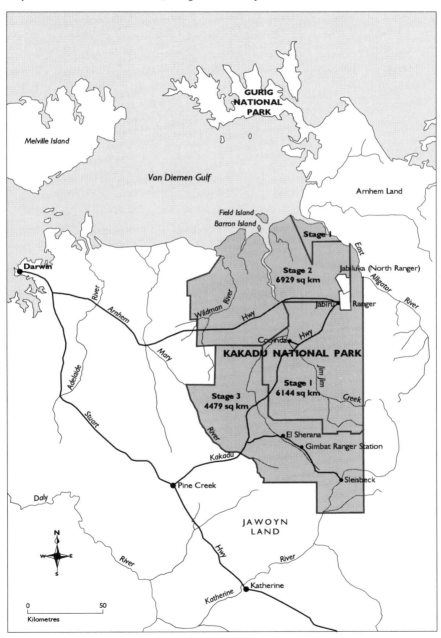

Source: Auslig ERA

In 1977, the Australian Liberal Prime Minister, Malcolm Fraser, and Deputy Prime Minister and Leader of the National Party, Doug Anthony, persuaded Galarrwuy Yunupingu and the Northern Land Council to consent to uranium mining at Ranger. If the Northern Land Council had not agreed, the Government could have obtained approval by the Governor-General making a proclamation declaring mining to be in the national interest, provided that the proclamation was passed by both Houses of Parliament. In August 1977, the Commonwealth Government approved the development of the township of Jabiru and Nabarlek uranium mine (a Queensland Mines Ltd project).

TERMS OF THE RANGER AGREEMENT

The November 1978 agreement between the Commonwealth Government and the Northern Land Council provides for rent and royalties to be paid, for environmental controls, Aboriginal employment and training, liaison between mining and Aboriginal interests, and education of mining employees about Aboriginal culture. An Aboriginal liaison committee was established comprising two representatives of Ranger and two members appointed by the Northern Land Council.

The authority to mine from the Commonwealth was granted in January 1980. ERA acquired all interests in the Ranger Project in 1980, and assumed total liability in respect of royalties. Royalties comprised 4.25 per cent of net sales revenue paid to the Commonwealth, which appropriates an equivalent amount to the ABR (see Figure 5.1). Net sales revenue comprises the value of ore extracted from the mine minus certain treatment and transportation costs. Another 1.25 per cent of net sales revenue is paid to the Commonwealth and appropriated to the Northern Territory Government. In addition, the Commonwealth levied a mining withholding tax of 5.8 per cent on the mining payment income of the ABR.[98]

The contents of the agreement have been summarised in an article by a senior public servant.[99] They cover a wide range of matters of concern to local Aboriginal people, addressing the following issues:

1.   Environmental aspects
2.   Liaison
3.   Employment and training
4.   Local business development
5.   Control of liquor
6.   Restricted areas

7. Rights of traditional owners
8. Sacred sites
9. Instruction in Aboriginal culture
10. Review of terms of agreement
11. Payments.

CONTRIBUTION OF ERA TO TOTAL ABR INCOME

Between 1981 and 1997, total royalty-equivalents for uranium mining paid to the ABR amounted to $144m, and ranged from $1.8m in 1980/81 to $14.1m in 1986/87. The royalty-equivalents included the sale of stockpiled uranium from the Nabarlek mine. On a percentage basis, uranium contributed 80 per cent of the ABR's income in 1986/87, and 7 to 28 per cent since then. For the nineteen years up to 1997, uranium royalties have contributed about 40 per cent of the ABR's income (see Graph 5.8). Royalty-equivalents are based on estimated royalty receipts for the following year, and therefore vary from Commonwealth appropriations.

The open pit mining of No.1 orebody commenced at Ranger in 1980 (see Map 5.2). Energy Resources of Australia (ERA) gained the Commonwealth and the joint venturer's interests in the project on 12 September 1980. An additional payment of $1.5m was made to traditional owners in 1981. ERA's 33 per cent shareholder, EZ, was taken over by North Broken Hill Holdings Ltd (NBH) in 1984. In 1988, NBH and Peko-Wallsend Ltd merged to form North Broken Hill Peko Ltd.[100] ERA was valued at $176m in 1989 and acquired by North Ltd, which owned 65 per cent of ERA. By 1990, Ranger and Nabarlek had a combined production of 4150 tonnes annually, valued at about $330m. In August 1991, ERA purchased the neighbouring Jabiluka Mineral Lease for $125m.

Ranger produced 4237 tonnes of uranium in 1997 (more than any previous year), and ERA now supplies 8 per cent of the western world's uranium needs. Ranger has become a major world source of uranium, and should produce until 2009. ERA's total workforce at Ranger has ranged from 167 to 406 employees, and was 233 in 1998, with minimal local Aboriginal employment. ERA's annual profit before income tax was $74m in 1997. Uranium has contributed substantially to ABR income (see Table 5.1 and Graph 5.1).[101]

ERA makes the following payments to the Commonwealth in connection with its Ranger royalty obligations:

Table 5.1 and Graph 5.1   Payments to the Aboriginals Benefit Reserve for uranium ($m)

YEAR 19–	URANIUM ERA ($m)
80/81	1.834808
81/82	2.883823
82/83	11.685890
83/84	13.541462
84/85	13.150664
85/86	13.802750
86/87	14.106926
87/88	12.427478
88/89	10.039276
89/90	9.223100
90/91	10.417118
91/92	6.983649
92/93	5.344029
93/94	4.531601
94/95	3.577281
95/96	4.669201
96/97	5.971412
TOTAL $m	144.190468

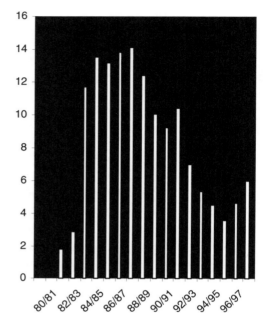

Source: ABR annual reports 1978–97

- $0.2m to the Northern Land Council;[102]
- 4.25 per cent of net sales revenue ($5.9m in 1996).[103]

In addition to payments to the ABR, ERA pays the following State royalties and environmental charges:

- 1.25 per cent of net sales revenue ($1.737m in 1996) pursuant to an agreement with the Commonwealth and the Northern Territory Government;
- 2 per cent of the payments received by ERA in respect of sales of uranium concentrates, to be credited to the Ranger Rehabilitation Trust Fund.[104]

ERA applied in 1996 to develop the Jabiluka/Ranger North mine, which is north of its Ranger mine, and submitted an Environmental Impact Statement in June 1997. The Minister for the Environment, Senator Robert Hill, announced that there did not appear to be any environmental issue that would prevent the preferred Jabiluka proposal from proceeding. ERA has consulted with the Aboriginal traditional owners.[105]

Figure 5.1   Distribution of Ranger ERA Ltd royalties under the *Aboriginal Land Rights (Northern Territory) Act 1976*

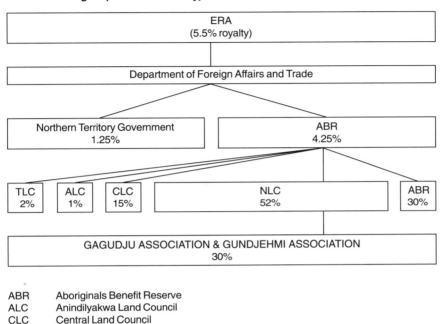

ABR   Aboriginals Benefit Reserve
ALC   Anindilyakwa Land Council
CLC   Central Land Council
NLC   Northern Land Council
TLC   Tiwi Land Council

THE GAGUDJU ASSOCIATION

The Gagudju Association was formed to receive royalty monies for mining at Ranger, but its membership has been a matter of some debate. The Kakadu region was initially defined as Stage 1 of Kakadu National Park (see Map 5.2). In 1977, the Ranger Inquiry land claim had identified 107 people as the traditional owners (by patrilineal descent) of eighteen clan territories in that area. Major community meetings were held in 1979 by the Northern Land Council, and resulted in a new census of 242 people and additional clans. The Northern Land Council field officer reported that 'the present members of the Association are all connected with the Ranger country, either through blood ties, intermarriage, clan relationship or some shared dreamings'.[106]

In 1980, 49 new members were admitted to the Gagudju Association, two-thirds of whom came from south of the Kakadu National Park. Admitting such new members was controversial, because mining royalties are known in the region as 'land money', and royalties are understood to flow to particular groups because of their ownership of particular tracts of country. Despite other adjacent groups attempting to gain membership, by the end of 1981 the composition of the association had been determined and membership had stabilised.

Since that time, the Gagudju Association has consisted of about 300 members. In 1982, about half the Aboriginal population of the Kakadu region (Stages 1 & 2) were members of the association. By 1986, this proportion had declined to 35 per cent, and it may now be slightly less because of internal Aboriginal immigration.[107]

Apart from direct payments in cash to members, housing, electricity, refrigeration, water, medical visits and food delivery were provided by the Gagudju Association on a camp basis, so that non-members living in members' camps or camps close to the mine also gained access to services. The *Aboriginal Land Rights (Northern Territory) Act* requires that royalties be paid either to traditional owners or to those who live near the area affected by the mining development.[108]

There appears to have been a long-standing concern among members of clans whose land is near the mine site that they should be better recompensed for the loss of their lands. In 1993, the Gagudju Association received $400,000 per annum as its share of the Kakadu National Park entry fee, which was then set at $8 per person. The traditional owners met and resolved that these monies should be directly distributed to eight clans, and not to the Gagudju Association. Entry fees for Kakadu National Park are now $15 per person, and entry fees paid to traditional owners have consequently increased.

In 1995, adult membership of the association totalled 240, and there were also 90 children who were members of the Gagudju Children's Trust. The association comprised both commercial and charitable purposes. There was Gagudju Association Incorporated and Gagudju Holdings Pty Ltd (Trustee), which was comprised of the Gagudju Children's Trust and the Gagudju Charitable Trust. The Charitable Trust principally involves the running of outstations. Its services include a workshop, a bus contract, a medical service, trades services and a buffalo farm.

Gagudju Enterprises Pty Ltd managed the commercial operations of Gagudju. Commercial activities include the Crocodile Hotel, which has 110 guest rooms, the Cooinda Lodge, which includes 48 lodge rooms and backpacker accommodation. They also include Yellow Water Cruises, the border store, the Mobil service station in Jabiru and the Daluk Daluk screen-printing operation. The Gagudju Association took on significant debt at commercial rates of interest in order to purchase some of these businesses. Some activities were not designed to make a profit but did have cultural significance. It has been found that the cost of (non-Aboriginal) wages and salaries has been high over recent years, in relation to the profitability of some of the enterprises.[109] A supplementary review to a 1996 study provided a general overview of the Gagudju Association's history and future options.[110]

The Gagudju Association's investment policies are in stark contrast to the Groote Eylandt Aboriginal Trust, which invested primarily in term deposits and government inscribed stock, and did not entertain bank borrowings. The Gagudju Association invested in local businesses with high visibility, and used borrowed funds. Interest on loans was high, as was the cost of employing non-Aboriginal staff. With the benefit of hindsight, a balanced investment policy might prove attractive to future royalty associations. A conservative but safe strategy would be to invest at least half of the available funds in government bonds, and, if the association wishes to do so, then invest the other half of available funds in profitable local businesses, free of debt.

It is important to bear in mind that the profitability of a business may turn on the buy-in price at which that business was obtained. Gearing is generally a much riskier strategy, and has not been adopted by other royalty associations, such as the Groote Eylandt Aboriginal Trust.

Under the 1978 agreement, Ranger royalty-equivalents paid to the ABR amount to 4.25 per cent. Ranger royalty-equivalents paid to the local land council, in this case the Gagudju Association, are 30 per cent of this amount, or 1.275 per cent of total value of production.[111] This amounted to $3.7m in 1982/83, but decreased to $2.1m in 1991/92 when the world price of uranium declined by some 30 per cent, and has remained below that level since then.[112]

In 1995, following representations from traditional owners, the Northern Land Council redirected royalty payments from the Gagudju Association to the Gundjehmi Association, which represents traditional owners near the mine site, and comprises about 10 per cent of the membership of the Gagudju Association.[113] Distributions were previously $500 per member per quarter, but in 1996 were $1000 per member every six months, and paid directly to Gundjehmi, which now has 25 members.

Jessie Alderson is the current Chair of the Gagudju Association, which received all royalties until 1995. In 1997, it paid each of its 400 members some $2000 a year, which allows many members access to social security. The Gagudju Association has invested the remainder in tourist and commercial ventures. It has also provided health, housing, education and outstation services. A report to the Kakadu Region Social Impact Study government review committee found that total payments to the Gagudju Association have amounted to $40m up to June 1997. The net value of investments in the Gagudju group had fallen from $7.9m in June 1993 to $6.2m in June 1996, and there was a deficit of $218,920 in that year.[114]

OTHER ASSOCIATIONS

Bill Neidjie is aged in his eighties and he is the senior traditional owner of Bunitj country, downstream from the Mirrar Gundjehmi extended clan. His family are pivotal to the Djabulukgu Association, which has been moderately successful in its aims to promote local small business, training and employment. It has received $68,000 per year from ERA's annual rental payment for the Jabiluka mining lease. He believes that future mining at Ranger North/Jabiluka is inevitable, and it is important that communities obtain the best possible protection in those circumstances.[115]

KAKADU REGION SOCIAL IMPACT STUDY

A major conclusion from studies of the effects of mining at Ranger is that paying royalty-equivalents is not sufficient to prevent communities suffering the ill-effects of mining operations, if other measures are not in place.

In financial terms, the Ranger uranium mine should have been the most favourable arrangement yet completed for Aboriginal people. At Ranger, as at Nabarlek uranium mine to the north, there was a comprehensive economic and social agreement made for the conduct of the mining project. However, there was a problem of implementation of the wide-ranging agreements, and academic studies suggest that many of the provisions in the agreement were not implemented.[116]

Jacqui Katona, of the Mirrar people, has told an Australian National University conference:

> There were many promises made to our people about the benefits of mining. Schools, housing, employment, health services and investments. We have no Aboriginal graduates of secondary education, housing is substandard, the vast majority of the community is unemployed, health services are minimal and those strategic investments are losing value each year. Consumption of alcohol and dependence on welfare are inescapable problems.[117]

Other Aboriginal traditional owners and journalists have publicised the detriment which their communities have suffered as a consequence of mining developments.[118] Their conclusions are supported by the reports of government committees.[119]

The Kakadu Region Social Impact Study was submitted to the Federal Government in July 1997. The Chair of the committee was Patrick Dodson.

The study concluded that Aboriginal people's socio-economic status in Kakadu may have stagnated over the past decade compared to other Northern Territory Aboriginal people. Aboriginal people at Kakadu occupy less than 8 per cent of local jobs. Few Aborigines are employed in tourism. In some years the Ranger mine has employed only one local Aboriginal person. Recently ERA has increased Aboriginal employment at Ranger, from an extremely low base. About half of all Aboriginal children aged four to eleven are enrolled at school. Housing is overcrowded, and in poor condition, and thereby creates major health risks. Alcohol is damaging the community. Aboriginal men who drink at the Jabiru and Gunbalanya (Oenpelli) sports and social clubs allegedly each consume an average of 67 cans of beer a week. According to a 1996 report on alcohol, the large scale of the Ranger mine has significantly added to the stress on local Aboriginal people. The report notes: 'Governments have been diligent when it comes to addressing environmental issues, but they have not been interested in social issues.' The company has also recently prohibited take-away sales of alcohol at the Jabiru Sports Club.[120] A survey completed in 1998 by ERA reported that nineteen of their employees (8 per cent of the workforce) were of Aboriginal descent. Most of these were not local people. A total of 45 Indigenous people were employed by the Gagudju Association and the Djabulukgu Association.[121]

It has been suggested that one way of ensuring that a comprehensive economic and social agreement for the conduct of a major mining operation is implemented, is to establish a unit charged with that task. Groups such as the Kimberley Land Council have set up monitoring units when agreements are entered into. The Northern Land Council had a uranium monitoring unit in 1979, but such units have often become diverted to more urgent tasks. A similar problem emerged following the Pancon/Koongarra agreement.

An additional problem that has emerged at Gagudju is defining the beneficiaries according to the *Aboriginal Land Rights (Northern Territory) Act*.[122] Justice Toohey noted that there is concern that the definition in the Act could lead to a relatively small number of Aboriginal people in the Northern Territory, who live in the vicinity of mining operations, receiving or benefiting from substantial sums under this section and under the mining agreement itself. The second Aboriginal Land Rights Commission report recognised the difficulty of identifying the area affected by mining operations, and recommended, as part of 'an arbitrary decision', that monies be distributed to communities within 60 km of a mineral lease. Justice Toohey noted that a mining operation may have less direct consequences and problems can arise in identifying the relevant incorporated communities and groups.[123] However, there is no simple formula for determining the appropriate recipient of royalty payments. A detailed consideration of all the facts is generally helpful, together with considering arrangements made in other areas and their outcomes.

NABARLEK AND QUEENSLAND MINES LTD, 1979 (NORTHERN TERRITORY)

TERMS OF THE NABARLEK AGREEMENT

Queensland Mines was established as a uranium exploration company in 1959. An agreement between Queensland Mines and the Northern Land Council to mine the small, rich Nabarlek deposit of western Arnhem Land was signed in March 1979, after the Ranger agreement was concluded in November 1978. Mining operations commenced in 1979 and continued for a nine-year period.

Summary of mining company and Aboriginal community relations

Location of mine	Nabarlek, western Arnhem Land, Northern Territory
Mining town	Jabiru
Name of company	Queensland Mines Ltd
Current parent company	-
Signatories	Commonwealth Government and Northern Land Council
Date of agreement	1979
Type of project	Nabarlek uranium mine
Description	Mining continued from 1979 to 1982, and the stockpile ran out in 1988. The deposit, of some 10,000 tonnes, comprised 2% U3O8.
Royalties: statutory	2.5%
negotiated	2.0%
(to area affected)	2.75%
Royalty association	Kunwinjku Association (1982–88). Approximate membership 1300 adults. Nabarlek Traditional Owners Association (1989–93). Approximate membership 100.
Scope of agreement	Royalties, environmental safeguards, training, employment and liaison.
Outcomes	Mining undertaken between 1979 and 1988. Environmental rehabilitation now completed.
Evaluation/studies	Kesteven 1983, O'Faircheallaigh 1988, Altman and Smith 1994.
Statutory land council	Northern Land Council.

With hindsight, the Nabarlek and Queensland Mines agreement and its implementation shows the importance of investing some of the funds gained from mining in long-term secure investments.

The summarised contents of the agreement between Queensland Mines and the Northern Land Council were published by a senior public servant in 1980. They relate to the following matters:

1.   Protection and rehabilitation of the environment
2.   Safety and health
3.   Liaison
4.   Employment and training
5.   Local business development
6.   Social club
7.   Permits to enter Aboriginal land
8.   Roads and buildings, etc.
9.   Payments.[124]

ESCALATING ROYALTY RATES

Aminco and Associates provided an unpublished report to the Northern Land Council on Nabarlek and uranium in Australia prior to the commencement of Ranger. The study assumed that the Australian Atomic Energy Commission would make payments to the Northern Land Council on a basis comparable to the Queensland Mines Ltd royalty, because s. 42 of the *Atomic Energy Act 1953/1966* provided for such compensation.

The Aminco study, which was undertaken on behalf of the Northern Land Council, identified that royalties should be paid by Queensland Mines Ltd in the following way:

Federal Government	2.5%	by ordinance
Stevens Estate	1.9%	by agreement
NLC Group	1.25%	by offer

The Aminco study suggested a sliding scale of royalties between 3.5 per cent and 6.8 per cent, depending on profitability.[125] This would allow for the statutory requirement of s. 50(b) of the *Northern Territory Mining Ordinance,* which requires that there be an additional 1.25 per cent royalty requirement in respect of Aboriginal reserves and this would be payable to Aboriginal people affected by the mining development. The study also found that Aboriginal working participation in the project would be a factor in determining efficiency and hence profitability.[126]

The published information on the 1979 Nabarlek agreement is that significant rent and up-front payments were included. Half of up-front moneys and rent were to be paid to traditional owners of the project area; the other half to traditional owners of the surrounding areas which would be affected by mining. There was also a statutory royalty of 2.5 per cent of production, and in addition a negotiated royalty of at least another 2 per cent. The maximum royalty-equivalent paid to the affected area was 2.75 per cent of production. These payments are illustrated in Figure 5.2.[127]

Mining commenced at Nabarlek in 1979, and 600,000 tonnes of uranium-bearing ore were stockpiled until 1982. The ore continued to be processed, while the stockpile remained, until 1988. The Nabarlek mine ceased operations in 1988, and the area was then rehabilitated. Queensland Mines Pty Ltd has been unsuccessful in locating any other uranium in the vicinity. The project lasted nine years, compared to the 30-year estimate for the Ranger mine. Royalty payments of $1.8m per annum were less than 20 per cent of the annual royalty-equivalent payments extracted from the Ranger mine. The population of the Kunwinjku Association, which received area-affected royalties between 1982 and 1987, is estimated to be some 1300 members, and average per capita payments did not exceed $1000 per annum during the life of the mine. However, the 50 traditional owners of Nabarlek did receive significant amounts of money through up-front and rental payments, and significant amounts between 1989 and 1993, when the deposit was being mined.[128]

FINANCIAL OUTCOMES OF MINING

A detailed study of the impact of Nabarlek mining moneys found that Aboriginal people of the Oenpelli area received $14m in royalties between 1979 and 1993. In Phase 1, beneficiaries who were traditional owners of the project area and of the area affected, numbering from 1200 to 1400, received $1.45m in agreement moneys. These were disbursed on cash payments and consumer goods, mainly vehicles.

In Phase 2, the Kunwinjku Association was established in January 1982 for 1300 traditional owners from Nabarlek, Aguluk and Wunyu. During the first six years (1982–87), the Kunwinjku Association received $8.3m, of which $2m was spent on vehicles and $2.8m on administration. Investments in a road contract, airline, abattoir, service station and barge incurred losses, and the Kunwinjku Association was wound up in March 1988. Over six years, the annual income of the association amounted to a notional $1.38m per annum for 1300 adult members, or $1064 each. Much less in fact was received because of the high cost of administration (34 per cent) and because investments decided upon by non-Aboriginal management failed.

In Phase 3, $1m was held in a trust account by the Northern Land Council in 1988. The Nabarlek Traditional Owners Association (NTOA) was incorporated on 5 April 1988, and received a total income of $3.3m until 1993. Membership comprised Nabarlek mine site traditional owners consisting of 49 adults and 34 children from five clan groups. In addition there was a supplementary list of 22 'gift people', that is, people who received regular cash distributions or 'gifts'. Expenditure slightly exceeded income during this period.

Of the $3.5m, $2.0m (57 per cent) was spent on vehicles and $1.0m (28 per cent) was spent on cash distributions. Expenditure was short term and oriented to consumer goods. A children's fund provided $9000 for each person when they turned eighteen years of age. This tended to be spent immediately by the recipient and their kin. Income during this period averaged $669,000 each year, or notionally $5400 per person after administration costs, which were fortunately reduced to 15 per cent.

Figure 5.2   Distribution of Queensland Mines Ltd royalties under the *Aboriginal Land Rights (Northern Territory) Act 1976*

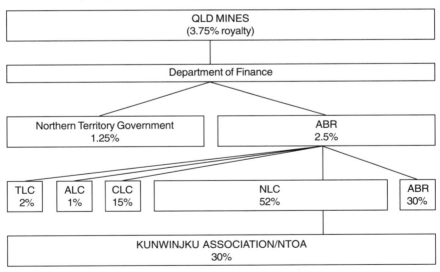

ABR   Aboriginals Benefit Reserve
ALC   Anindilyakwa Land Council
CLC   Central Land Council
NLC   Northern Land Council
TLC   Tiwi Land Council

Table 5.2 and Graph 5.2   NTOA (Nabarlek Traditional Owners Association) income and expenditure 1989–93

YEAR 19–	Income ($m)	Expend. ($m)
88/89	1.108	0.778
89/90	0.656	0.497
90/91	1.084	0.755
91/92	0.227	1.131
92/93	0.272	0.363

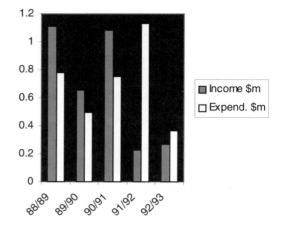

Source: Altman and Smith

Training and employment were not consistently monitored by the Northern Land Council or any other party to the Nabarlek agreement. The Nabarlek Traditional Owners Association only erratically pursued the potential economic opportunities available via the agreement.[129] Short-term investments have included purchasing vehicles, which have provided access to specialist health services, transport to ceremonies and funerals, to relatives and for hunting bush foods. However, the review found that it would have been desirable that some funds had been invested for the long term. Altman and Smith concluded their evaluation as follows:

> the current financial policy of a number of royalty associations in the Northern Territory specifies that at least 50 per cent of income must be invested. Statutory or constitutional guidelines (as found in North America and in New South Wales land rights legislation) are essential, as is expert financial advice, especially if concern exists among members about the risks associated with investment.[130]

MEREENIE AND MAGELLAN PETROLEUM AUS. LTD, 1981 (NORTHERN TERRITORY)

Further south, in Central Australia, the land is sparsely settled. Oil, gas and gold have been mined under various agreements negotiated by the Central

Summary of mining company and Aboriginal community relations	
Location of mine	Mereenie
Mining town	Fly in–fly out to Alice Springs
Name of company	Santos Ltd (65%) and Magellan Petroleum Aus.
Current parent company	Santos & Magellan Petroleum Corporation
Signatories	Central Land Council and Santos/Magellan
Date of agreement	1981
Type of project	Mereenie and Magellan Petroleum oil and gas
Description	Magellan signed an agreement in 1981 for oil and gas exploration at Mereenie. Major Northern Territory supplier. Magellan's total sales revenue was $17.5m from Mereenie in 1997.
Royalties: **statutory**	10.0%
negotiated	1.5%
(to area affected)	4.5%
Royalty association	Ngurratjuta Association (Western Arrente and Luritja people).
Scope of agreement	$0.5m up-front payment. Mining, environmental and sacred site protection and some contract employment.
Outcomes	$1.5m per annum paid in oil royalty equivalents for local land councils since 1993. 50% of local royalties invested in Alice Springs real estate etc.
Evaluation/studies	Marshall 1994.
Statutory land council	Central Land Council.

Land Council and benefiting both local communities and often small mining and oil companies as well. Gas and oil were discovered in the Amadeus Basin at Mereenie on the Haasts Bluff reserve in 1964, and at Palm Valley in 1965. The Mereenie oil field is some 120 km and the Palm Valley gas field is some 100 km west of Alice Springs, on Western Arrente and Luritja land (see Map 5.3). It is likely that gas reserves in the basin will last between 50 and 100 years. Traditional owners receive a small amount of royalties from the Mereenie and Palm Valley gas fields. The fields power Alice Springs, Darwin and the McArthur River and Mt Todd mining developments.[131]

THE MAGELLAN AGREEMENT

The Magellan agreement shows how difficult it is to accurately estimate the income from a mining venture in advance, because in this case oil production was less than one-sixth of what had been estimated on commencement. Magellan Petroleum and the Central Land Council signed the Magellan agreement for oil and gas exploration at Mereenie in 1981 under the auspices of the *Petroleum (Prospecting and Mining) Act 1978*. This Act specifies that statutory royalties for petroleum or gas production be at the rate of 10 per cent *ad valorem* (based on production), which is the same rate as specified in the *Petroleum and Mining Ordinance 1954*. The royalty rate for mining oil is higher than the royalty rate for extracting minerals to allow for the fact that production costs for oil and gas are lower compared with the costs of extracting base metals. The 1981 agreement between the Magellan consortium and the Central Land Council included an up-front payment of $500,000 which was paid to traditional owners, who are Western Arrente and Luritja people. The negotiated royalty of 1.5 per cent is *ad valorem* of the gross value of the crude oil, petroleum and natural gas produced. In addition, a statutory royalty is payable on petroleum of 10 per cent *ad valorem*.[132]

The Commonwealth has approved the agreement between the oil companies and the Central Land Council.[133]

Magellan Petroleum Australia Ltd is an Adelaide-based company chaired until 1997 by Benjamin Heath for the previous 48 years. The continuity of direction over such a long period may be a factor in Magellan conducting successful operations with Aboriginal people in the Northern Territory. Magellan Petroleum Australia Ltd is 50.66 per cent owned by the Magellan Petroleum Corporation of the United States.[134]

Mereenie field is the major source of Magellan's oil and gas production. Between 1986 and 1997, Mereenie Oil's annual oil production ranged from 0.5m to 1.2m barrels. Cumulative oil production amounted to 10.7m barrels.[135] Oil production was less than one-sixth the amount that had been estimated on commencement in 1981. Total royalties have been substantially less than was estimated in 1981. Total Aboriginals Benefit Reserve royalties were $15.5m for oil and $16.3m for gas from 1984 to 1997 (see Graphs 5.3 and 5.4). This was much less than the Department of Aboriginal Affairs estimated total royalties payable of $192m, which assumed a total production of $4m barrels of oil a year over fourteen years. [136]

THE NGURRATJUTA ASSOCIATION

The Ngurratjuta Association of the Western Aranda is one of the most successful of the royalty associations. An evaluation undertaken by a former manager of the Ngurratjuta Association described an impressive investment record despite a modest income for this organisation. However, the evaluation also found that there must be appropriate structures to manage royalty funds, and that such structures should be Aboriginal-controlled organisations with

Table 5.3 and Graph 5.3   Payments to the Aboriginals Benefit Reserve for oil ($m)

YEAR 19–	OIL MEREENIE ($m)
84/85	0.431413
85/86	2.945022
86/87	1.298878
87/88	1.105131
88/89	0.180317
89/90	0.334982
90/91	0.636943
91/92	0.470259
92/93	0.912145
93/94	1.210215
94/95	1.468019
95/96	1.701949
96/97	2.825761
TOTAL $m	15.521034

Source: ABR annual reports 1978–97, and *Hansard,* 25 November 1997

policies and guidelines on investment, distribution of royalty moneys, and saving and expenditure of the fund.

The Central Land Council established the Ngurratjuta Association in 1985. The Association receives the 30 per cent of area-affected monies payable under the *Aboriginal Land Rights (Northern Territory) Act 1976.* The Mereenie affected area stretches from Papunya to Kings Canyon, and from Iwupataka (Jay Creek) to Ilpili, west of Ntaria (Hermannsburg).

Palm Valley, on the other hand, is restricted to the area close to the south-east of Ntaria and the outstations of Ntaria which are serviced by the Tjuwanpa Resource Centre. In total the Ngurratjuta Association comprises some 70 member communities representing in all 1500 people. Negotiated payments have been made to traditional owners. Statutory royalties are paid to the Ngurratjuta Association, which has designated in its constitution that these moneys are to be spent on community purposes. The Ngurratjuta Association's management committee decided on a policy that, after deducting management expenses, 50 per cent of royalty income would be designated for long-term investment. The other 50 per cent would be paid to community trust accounts for all those living on Western Arrente and Luritja lands (see Map 5.3).

Between 1985 and 1994, principal investments included a block of flats in Alice Springs and other residential property which was used for staff housing. There was also a commercial property in Alice Springs, which housed the Ngurratjuta Association's office; Ngurratjuta Air, a small airline service; investments in shares, mortgage trusts and unit trusts; and Albert Namatjira paintings, housed at the Araluen Art Centre in Alice Springs. Mereenie area-affected income has totalled $4.47m ($372,000 per annum during this period). The impressive investment record despite a modest income can be attributed to the wisdom of the Western Arrente and Luritja people, and to the dedication of the Ngurratjuta Association's company secretary, who worked for the organisation between 1985 and 1995.[137]

Between 1996 and 1998 the Ngurratjuta Association had sold their block of flats, residential property, shares and mortgage trusts. They had $0.8m equity in a commercial investment property and undertook an urban subdivision in a joint venture. They owned three planes, including a thirteen-seater aircraft, valued at $2m, and the Glen Helen tourist resort, 130 km west of Alice Springs. Total assets amounted to $5m and total debts to $1m. Aboriginal people are employed as Chair, deputy Chair, Chief Executive Officer and Company Secretary. In March 1998, the grandchildren of the late Albert Namatjira and their relatives painted some 100 canvases of dot and landscape paintings for an art exhibition in Alice Springs. The Ngurratjuta Association's philosophy is to engage in joint ventures where their interests and security can be guaranteed, but another party with a proven track record can introduce expertise.[138]

PALM VALLEY AND MAGELLAN PETROLEUM AUS. LTD, 1982 (NORTHERN TERRITORY)

Gas was discovered in Palm Valley in 1965 (see Map 5.3). The agreement made between the Magellan consortium and the Central Land Council for Palm Valley in 1982 was similar to Mereenie, involving payment of an up-front $500,000, paid to the traditional owners, and a negotiated royalty of 1.5 per cent of the gross value of all natural gas and other petroleum products, equally distributed among 1000 traditional owners.

The Palm Valley Pipeline Agreement with the Northern Territory Government was negotiated in 1995 to cover the following 27 years.[139] It guaranteed an up-front payment of $30,000 and an annual rental of $5000, indexed to the Australian Bureau of Statistics National Consumer Price Index. Santos and Magellan signed an agreement in 1995 with the Northern Territory Government signing on behalf of that government's company

Summary of mining company and Aboriginal community relations

Location of mine	Palm Valley, central Northern Territory
Mining town	Fly in–fly out to Alice Springs
Name of company	Santos & Magellan Petroleum Aus. (51%)
Current parent company	Santos & Magellan Petroleum Corporation
Signatories	Central Land Council and Magellan/Santos
Date of agreement	1982
Type of project	Palm Valley and Magellan Petroleum gas project
Description	Magellan signed an agreement in 1982 for oil and gas exploration in Palm Valley. Major gas supplier for Alice Springs and McArthur River lead-zinc mine. Magellan's sales revenue from Palm Valley in 1997 was $8.2m.
Royalties: statutory	10.0%
negotiated	1.5%
(to area affected)	4.5%
Royalty association	Five groups of traditional owners, mainly living at Ntaria (Hermannsburg).
Scope of agreement	$0.5m up-front payment. Mining, environmental and sacred site protection. Palm Valley Pipeline Agreement covers the period from 1982–2009.
Outcomes	$1.6m per annum paid in oil royalty-equivalents for local land councils since 1993.
Evaluation/studies	Marshall 1994.
Statutory land council	Central Land Council.

Table 5.4 and Graph 5.4   Payments to the Aboriginals Benefit Reserve for gas ($m)

YEAR 19–	GAS ($m) PALM VALLEY
84/85	0.311499
85/86	0.141060
86/87	0.410292
87/88	1.050735
88/89	1.284216
89/90	1.928807
90/91	1.746840
91/92	1.795095
92/93	1.554721
93/94	1.819693
94/95	1.537341
95/96	1.300099
96/97	1.455299
TOTAL $m	16.335697

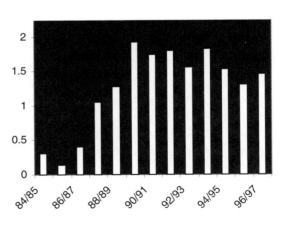

Source: ABR annual reports 1978–97, and *Hansard*, 25 November 1997

Gasgo. Gasgo will purchase 25 petajoules of gas over fifteen years in order to service the Alice Springs and McArthur River mining projects.[140]

Magellan Petroleum Australia Ltd owns Magellan Petroleum (Northern Territory) Pty Ltd. This company in turn owns 51 per cent of the Palm Valley gas field, which comprises the 615 sq km Palm Valley lease, as well as 35 per cent of the two Mereenie leases covering 281 sq km and 34 per cent of the Dingo lease covering 468 sq km. A statutory government royalty of 10 per cent of the well-head value of gas and oil is levied on each of these leases (see Appendix A). In addition, the two Mereenie leases and the Palm Valley lease are subject to overriding royalties aggregating 6.3 per cent, and the Dingo exploration licence is subject to overriding royalties aggregating 4.8 per cent. Magellan's income from the Palm Valley field was $8.2m in 1997.[141] Gas production was higher at Palm Valley than at Mereenie. However, at Mereenie, oil production has proven to be more lucrative.

ARGYLE AND RIO TINTO LTD, 1982 (WESTERN AUSTRALIA)

> Those diamonds are from the Barramundi, where it left its fat in the Dreamtime…The government should send back half of the money for the blackfella and half the money for the *kartiya* [non-Aboriginal].
>
> Jack Brittain, Kimberley traditional owner[142]

The Argyle project is located some 80 km south of the town of Kununurra, in the east Kimberley region of Western Australia (see Map 1.1). It is likely that some 3000 Aboriginal people live in Kununurra, Wyndham, Halls Creek, Warmun (Turkey Creek), Doon Doon, and Mandangala (Glen Hill). John Toby was a member of the Warmun community, whose traditional lands included the site for a diamond mine. On discovering that Conzinc Rio Tinto Australia (CRA) had commenced exploration work on his land in May 1980, he commenced legal proceedings against that company.[143]

The unwillingness of the Western Australian Government in 1978–80 to make any concessions for Aboriginal people with respect to mining on their land attracted major controversy. The controversy also encouraged the Commonwealth Government to pass the *Aboriginal and Torres Strait Islander Heritage Protection Act 1984,* which provided protection to significant Aboriginal sites. Quotes from Aboriginal people directly affected by mining relate an acute and articulate understanding of contemporary poor arrangements for sharing the potential benefits of a major world mining

Summary of mining company and Aboriginal community relations	
Location of mine	Argyle, east Kimberleys, Western Australia
Mining town	Fly in–fly out Perth
Name of company	Argyle Mining
Current parent company	Rio Tinto Ltd (60%) and Ashton Mining Ltd
Signatories	*WA Diamond (Ashton Joint Venture) Act 1981*
Date of agreement	1981
Type of project	Argyle diamond mine, Kimberleys, Western Australia
Description	Open-cut mine, producing 42m carats, or 35% of world's diamonds. Contributed $47m to Rio Tinto and $21m to Ashton's profits in 1996.
Royalties: statutory	Nil to Aboriginal people
negotiated	-
(to area affected)	-
Royalty association	-
Scope of agreement	CRA and six traditional owners, 1980. $0.4m per annum 'good neighbour' payments by CRA. Other benefits included scholarships and apprenticeships.
Aboriginal/total employment	33 out of 824 in direct Argyle employment, 60 Aboriginal people employed in businesses supported by Argyle in February 1998. By April 1998, 35 of 400 employees were Aboriginal.
Outcomes	Arrangements recognising some compensation have been negotiated, despite State legislation.
Evaluation/studies	Dillon 1991.
Native Title Representative Body	Kimberley Land Council.

development with local Indigenous people. For instance Tim Timms said: 'They could give every community everywhere something. That would be good. It would make people happy instead of going on fighting with these mining *kartiya*.' Rammel Peters said: 'The newspapers say CRA is getting $400m [from the mine]. They are going to give us something like a cigarette paper to a cigarette packet...we are asking for an extra quid so we can split it among the small [outstations] communities to level things.'[144]

An exploration program had commenced in the region in 1972. Laboratory testing in 1979 provided evidence of diamond-bearing rocks from Smoke Creek in the Kimberley region. It was subsequently found that some 49 Argyle 'pipe' structures, in which diamonds occur as a result of deep volcanic activity, cover an area of approximately 45 ha with proven ore reserves of some 61m tonnes containing 6.8 carat per tonne. Although the amount of diamond contained in the 'ore' is small, varying from one part per 100m to one part per million, the Argyle deposit is of major world significance.[145]

Sir Charles Court, then Premier of Western Australia, agreed to mining exploration in 1978 and 1980 at Noonkanbah in the Kimberley region where the Yungngora community lived south of Lake Argyle.[146] Drilling commenced at Argyle in 1980, and in 1985 Argyle Diamond Mines Pty Ltd commenced as a major mine. Mining at the current pit will continue until 2003.[147]

Argyle produces some 35 per cent of the world's diamond output. The Argyle mine contributed $47m to CRA's profits in 1996.[148] State Government policy has been that the State, rather than Aboriginal communities, would receive any royalties paid by mining companies.[149] Aboriginal people and their representative bodies, such as the Kimberley Land Council, have strongly opposed the fact that no royalty-equivalents are paid to Aboriginal land owners for mining in Western Australia.

Argyle is important as it employs Aboriginal people. In 1998, 35 of its 800-strong workforce were Aboriginal.[150] Apart from some 50 senior staff, most workers are flown in from Perth on a fourteen-day cycle, and live in a fully serviced mining compound when they are working on site. In 1994, 100 of 1006 employees were Aboriginal. Argyle was supporting the development of community-based Aboriginal enterprises at that time.[151] In 1996, 60 of 600 employees were Aboriginal.[152] In the following two years, Argyle directly employed between 33 and 36 Aboriginal people, even though the total workforce was reduced to 400 in April 1998. Argyle also supported an additional 31 Aboriginal people who worked in four businesses which have contracts with Argyle. They are the Dawun Gidja Culture Group, Wurreranginny Contractors, JNM Contracting and Warmun Plant Hire. In addition, Doon Doon Pastoral Company, Glen Hill station and Djuwarlu Store have a combined Indigenous workforce of 29, and undertake some contracting work with Argyle.[153]

THE GLEN HILL (OR ARGYLE) AGREEMENT

The main lesson of the Argyle agreement is that Aboriginal people turned nothing into something during the course of negotiations. The Glen Hill (or Argyle) agreement was negotiated in Perth in July 1980 between six Aboriginal people and the mining company CRA. The six Aboriginal people have traditional interests on Lissadell station near Lake Argyle.[154] In return for some financial payments, the Aboriginal people who signed the agreement agreed not to oppose exploration or mining of the Argyle deposits. John Toby and his close kin were paid $200,000 for the first year (1980) and $100,000 per year in following years during the mining and exploration period.[155] CRA paid financial benefits to the Mandangala community, and at a later stage to the Warmun and Doon Doon communities. In 1987, Turkey Creek's total income was probably $1,040,000, which was supplemented by $430,000 in 'good neighbour' payments from CRA. These arrangements were initially for a five-year term, and were later extended.[156]

Other benefits offered were four to six Aboriginal bursary scholarships and 25 trainee positions including apprenticeships each year. English language training was provided, and some elders were engaged in cross-cultural awareness. Aboriginal tourist projects and pastoral industries were supported, and contracts were let to the Mandangala and Wurreranginy Aboriginal Corporations. It was agreed that significant sites would be protected.[157]

Aboriginal people turned nothing into something, as they had no veto right, and later the Argyle mining venture did provide some benefits for Aboriginal people. The requirements of the *Diamond (Ashton Joint Venture) Agreement Act 1981* (WA) stated that Argyle Diamond Mines Pty Ltd must submit a document to the State Government which reported on its self-monitoring on the effects of the mine. There was no provision for consultation with the traditional owners, or for an acceptable authority such as the Western Australian Museum to undertake monitoring.

JABILUKA (RANGER NORTH) AND PANCONTINENTAL LTD, 1983 (NORTHERN TERRITORY)

Jabiluka is one of the largest uranium deposits in Australia. When built it will comprise an underground mine and complex mining infrastructure.

Although the Jabiluka/ Ranger North mine is financially lucrative, and a production-based royalty of 5.75 per cent would be the highest royalty-equivalent paid in Australia, local Aboriginal people see the social problems introduced by mining as a formidable obstacle.

The Northern Land Council, for the Aboriginal people in western Arnhem Land, and a mining company, Pancontinental Ltd initiated a third uranium mining agreement in July 1982. Following the conclusion of the agreement between the Gagudju people and the Ranger Mining consortium, the traditional owners of Jabiluka/Ranger North, represented by the Northern Land Council, began formal negotiations with Pancontinental Mining Company and reached agreement in 1983. A Labor government introduced a moratorium on new uranium mines, and Jabiluka Ranger North had not commenced production in 1998.

Summary of mining company and Aboriginal community relations	
Location of mine	Jabiluka uranium prospect
Mining town	Jabiru
Name of company	Pancontinental Ltd
Current parent company	North Ltd
Signatories	Northern Land Council and Pancontinental
Date of agreement	1983
Type of project	Jabiluka (Ranger North) uranium mine
Description	90,000 tonnes U3O8, 'the world's largest undeveloped deposit' (estimated value of $8 billion).
Royalties: statutory	2.5%
** negotiated**	2.5%
** (to area affected)**	2.2%
Royalty associations	Djabulukgu Association (80%), Gagudju (10%) Kunwinjku (10%).
Scope of agreement	ERA has commissioned an environmental impact statement.
Outcomes	-
Evaluation/studies	Levitus 1997 social impact study, and 1997 EIS.
Statutory land council	Northern Land Council.

The financial arrangements of the 1983 agreement have been published. There was to be an up-front payment of $1m on the Minister granting approval for the mine to proceed. There were to be payments of $0.8m over four years for Northern Land Council administration. An amount of $1.2m was to be paid after sale of 3000 tonnes of yellowcake per annum for the first five years of the project. As well, there was to be a payment of $1.2m per annum for three years commencing one year after the project received approval, and $3.4m on commencement of production of yellowcake.

The total production-based royalty payable by Pancontinental was to be 5.75 per cent. One and a quarter of this would be payable by the Northern Territory Government in lieu of royalties, 4 per cent would be paid to the Aboriginals Benefit Reserve, and 0.5 per cent would be paid to traditional owners of the project area. After ten years the negotiated royalty paid to traditional owners would increase to 1 per cent, providing a total royalty of 6.25 per cent.[158]

In 1983, it was estimated that $13.3m per annum would flow to Aboriginal people in the first ten years of the project, with $11.8m going to the ABR and $1.46m going to traditional owners. The amount paid to traditional owners was to increase to $2.7m after ten years. An agreement was signed that 80 per cent of agreement moneys, including negotiated royalties, would be paid to three royalty associations. The associations were the Djabulukgu Association (although only 20 per cent of their share would be spent at the discretion of the members of that association), 10 per cent was to be paid to the Gagudju Association, and 10 per cent was to be paid to the Kunwingku Association. In this way, payments would be distributed to both traditional owners and to some extent to those people living in the region of the mine.[159] Pancontinental was sold to ERA, which in turn was acquired by North Ltd in 1989.

The 1983 agreement between Pancontinental and the Northern Land Council was to be one of the highest paying royalty agreements yet concluded with Aboriginal people. Pancontinental specified in the agreement that traditional owners could only spend the money on eighteen specific functions. Many of the functions would normally be provided by government, for example sporting facilities, educational scholarships, libraries, community halls, basic utilities, water, power and sewerage, funding of Aboriginal Parks and Wildlife Services to operate in the Northern Territory, outstations, transportation systems, communications systems, group health insurance and hospitals.

THE CURRENT POSITION

Mining did not proceed in 1983 because the Federal Labor government had a moratorium on new uranium mines. The Coalition government, elected in 1996, wishes to expedite mining and initiated an environmental impact statement on mining at Jabiluka/Ranger North. According to a confidential government briefing paper which appeared in the press, ERA should not rely on the 1983 agreement between Aborigines and former leasehold Pancontinental Mining Ltd, and would need to obtain consent from traditional owners before Jabiluka could proceed.[160] A point at issue is that ERA's preferred current position is that it wishes to proceed with underground mining at Jabiluka, but it wishes to mill Jabiluka product 20 km to the north at Ranger, where it has built facilities. The Northern Land Council must make a determination as to whether ERA's current preferred position is a change in 'concept of design and operation' to that proposed under the 1982 agreement. If it is a breach of that agreement, the agreement will need to be renegotiated.[161]

Environmental and Aboriginal social impact studies have been completed for the proposed Jabiluka mine. Although the Mirrar, who are the traditional owners of the land around Jabiluka, appear to be bound by the 1982 agreement made under the *Aboriginal Land Rights (Northern Territory)*

Act, they also investigated the possibility of making a native title claim to the site, which would trigger new negotiation processes.[162]

In 1998, ERA said that although it would prefer to mill product at the Ranger mill, if permission was not granted it would build a $100m mill at Jabiluka, and that Jabiluka is expecting to be producing by the year 2000.[163]

THE VIEWS OF JABILUKA TRADITIONAL OWNERS AND ENVIRONMENTALISTS

In October 1997 the Federal Government granted approval for Jabiluka to proceed provided specified environmental standards were met. Environmental groups spent two hours at the annual general meeting of ERA raising questions, and in April 1998 commenced a protest at the mine site. They are concerned that environmental standards have been set too low. Bill Neidjie is the senior traditional owner of Bunitj country, downstream from Jabiluka. He is concerned about the possibility of low-level toxic water poisoning people and their environment in the long term. As he says, 'water might not kill now, might kill slowly, in 100 years'.[164] Yvonne Margarula, the senior traditional owner in the Mirrar Gundjehmi clan, is among many Aboriginal spokespersons who have expressed concerns about the future environmental effects, which will remain with their community indefinitely.

Moreover, her experience to date has shown that mining and the present structuring of royalty payments have exacerbated alcoholism in the community. Yvonne Margarula's father died of cirrhosis of the liver, and her only brother was stabbed to death when he tried to break up a fight involving alcohol: 'I do not want to see that happen, Jabiluka mine, same like Ranger mine, causing those problems.'[165]

THE GRANITES AND NORMANDY NORTH FLINDERS MINES LTD, 1983 (NORTHERN TERRITORY)

Goldmining has been the only major industry to develop in the remote and isolated Tanami region of the Northern Territory, 500 km north-west of Alice Springs. In 1910, large numbers of goldminers occupied the region. Pastoral leases were first established in 1924. During a severe drought, conflict between Warlpiri and pastoralists resulted in the killing of one pastoral worker on Coniston station, and reprisals in which at least 31 Warlpiri were killed in the Coniston massacres of 1928.[166]

Small-scale goldmining continued on the Tanami field until the 1950s and at the Granites until 1984. In 1977, the Warlpiri land owners lodged a

Map 5.3   Mining in central Northern Territory and Aboriginal Australia

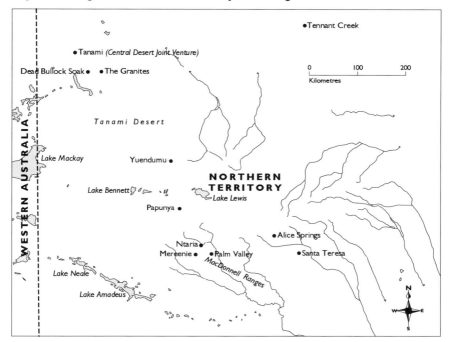

Source: Acacia Resources, Horton

claim to 290,000 sq km of the Tanami region under the *Aboriginal Land Rights (Northern Territory) Act,* and were successful in regaining title to their land. Such ownership strengthened the Warlpiri's hand in negotiating for mining on their land.

Mining presents the Warlpiri with a dilemma. It expands non-Aboriginal interests on already vulnerable communities, but it also offers scope for increased income and thereby support for outstation and homeland projects, and access to new goods and services.[167]

NORTH FLINDERS MINES

North Flinders Mines has concluded several successful agreements with Central Australian Aboriginal communities. The agreements include financial payments, protection of sacred sites, community assistance and some employment and training. Agreements have also been made with Warlpirri Aboriginal land owners north-west of Yuendumu (see Map 5.3).

Summary of mining company and Aboriginal community relations	
Location of mine	Tanami Desert
Mining town	Fly in–fly out Alice Springs
Name of company	Normandy North Flinders Mines Ltd
Current parent company	Normandy Mining Ltd (80%)
Signatories	Normandy North Flinders Mines Ltd and Central Land Council
Date of agreement	1983
Type of project	Yuendumu and North Flinders Mines goldmining
Description	Underground and open-cut gold producer which acquired the Granites tenements in 1976. $38m net profit from $138m total sales in 1997. Reserves of 1.3m ounces, mostly at Callie and Dead Bullock Soak.
Royalties: statutory	Approximately 18% of profits paid to the ABR
negotiated	1.5% of turnover
(to area affected)	1.5%
Royalty associations	Janganpa Association. Membership some 1200 adults.
Scope of agreement	Company gained secure lease over 20 sq km, and exploration licences over a further 5000 sq km, in return for royalties, protection of sacred sites, reasonable assistance to Aboriginal people, training and employment.
Outcomes	$1m to $2m per annum paid in royalty-equivalents during the 1980s to Janganpa and other royalty associations. Between 8 and 16 Aboriginal people are employed in a 200-strong workforce.
Evaluation/studies	Howitt 1991.
Statutory land council	Central Land Council.

North Flinders Mines Ltd was founded in 1969 to prospect the Flinders Ranges of South Australia, and is still Adelaide based. In 1975 it explored the Tanami region, and acquired tenements to the Granites area in 1976, prior to the Warlpiri people's successful claim under the *Aboriginal Land Rights (Northern Territory) Act*.

In 1982, North Flinders Mines commenced negotiations for a larger mining lease and a treatment area for the Granites. In 1983 it concluded negotiations with the Northern Territory Government and with the Warlpiri Aboriginal land owners to mine the Granites and its abandoned mine workings. In 1984, the company developed a small high-grade underground mining operation, and began producing gold in 1986. The major financial provisions of this agreement were:

- an initial payment of $350,000 to traditional owners;
- payments of $55,000 each six months from the commencement of gold production, plus an additional amount if the gold price exceeded $400

per ounce. Such amounts were not to exceed the equivalent of 1.5 per cent of the gross value of gold produced at the mine.[168]

In addition to financial payments, North Flinders Mines agreements with the Warlpiri included some development at Yarripirri, protection of sacred sites, provision of assistance to Aboriginal people, and some employment and training. The project proceeded as a fly in–fly out operation based in Alice Springs. Rapid development of goldmining has provided some Warlpiri with significant funds, however development has brought with it much social and economic change for the Warlpiri, with consequent disruption. In 1997 and 1998, eight to sixteen Warlpiri people (comprising between 4 and 8 per cent of the total workforce) were employed at the Granites Mines.[169]

ROYALTY-EQUIVALENTS AND OTHER PAYMENTS

Over $25m, or an average of some $2.8m each year, has been paid in goldmining royalty-equivalents to Northern Territory Aboriginal people since 1988, by way of Commonwealth transfers to the Aboriginals Benefit Reserve. Because of the structure of the Aboriginals Benefit Reserve, only 30 per cent of royalty-equivalent (s. 64(3)) payments, that is $0.74m, are paid to local land councils. If this amount is distributed to 1200 adult household heads equally, each household would receive $617.

In addition to these statutory payments to local land councils, there are negotiated payments. When received by the land council, they must be paid to an incorporated Aboriginal association.

The Janganpa Association received negotiated royalties for the first four years of operation. As shown in Table 5.5, this averaged $0.66m each year.

Table 5.5 and Graph 5.5   Janganpa Association negotiated royalties 1985–90 ($m)

YEAR 19–	JANGANPA ($m)
85/86	0.27
86/87	0.20
87/88	0.87
88/89	2.11
89/90	1.14

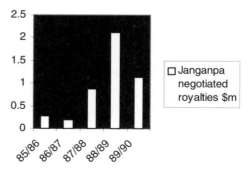

Source: Central Land Council's annual reports 1987–1989.

In the five years to June 1990, negotiated royalties paid to the Janganpa Association totalled $4.7m. Of this amount, $4m was paid out between 1985/86 and 1990/91 to the Janganpa Association and the Warlpiri Charitable Trust.

Although an average annual payment of $0.66m is significant given the poverty of the Warlpiri, it must be remembered that there have been 1200 adult traditional owners identified. If all monies were distributed equally, annual payments would only amount to $550 per adult. The Central Land Council followed Janganpa's instructions and distributed most payments to household heads. These people have many social obligations to relatives, including those who do not live in areas close to mining activities. For most people these payments give them one of their few opportunities to purchase large consumer items, such as video players, or vehicles if resources are pooled.[170]

In addition, the Warlpiri Aboriginal Corporation received some compensation for mineral exploration. Individual corporate bodies that receive funds for mining determine how to invest those funds. Since 1990, royalty-equivalent payments have been made to several Warlpiri royalty associations. But again, one can conclude that vast wealth is not being transferred to Aboriginal land owners in the Northern Territory through goldmining, and they do incur social and environmental costs for allowing mines to proceed on their lands.

MINING PROSPECTS

Following the grant of the Granites goldmining lease in 1983, North Flinders opened pit and other underground operations at the Granites, together with milling facilities. North Flinders was granted a second goldmining lease at Dead Bullock Soak, 45 km to the west, in 1991. Dead Bullock Soak contains the rich Callie deposit and is now the main source of North Flinders Mines product. Both the Granites and Dead Bullock Soak are in the Tanami Desert (see Map 5.3).

Gold produced by North Flinders Mines increased from 109,000 ounces in 1991 to 237,000 in 1997 at an average realised price of $587 per ounce. Total gold sales were $138m, and there was a profit after tax of $38m in 1997. Provision for payments made to land owners and other associated persons in that year were $2.1m, and provision for government royalties on sale of gold were $4.9m.[171] Some of the completed open cuts at the Granites will be used for the disposal of tailings. Waste rock dumps were shaped and revegetated at Dead Bullock Soak. [172]

Table 5.6 and Graph 5.6   North Flinders payments to Aboriginal land owners 1991–96

YEAR 19–	NORTH FLINDERS	s. 64(3) ($m)
91/92	0.934	0.969
92/93	1.184	1.027
93/94	1.887	1.959
94/95	1.727	2.130
95/96	1.802	1.680

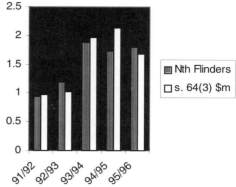

Sources: North Flinders Mines Shareholders report 1991–96; Central Land Council annual reports 1991–1996

North Flinders has a large area of exploration licences (7819 sq km) and applications (5824 sq km) on Aboriginal land.[173] North Flinders Mines Ltd signed a further agreement on 27 August 1993 in respect of six exploration licences. This added a further 3000 sq km of Aboriginal land held under exploration licences by North Flinders Mines. North Flinders Mines spent over $10m exploring on Aboriginal land in 1993–94. The *Granites Exploration Agreement Ratification Act 1994* granted North Flinders Mining the right to explore for ten years subject to certain terms and conditions.[174]

North Flinders Mines operated six exploration agreements negotiated with land owner groups and the Central Land Council, using periodic liaison

Table 5.7 and Graph 5.7   Payments to the Aboriginals Benefit Reserve for gold ($m)

YEAR 19–	GOLD ($m)
88/89	3.010186
89/90	2.243791
90/91	3.880800
91/92	0.177355
92/93	1.167096
93/94	3.904854
94/95	4.276158
95/96	1.569352
96/97	4.996010
TOTAL ($m)	25.225602

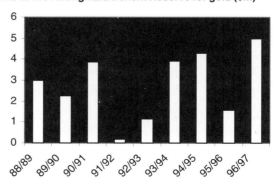

Source: ABR annual reports 1978–97, and *Hansard*, 25 November 1997

meetings to advise land owners of progress, sacred site clearances, and other approval procedures. 'As a result of exploration activities, culturally significant sites were protected, new water sources were made available; and landowners gained access to their traditional country.'[175] North Flinders' success would appear to be due to both its efficiency as a goldminer and its investment in recognising the rights and interests of Aboriginal land owners over a twenty-year period.

By 1994, the Central Land Council had successfully negotiated fourteen exploration agreements for 35 mineral exploration licences and one oil and gas exploration permit covering 40,000 sq km of Aboriginal land, with companies such as Sons of Gwalia, Zapopan, Santos, Magellan Petroleum, Otter NL/Shell Billiton. In one case, a company owned by traditional Aboriginal land owners (Kumapula Pty Ltd) has taken out exploration licences.

OTHER EXPLORATION

A Tanami joint venture with three companies, Zapopan, Kumagai Gumi and Henry & Walker, negotiated exploration over 7400 sq km in 1988. Their exploration agreement provided for protection of sacred sites, Aboriginal employment, environmental protection, control of guns and alcohol, entry permits, and restrictions on treatment plants.

The western Tanami has continued to be prospective. In December 1997, the Central Land Council and traditional owners signed five exploration agreements with Otter Gold NL, Aberfoyle Resources Ltd and Adelaide Resources NL, covering 2900 sq km. The total land covered by exploration and mining in the Northern Territory central region amounted to 83,000 sq km in 1998, and of that 35,000 sq km is currently on Aboriginal-owned land. It is therefore reasonable to conclude that the *Aboriginal Land Rights (Northern Territory) Act* has not prevented exploration and mining on Aboriginal land. In fact long-experienced observers have concluded that the Act provides an efficient model for the interaction of Aboriginal land owners and mining companies which has delivered certainty to both parties.[176]

CARE OF THE LAND

Most modern mining agreements include, at the request of Aboriginal people, references to environmental management. Printed on the letterhead of the Central Land Council is the statement in fourteen Central Australian languages, 'the land is always alive'.

The Central Land Council's submission to the Review of the *Aboriginal Land Rights (Northern Territory) Act 1976* conducted in 1998 makes clear in a vivid and practical way how Aboriginal people are concerned for the land, and how they act on those concerns. Aboriginal people care for the land for environmental and religious reasons, to protect the integrity of sacred sites and dreamings. The Central Land Council states:

> Whereas non-Aboriginal people see physical features for what they are—a hill, claypan or group of trees, traditional Aboriginal owners see the physical features as special places or sacred sites linked together by Dreaming paths. The pathways and places for a cultural map recording the routes along which Dreaming Beings travelled, the locations of events that happened along the way, and where the Beings reside today. This cultural information is recorded in different media like song, dance, designs and objects, just to mention a few.

In practical terms this means that the Warlpiri do not want the flat nature of their landscape disturbed. They want to be able to see the Dreaming paths over long distances, and want a mine to be unobtrusive. They have limited to 15 metres the height on waste dumps, and positioned them so that traditional owners can follow a line of a ridge. They ensure that larger trees or stands of trees are left around the mine. Sometimes a cultural item, such as an old dwelling or windmill, will be retained, because they recall old days when Warlpiri worked in those places. The mining company is responsible for 'cleaning up the mess' and 'putting the plants back' around a former mine.

Open pits, tailing facilities and waste dumps are important, for Warlpiri are rightly concerned that the use of cyanide in gold recovery does not pollute ground water, or poison wildlife or people in the long term. Dead birds or animals near a mine cause concern. Warlpiri have requested safety berms of 2 metres in height around some pits, and culturally appropriate signs of symbols and writing, warning of mine dangers. If a mine worker, Aboriginal or non-Aboriginal, is killed or injured from cyanide poisoning or any other cause, Warlpiri land owners are distressed. They have cultural responsibility for their land, and feel deep personal responsibility. Sometimes cyanide pellets have fallen off trucks onto roadways. Once an old Aboriginal man ate white surface crust on a tailings dam, thinking it was salt. 'A miner grabbed him by the ankles and swung him around and around until he vomited.' The story is told in a humorous way, but with a serious concern. Aboriginal people now have a 'collective wisdom' about the poisonous nature of cyanide tailings, which is likely to remain long after the mines have closed.[177]

YUENDUMU MINING COMPANY

The Yuendumu Mining Company is the first Aboriginal-owned mining company. It was originally set up for the purpose of employing local people in finding and exploiting copper and wolfram deposits in the Yuendumu and Mt Doreen area. Large numbers of Aboriginal people were employed in prospecting in early years.

The Yuendumu Mining Company's directors comprise Warlpiri Aborigines living at Yuendumu, a settlement 300 km south-east of the Granites. It was formed in 1969 and has 300 Aboriginal shareholders and a small number of non-Aboriginal people who are long-term residents of Yuendumu. Harry Nelson Jakamarra, a director of the company, and Darby Ross Jampijimpa, a traditional owner of the Tanami area concerned, are currently involved in an exploration venture.

Perceived benefits from mining and increasing aspirations for self-management led to the Yuendumu Mining Company taking out two mining exploration licences to explore for gold in 1996. Recently it has formed joint ventures with Normandy Mining Ltd. A second agreement undertook exploration in partnership with Posgold. Together, the agreements cover 2400 sq km of the Tanami Desert. The company also successfully operates a store, a workshop and earth-moving contracts.[178]

The Yuendumu Mining Company's exploration arm currently employs two Aboriginal people in a joint venture with Normandy Mining Ltd. They are hired out as field hands to other mining and exploration operators. On occasions, teams of four Aboriginal people have been hired out for periods of up to four months. Staff of the Yuendumu Mining Company believe that an effective education system will improve employment prospects. Other prerequisites for greater Aboriginal employment at mine sites include accommodation for families, and a mentoring system for Aboriginal employees.

An associate of the company has published on Aboriginal employment in mining. He found that it is more likely for Aboriginal people of Central Australia to be employed in exploration than in mining. Because of a communal lifestyle and pooling of resources, and a welfare support system, money is necessary and sought after, but not necessarily associated with a work ethic. Aboriginal people employed in exploration are intelligent and seek escape from the boredom of settlement life. Some take on work for friendship for the people they are working with. Cultural and ceremonial business sometimes must be accommodated in a work program. Skills are usually picked up quickly if the purpose behind the skills is explained. Nearly all young men have better geographic, directional and observational skills than non-Aboriginal people. Incentives such as Aboriginal pride and prestige should be taken into account in work programs. Older people should be included in any consultations and encouraged in their 'vision'. A pool of employees to draw from at different times is far more practicable than expecting regular employees. Aboriginal people will set greater store in personal relationships than in job responsibilities. Organisations have sometimes successfully hired young Aboriginal workers and also employed two senior men who had traditional links with the area being explored. The key to a successful program is building relationships between company staff and Aboriginal employees.[179]

CONCLUSIONS

The Yuendumu Mining Company's conclusion that relationships between company staff and Aboriginal communities are important also holds true for the two companies that are currently mining in Central Australia, North Flinders and Normandy Mining Ltd.

Goldmining under the *Aboriginal Land Rights (Northern Territory) Act* at the Granites, in the western Tanami Desert of Central Australia, has occurred since 1984. Under their agreement with North Flinders Mines the Warlpiri gained protection of sacred sites, provision of some assistance and some employment and training. Several factors can be attributed to North Flinders Mines' accessibility to Aboriginal people. The company is Adelaide based, and has been dealing with Central Australian people for over twenty years. It prides itself on being courteous and fair in its dealings with land owners. Payments to land owners amount to about 1.4 per cent of total receipts, in addition to royalties that amount to 3.4 per cent of total receipts.

Trevor Ireland, General Manager of North Flinders Mines, has publicly supported Aboriginal land rights. In his address to the Mineral Council of Australia, he said:

> the *Aboriginal Land Rights (Northern Territory) Act* has delivered genuine protection of landowners' cultural interests, and significant economic benefits to them, at some cost to the industry. This accommodation of landowner interests is long overdue in this country, is consistent with the spirit of reconciliation, and accords with majority public opinion in Australia in the 1990s.[180]

In 1991, Normandy Mining Ltd purchased 49 per cent of North Flinders Mines, and increased this to an 80 per cent interest in 1998. Normandy's

Graph 5.8 Payments to the Aboriginals Benefit Reserve for all minerals (1996/97) ($m)

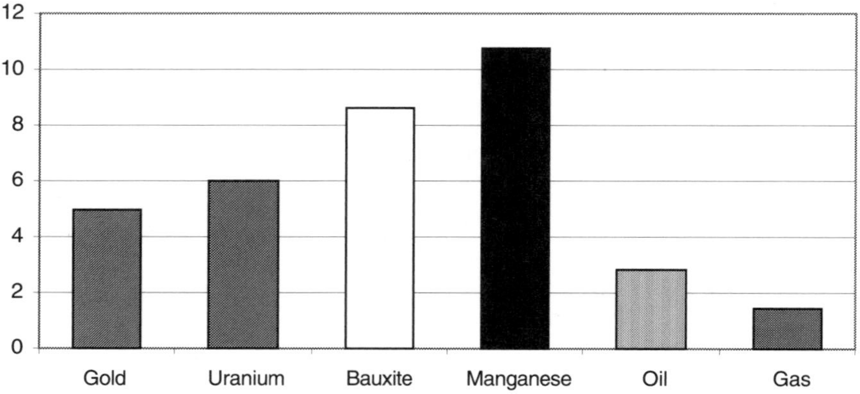

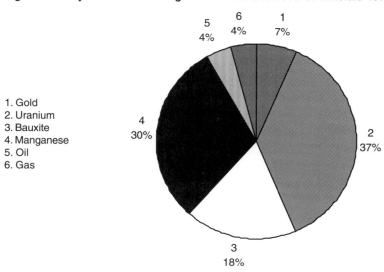

12
10
8
6
4
2
0
Gold
Uranium
Bauxite
Manganese
Oil
Gas

Source: ABR annual reports 1978–97, and *Hansard*, 25 November 1997

head office is also in Adelaide, and it also prides itself on establishing a special relationship with Aboriginal people and joint development of appropriate programs. Normandy's employment and training programs at Woodcutters near Darwin, and at Tennant Creek, some 500 km east of the Granites, are discussed in Chapter 6.[181]

Figure 5.3 Payments to the Aboriginals Benefit Reserve for all minerals 1978–97

1. Gold
2. Uranium
3. Bauxite
4. Manganese
5. Oil
6. Gas
1
7%
2
37%
3
18%
4
30%
5
4%
6
4%

Source: ABR annual reports 1978–97, and *Hansard*, 25 November 1997

Table 5.8   Payments to the Aboriginals Benefit Reserve for all minerals 1978–97 ($m)

YEAR 19–	GOLD (NTH FLINDERS)	URANIUM (ERA)	BAUXITE (NABALCO)	MANGANESE (GEMCO)	OIL (MEREENIE)	GAS (PALM VALLEY)	TOTAL
78/79			0.565201	0.570619			1.135820
79/80			0.897140	1.186932			2.084072
80/81		1.834808	1.079469	1.183675			4.097952
81/82		2.883823	1.798773	1.102482			5.785078
82/83		11.685890	4.736264	1.189368			17.611522
83/84		13.541462	2.241494	1.281043			17.063999
84/85		13.150664	2.377959	1.835654	0.431413	0.311499	18.107189
85/86		13.802750	2.320873	2.335442	2.945022	0.141060	21.545147
86/87		14.106928	2.123290	1.963876	1.298878	0.410292	19.903262
87/88		12.427476	2.383395	1.841183	1.105131	1.050735	18.807922
88/89	3.010186	10.039276	2.420480	1.894181	0.180317	1.284216	18.828656
89/90	2.243791	9.223100	2.738117	17.833539	0.334982	1.928807	34.302336
90/91	3.880800	10.417118	2.686177	13.907701	0.636943	1.746840	33.275579
91/92	0.177355	6.983649	2.488092	22.217281	0.470259	1.795095	34.131731
92/93	1.167096	5.344029	2.454671	7.156991	0.912145	1.554721	18.589653
93/94	3.904854	4.531601	10.452868	10.376888	1.210215	1.819693	32.296119
94/95	4.276158	3.577281	9.899198	7.950697	1.468019	1.537341	28.708694
95/96	1.569352	4.669201	7.393211	9.868193	1.701949	1.300099	26.502005
96/97	4.996010	5.971412	8.631664	10.791372	2.825761	1.455299	34.671518
TOTAL $m	25.225602	144.190468	69.688336	116.487117	15.521034	16.335697	387.448254

Source: ABR annual reports 1978–97, and *Hansard*, 25 November 1997

SHARING THE NORTHERN TERRITORY'S MINERAL RESOURCES

The *Aboriginal Land Rights (Northern Territory) Act* has provided a model for an efficient and fair interaction between Aboriginal land owners and mining companies. The Central Land Council has concluded that:

> A delicate balance currently exists between traditional Aboriginal owners' rights to enjoy their land and control access, as against the needs of the mining industry for security and certainty of access to land for the discovery and development of resources. On Aboriginal land the mining industry gets the certainty it desires to enable it to secure the level of investment it requires. Aboriginal people get recognition, control and benefits from mining on their land where they choose to participate.[182]

It is only in the Northern Territory, and then only since 1976, that mineral royalty-equivalents of any note have been paid to Aboriginal land owners in Australia. On a current annual basis, manganese and bauxite are greater providers of wealth than uranium. Gold, oil and gas provide a little over $1m a year each. Uranium has provided the largest amount (37 per cent) of payments to the Aboriginals Benefit Reserve during the past twenty years. The second largest source of payments has been manganese (30 per cent). This is followed by bauxite (18 per cent), with gold (7 per cent), oil (4 per cent) and gas (4 per cent) of less importance (see Figure 5.3).

Although the moneys paid in royalty-equivalents are significant, and welcome, they have not solved the poverty of the great majority of Northern Territory Aboriginal people. And compared with North America and New Zealand, there has not been a dramatic increase in the training and employment skills of many Aboriginal people in most locations. Some Aboriginal people have gained skills, training and jobs at Mt Todd, near Katherine, at Tennant Creek and at the Central Desert Joint Venture in the Tanami Desert. In the Pilbara, Western Australia and Hopevale, North Queensland a significant number of Aboriginal people have gained training and employment in mining ventures.[183] The lessons for the future, taking into account overseas experience, would seem to point to the benefit of negotiating an agreement which provides specific details of a comprehensive package of benefits. The benefits should empower an Aboriginal community faced with a major mining development on their lands, so that they can gain the complex range of skills which are necessary if that community is to benefit from that development. The sorts of measures which have worked, in certain instances in Australia, and in North America and New Zealand, are discussed in Chapter 8.

HOPEVALE COMMUNITY AND MITSUBISHI LTD, 1992 (QUEENSLAND)

The *Aboriginal Land Rights (Northern Territory) Act 1976* provided substantial benefits which allowed Northern Territory Aboriginal people to negotiate with mining companies after 1976. A stronger agreement was negotiated for the benefit of Aboriginal people in Hopevale, Queensland, with the assistance of negotiators who had worked in the Northern Territory and overseas. Negotiations conducted by the Hopevale community mark a new era of native title. Cape Flattery is 50 km from Hopevale, on the eastern side of Cape York Peninsula, 200 km north of Cairns. A Lutheran mission was established at Hopevale in 1886. Under the *Community Services (Aborigines) Act 1984* Hopevale became a Deed of Grant in Trust (DOGIT) community with a self-managing community council.

Summary of mining company and Aboriginal community relations	
Location of mine	Cape Flattery Silica Mine
Mining town	Fly in–fly out Cairns
Name of company	Mitsubishi Australia Ltd
Current parent company	Mitsubishi Japan Ltd
Signatories	Queensland Government and Mitsubishi Australia.
Date of agreement	1992
Type of project	CFSM (Mitsubishi) silica mine near Hopevale
Description	Silica mine operating since 1970 which required renewal of lease in 1990.
Royalties: statutory	Queensland Government
negotiated	Production-based royalty of 3%
(to area affected)	3%
Royalty association	Hopevale Community Council
Scope of agreement	Production-based royalty, some training, employment and occupational health provisions negotiated on renewal.
Outcomes	Training and employment, including management roles.
	46 out of 104 employees were Indigenous in 1998. 'The mine is part of the community.'
Evaluation/studies	O'Faircheallaigh 1995; O'Faircheallaigh and Holden 1995.
Native Title Representative Body	Cape York Land Council.

The Hopevale negotiations provide some guidelines on how to negotiate successfully with an Aboriginal community, and on helpful models of organisational support. Cape Flattery Silica Mines (CFSM) is 100 per cent owned by the Mitsubishi Corporation of Japan, and has operated a silica mine at Cape Flattery since 1970. By 1990, CFSM needed an additional lease to support its operation, as its existing leases were due for renewal.

Under Queensland's *Mineral Resources Act 1989*, mining leases cannot be granted over Deed of Grant in Trust land without the consent of the Aboriginal trustees of the land or the Governor-in-Council. If there is no agreement, the matter is arbitrated by the Mining Warden. Dr C. O'Faircheallaigh was engaged by the community council to assist in negotiating an agreement with CFSM, and the project team interviewed half the adult population of Hopevale, as well as using community television. Three young people from the community assisted in gathering information for the negotiations. They submitted a report to the community council and set out the record of mining impacts. The results were drawn on in negotiations with Mitsubishi.

Formal public meetings were not used much for negotiating purposes as they screened out the elderly, women and teenagers. The contribution of these groups to decisions is very important. However, it was found that public meetings are essential if time is limited. The current style of many community meetings with officials and companies involves non-Indigenous people spending half an hour providing technical information. The response is often silence, then a few speakers from the community just talk about their special interests. It was found that three one-hour meetings over a period of at least two or three days is far preferable.

During the course of O'Faircheallaigh's study, information was obtained for an environmental data base, including information on Mitsubishi's 2400 subsidiaries, information of tonnage of sand sold, and the profitability worldwide of these operations.

Although equality of negotiating positions is probably impossible, it is fairer if an Aboriginal community has basic information and at least some access to expert advice. However, such support is expensive. There was no Queensland Government assistance for Aboriginal people with mining negotiations until Environmental Safeguards Impact Assessments were partly funded in 1993, by means of $2000 per negotiation. Since 1992, ATSIC has allocated significant funds to the Cape York Land Council for the prosecution of native title claims and negotiating mining agreements. The mining company CFSM also provided funds for Hopevale to conduct negotiations, which enabled the community to employ a legal adviser. Often there are several sets of negotiations, covering various areas, which are required to complete an agreement. Time may be a valuable resource, and it was used at Hopevale to secure an agreement from CFSM. It was found to be particularly valuable if there is an institutional structure, such as:

1. a regional land council;
2. a community land council;
3. a private law firm.

The advantage of a regional land council is that it guarantees a sufficiently large range of skills and specialised staff to accumulate expertise. Some mining companies in the past have asserted that regional land councils are 'inefficient' or that they 'get in the way of an agreement'. In fact it was found at Hopevale that they were of tremendous assistance to Aboriginal people involved in negotiation. However, it is important to have clear communication with advisers. A coherent negotiating team is needed; it must have good rapport, internally with its own members, and externally with community members, governments and mining company officials.

At Cape Flattery, three people in the community and three people in the company formed a monitoring unit. The company paid a set amount each year for monitoring the implementation of the agreement. There is a wide variety of agreements and processes are needed for brokering them.

The 1992 agreement between Hopevale Council and CFSM provided the following benefits.

Royalties

Under pre-1992 compensation arrangements, Hopevale residents received a *profit-based* royalty which yielded little and sometimes no income because of transfer-pricing arrangements between Mitsubishi and its subsidiaries.[184] Under the 1992 agreement, it was agreed that a *production-based* royalty of 3 per cent was to be provided by Cape Flattery Silica Mines to the Hopevale Community Council. In 1995, the Hopevale Community Council received $600,000 per annum mining royalties from Mitsubishi; 200,000 tonnes of material were expected to be extracted each year for the next 100 years from the Cape Flattery area.[185]

Employment and occupational health

Aboriginal people have undertaken many of the mining and milling jobs in the past. Under the new agreement, these opportunities were extended, and there was an emphasis on the employment of Hopevale women, as none had been employed up to 1992. An Aboriginal liaison officer was appointed to implement agreed recruitment procedures. There were regular X-ray checks to monitor the effect of silica dust on employees.

Accommodation

Sometimes concessions that have a small financial cost can be of particular significance to Aboriginal workers. For instance, the company agreed to renovate some dilapidated accommodation at the mine site, so that families could visit local workers employed there.

Training

The 1992 agreement extends training and employment provisions to local Aboriginal people, and provides for two apprenticeships a year for four years, after which eight apprentices will be maintained permanently. It provides for college or university bursaries. Training programs were also provided to enable Hopevale residents to attain senior management positions.

OBJECTIONS TO THE AGREEMENT

During the early phase of native title, differences between groups emerged at Hopevale. This was particularly the case for traditional land owners who wished to assert their rights over 'historical' peoples who had moved into Hopevale since the mission was established in the nineteenth century. For instance in 1994, Gordon Charlie of the Dingaal clan lodged a native title claim over Cape Flattery and Lizard Island. This is the site of the mine, and this claim was accepted for adjudication. The area of the claim was 300 sq km. Stan Darkan, a traditional owner of the Hopevale township site, lodged a claim on behalf of the Dhubbi-Warra clan for land around the township and this was also accepted for adjudication. Dhubbi-Warra consider that some seven of the major clan groupings at Hopevale are traditional, and another thirteen are 'historical', having migrated to the former mission settlement during the past 70 years. The Cape York Land Council has mediated differences between various Hopevale groups. The determinations arising from native title claims in North Queensland, such as with CFSM at Hopevale and Alcan north of Weipa (Chapter 7), will influence native title agreements made in other parts of Australia.

HOPEVALE'S SUCCESS

O'Faircheallaigh and Holden provide a detailed account of the economic and social impact of mining and its historical context. They note that Aboriginal people at Hopevale perceive the mine as theirs. There have been a series of strategies over many years to make the mine successful in Aboriginal terms. Aboriginal role models are important. There were Aboriginal supervisors involved from an early period. The technology for the mine has evolved gradually. For ten years after 1981 Aboriginal employment ranged from 25 to 36 in a total workforce of 59 to 84.[186]

The Cape Flattery Silica Mines now employs between 46 and 49 Aboriginal employees, and is now the highest direct employer of Aboriginal people of any mining operation in Australia. In percentage terms, its success is even more noteworthy, for about 45 per cent of the total workforce are Aboriginal people. The company attributes this success to having a very close relationship with the community for some 30 years, and in fact, to the mine 'being part of the community'. All employees, including Aboriginal people, work 55 hours over eight days, then rest at Hopevale for six days. Hopevale is 160 km away by road, but travel is by aircraft, and takes eleven minutes. About 30 per cent of supervisors, 75 per cent of mine mill workers and 50 per cent of wharf workers are Aboriginal people. All employees have three to four days of training each year, with literacy and numeracy development incorporated into it. It is planned to convert to school-based curriculum in Cooktown. There is low turnover among Aboriginal staff; the average period of employment is four years. An Aboriginal employee retired in 1998 after 25 years service. Cape Flattery Silicon Mine management are in demand as speakers to mining and Aboriginal groups.[187] The series of strategies implemented at Hopevale's mining venture has been influential in developing the Napranum and Alcan agreement signed in 1997, and discussed in Chapter 7.

6 Post-Mabo mining agreements 1993–1996

The *Mabo (2)* High Court judgment in 1992 did not refer to mining, as there is no mining on Murray Island. It did, however, introduce native title into common law in Australia. All Australians now know that Indigenous peoples are 'entitled as against the whole world to possession, occupation, use and enjoyment of their lands'. Following this judgment there was a more helpful environment to encourage mining companies to make agreements with Indigenous people, if they had not already done so under the *Aboriginal Land Rights (Northern Territory) Act.*

In the four years following the *Mabo (2)* judgment, at least eight agreements were made over the exploration and mining of land subject to native title claim in the Northern Territory, Western Australia and South Australia. Native Title Representative Bodies have rapidly gained expertise in negotiating and making agreements which will provide some benefits to Aboriginal people from a mining project.

Since the passage of the *Native Title Act*, resource developers have increasingly recognised that native title parties are not anti-development. With the incentive of returns from commercial activity on land that might have native title over it determined, Indigenous people have often been pro-development. Indigenous interests are increasingly accepting that the expectations of profits are a prerequisite for investment. Through their Native Title Representative Bodies they are seeking a fair share of those profits. Creative forms of joint venturing under a native title regime have already occurred with native title stakeholders, for example with tourism in the Cairns region, real-estate development in Broome and mining contracts at Mt Todd and McArthur River. The 'right to negotiate' provisions of the current *Native Title Act* are in fact less confrontationist than the more powerful de facto property rights contained in a 'right of veto' or 'right of consent' available under the *Aboriginal Land Rights (Northern Territory) Act.*

THE JAWOYN AND ZAPOPAN LTD, 1993 (NORTHERN TERRITORY)[188]

The Jawoyn people came to national prominence when they protested against mining in Coronation Hill in the Northern Territory, and obtained Federal Government agreement not to mine at that site. Since then, one of the most comprehensive agreements has been made by the Jawoyn people for mining on their land near Katherine, south of Kakadu National Park in the Northern Territory (see Map 5.2). It does not involve royalties and has been operating to the satisfaction of both traditional owners and mining companies managing the project.

When Zapopan NL undertook exploration for gold on Jawoyn land in 1991 and 1992, the Jawoyn were keen to ensure that appropriate agreements could be negotiated. Following *Mabo (2),* the Jawoyn Association convened a meeting between Zapopan and the Commonwealth and Northern Territory Governments, and said it would lodge a native title claim unless local Aboriginal people were given substantial benefits from any mining project, specifically jobs and land.

Summary of mining company and Aboriginal community relations	
Location of mine	Mt Todd, Northern Territory (Top End)
Mining town	Commute to Katherine
Name of company	Zapopan Ltd
Current owner	Pegasus Ltd (USA) (in receivership)
Signatories	Jawoyn Zapopan and Northern Territory Government
Date of agreement	1993
Type of project	Goldmine of low-grade ore
Description	Open-pit extraction between 1993 and 1997
Royalties: statutory	Approximately 18% of profits paid to Northern Territory Government
negotiated (to area affected)	Nil royalties paid to Aboriginal people -
Community association	Jawoyn Association and traditional land owning clans
Scope of agreement	Various titles to land and other cultural, employment, training and housing benefits
Outcomes	Jawoyn gained 4,360 sq km land, $1m of housing, and employment and training. In 1995, Aboriginal people comprised 27% of the workforce. In 1997, 43 of 327 employees were Aboriginal people. Non-Aboriginal employees undertook cross-cultural training.
Evaluation/studies	Altman 1994.
Statutory land council	Northern Land Council.

THE 15 JANUARY 1993 AGREEMENT BETWEEN JAWOYN, ZAPOPAN AND THE NORTHERN TERRITORY GOVERNMENT

Under the Mt Todd agreement, which was signed on 15 January 1993, the Jawoyn gained Northern Territory title to land, with no mineral rights, and title to Eva Valley pastoral lease, which is now Aboriginal land under the *Aboriginal Land Rights (Northern Territory) Act 1976*. John Ah Kit was Director of the Northern Land Council in 1983-90, and Executive Officer of the Jawoyn Association in 1993. He negotiated with Zapopan NL Mining Company in the Northern Territory. The Northern Territory Government also signed the agreement. John Ah Kit described in detail how the Jawoyn negotiated their agreement:

> Christmas 1992, we heard on the grapevine that there were going to be licences issued to Zapopan NL, and we wrote quickly after having our meeting with the executive to the Prime Minister and the Minister for Aboriginal Affairs and gave them forewarning that, if they weren't to come and sit down at the table about the Mt Todd negotiations, that we'd see them in court. That action prompted them to get to the table very quickly, and we began the process of working out what the Jawoyn wanted to reach from this agreement—if an agreement was to be put in place...

John Ah Kit noted that the Jawoyn leadership consulted the traditional owners on a weekly basis during the negotiations with governments. He continued:

> We've had no luck with the Commonwealth Government in the negotiations about environmental standards and we feel that we were let down there. But the things that we managed to get out of the agreement were: the land claim that was over Eva Valley Station on Jawoyn country where we have the tourism—we managed to get 2800 sq km coming back to us as Commonwealth inalienable freehold title, not Northern Territory freehold. That way, we skirted around running a land claim and going through all those heartaches of taking people out bush and proving their country. They tried to sell us on Northern Territory freehold. We wouldn't accept it. So I think that, in itself, is a precedent that people should be mindful of—if you've got something that you wish to develop, and in turn some Government is looking for some positive response from you, then a precedent in that area certainly has been set.
>
> We were able to get other areas round Mt Todd and Mt Todd itself back under Northern Territory freehold title. We were able to stitch up most of our land tenure problems. We felt that if we don't secure our

land needs and get titles, then obviously it's going to be harder to develop economic enterprises.

If people wish to start developments on Aboriginal land, especially with Jawoyn, we certainly appreciate them writing to us with well-thought-out and documented proposals. Then we can begin the negotiation process. If we think they are not genuine, then we turn them away very quickly.

I think Mabo's just the foot in the door and we're on our way. It's taken a long time, but we'll get there because, I believe, time's on our side. Governments need to realise that we've been around for a long time and we're not in a hurry to go away. This is our country.[189]

The Jawoyn had played a major role in halting the Coronation Hill development. This emphasises the importance of the agreement for Mt Todd, where mining did proceed as part of a comprehensive agreement on Aboriginal terms. The agreement was criticised because royalties or environmental protection, although sought, were not provided, and because most of the benefits are provided by governments, and may have been provided irrespective of mining development.[190]

A closer examination five years later reveals that there was environmental protection, and the Jawoyn were particularly astute in structuring land benefits and other businesses so that if the mine ceased production, it would not affect other assets gained by the Jawoyn.

The benefits of the agreement can be listed under a number of headings.

Land

Title to Werenbun/Barnjarn (1368 sq km) as Northern Territory freehold, and title to Eva Valley pastoral lease (2926 sq km), as Aboriginal freehold under the *Aboriginal Land Rights (Northern Territory) Act* were transferred to Jawoyn people. Title to Catfish Dreaming (2 ha) and the Conservation Land Corporation Block (803 sq km) were also transferred to Jawoyn people.

Environment

Zapopan were required to recognise Jawoyn attachment to their land, in the planning, development and decommissioning of the mine, including sacred site avoidance. The company has provided written undertakings that it will operate according to environmental guidelines contained in Mineral Leases.

Culture

Zapopan undertook to design work practices to allow Aboriginal employees to carry out cultural obligations, and ensured all non-Aboriginal staff undertook cross-cultural training. The Conservation Commission of the Northern Territory agreed to contract cultural advice from the Jawoyn Association and pay the association $30,000 per annum for these services.

Employment and training

Zapopan undertook to employ an Aboriginal employment and training officer at the Jawoyn Association. Five other Aboriginal people filled initially designated positions at Zapopan, which also established an employment and training committee, to identify local employment opportunities for Jawoyn. By 1995, Jawoyn comprised 27 per cent of the workforce. This dropped to 13 per cent (43 out of 327) in 1997. The mine closed in November 1997.

Non-Aboriginal employees of Jawoyn were obliged to participate in a cross-cultural training and education program developed in consultation with the Jawoyn Association.

Housing

The Northern Territory Government undertook to fund housing, water, and power for Werenbun outstation, which is just south of Mt Todd project. The Jawoyn gained $1m worth of housing and water supplies for Jawoyn people.

Tourism

The Jawoyn gained $60,000 for capital works for tourist accommodation at nearby Eva Valley station. The Nitmiluk Visitor Centre was transferred to the Jawoyn Association, which was contracted to provide cultural advice at the centre. Annual rent paid to the Jawoyn for Nitmiluk National Park lands increased from $115,000 to $140,000.

CONCLUSION

There was positive press coverage of the 1993 and 1996 agreements. Aboriginal employment was particularly emphasised at Mt Todd. Whereas in the Northern Territory mining industry in general, about 4 per cent of the workforce were reportedly Indigenous, at Mt Todd it ranged up to 32 per cent.[191] The lesson from the initiatives of the Jawoyn appear to be that both financial capital and human capital are necessary for regional economic development. Active Indigenous participation is necessary in resource development, and the Jawoyn have provided a model of how this can be achieved.[192]

Zapopan was purchased in full in 1995 by Pegasus Inc of the United States, a company that specialises in extracting gold from low-grade deposits.[193] Following a decline in world gold prices, the Pegasus Mt Todd Goldmine closed at the end of 1997.[194] The Jawoyn did not have a stake in the Mt Todd goldmine. The closure of Mt Todd has affected them, but not in direct financial ways as they had structured their businesses so that the closure of the mine would not affect the assets they hold elsewhere.

As it was, they gained ownership of some 5097 sq km of land, housing, water, and economic opportunities from tourist, employment and training ventures. The Jawoyn example seems to reinforce the need for comprehensive, well-thought-out mining agreements and good corporate and tax advice. Without training, education and skills, mining royalty-equivalents by themselves are not enough. Aboriginal people are justifiably proud of the outcome, as John Ah Kit makes clear.

OTHER JAWOYN BUSINESS JOINT VENTURES

The Jawoyn have created other local economic opportunities for Aboriginal people, particularly in tourism, contract mining and mining exploration. Since the negotiation of their agreement with Zapopan, the Jawoyn have formed an exploration company which is prospecting south of Coronation Hill. Jawoyn is involved, through Barnjarn Mining Company, with two joint venture exploration projects with Northern Gold and Pegasus Australia. Joint ventures also exist with a number of other companies. On 3 September 1996, the Jawoyn Association signed a joint venture agreement with the Henry Walker group and the Aboriginal and Torres Strait Islander Commercial Development Corporation to undertake contract mining. Aboriginal interests are represented by the Mirrkworlk Joint Venture, which is owned 50 per cent by the finance company Henry Walker, 25 per cent by ATSIC's Commercial Development Corporation, and 25 per cent by the Jawoyn's Gunyilli Mining Company. The Jawoyn share of $10m in capital is being funded though a fully commercial loan from the Commercial Development Corporation.[195]

THE JAWOYN PHILOSOPHY

The Jawoyn leader, John Ah Kit, further identified the Jawoyn approach in a speech he gave to the Committee for the Economic Development for Australia, in which he said in part:

> What is not recognised by business leaders is that Aboriginal leaders have shareholders that must be accommodated, and whose futures must be assured before they will agree to decisions that will affect their lives and those of their children. In a very real sense, I believe Zapopan recognised that, and the results can be seen in Jawoyn dealings with the Mt Todd mine since the agreements signing.
>
> Firstly, the interests of business and Aboriginal people are reconcilable where there is a genuine commitment on both sides to sit down and talk as equals, resolve potential conflicts, and develop arrangements that are mutually beneficial...
>
> Second, the interests of business and Aboriginal people can be mutual. All of us—Aboriginal and non-Aboriginal—have much the same concerns for a secure economic future for ourselves and our children. There are enormous opportunities waiting for all of us to do business. Aboriginal people are just as keen to talk constructively about such opportunities as the next person and we know the benefits of commercial cooperation.
>
> Finally, Aboriginal people must be capitalised so they can take up their role in the broader economy.
>
> For many Aboriginal people, this involves the return of a land base.
>
> Those who oppose the establishment of the Land Acquisition Fund might do well to consider what the Jawoyn people have achieved in a very short time through the land base they won back through both the land claim and native title processses. The Jawoyn have been able to begin along the road to establishing an Aboriginal-controlled capital base, building employment, and investing in the future for their people.[196]

GURDANDJI (McARTHUR RIVER) AND COMMONWEALTH GOVERNMENT, 1994 (NORTHERN TERRITORY)

North of Katherine, on the Gulf of Carpentaria, there has been another major mining agreement (see Map 4.1). The Commonwealth Government

Summary of mining company and Aboriginal community relations	
Location of mine	McArthur River
Mining town	Commute to Katherine
Name of company	McArthur Joint Venture
Current parent company	MIM Holdings Ltd (70%), ANT (Japan) (30%)
Signatories	Gurdandji-Binbinga, Northern Land Council and Commonwealth Government.
Date of agreement	1994.
Type of project	McArthur River lead, zinc, silver mine.
Description	Large lead zinc mine, planned to generate $250m a year.
Royalties: statutory	Nil to ABR
negotiated	-
(to area affected)	-
Royalty association	-
Scope of agreement	Pastoral property gained by Commonwealth grant. MIM awarded commercial contract work to local Aboriginal people in joint venture arrangement.
Outcomes	Commercial opportunities. Joint ventures with Burns Philp and ATSICDC.
Evaluation/studies	-
Statutory land council	Northern Land Council.

played a leading role in bringing parties together, although in the event neither MIM (Mount Isa Mines) Holdings Ltd nor the Northern Territory Government were a signatory to the agreement.

McArthur River at Borroloola, some 720 km south-east of Darwin, has one of the world's largest zinc, lead and silver deposits. Minerals were discovered there in 1955 in the territory of the Binbinga, which is intersected by McArthur River and the township of Borroloola. The principal reason why development did not occur until 40 years after discovery was that MIM did not develop the use of fine-grinding for minerals until 1990. Following the development of new extraction methods by MIM in 1990, a mining development received Commonwealth and Territory government approval in 1992.

The mine was officially opened on 6 September 1995 and it was estimated that it should be in production for twenty years.[197] Zinc, lead and silver were permitted to be mined there despite concerns of Aboriginal people that, although the project is not located on land owned by Aboriginal people under Australian law, there would be effects from the mine on their society and country. Up to 1.5m tonnes of ore will be extracted annually from the underground mine, to produce 350,000 tonnes of concentrate containing 160,000 tonnes of zinc, 45,000 tonnes of lead and 1.6m ounces of silver.

The McArthur River Mining joint venture is 70 per cent owned by MIM Ltd and ANT Minerals own the balance.[198] It was estimated that the mine would generate $200m to $300m a year in export revenue. It is managed by McArthur River Mining Pty Ltd, which is a wholly owned subsidiary of MIM Holdings Ltd.

Although neither the port nor the mine areas are on land owned by Aboriginal people under the *Aboriginal Land Rights (Northern Territory) Act,* MIM was keen to secure the agreement of Aboriginal people to the development. During 1993 the Northern Land Council and the Gurdandji traditional owners attempted to negotiate an agreement for mineral development with MIM.

THE MARCH 1994 GURDANDJI AND MIM AGREEMENT

The Gurdandji-Binbinga, who are the traditional landowners of the port and mine area of this mineral deposit on McArthur River station, entered into an agreement with the Northern Land Council and the Commonwealth Government in March 1994. It essentially comprised the purchase of some lands and a barge contract.

The agreement ensured the purchase of Bauhinia Downs station by the Commonwealth, for the benefit of the Gurdandji people. In return, the Commonwealth received assurances that Anyula-Mara and Gurdandji native title holders would not seek compensation from the Commonwealth for the issue of title by the Northern Territory Government to the mining company for the port and mine site area. However, local people have not withdrawn native title claims to off-shore islands.[199]

The Commonwealth also agreed to provide the funds for training employees at the mine. Under the agreement, some economic opportunities will also be provided at McArthur River to the Gurdandji-Binbinga.

Just as for the Jawoyn at Mt Todd, agreement for the purchase or transfer of land has led to other commercial opportunities for the Gurdandji of Borroloola. Subsequent to the 1994 agreement, MIM awarded a contract to barge McArthur River mine concentrates, on a commercial basis, to a joint venture established by Burns Philp Shipping and the Aboriginal and Torres Strait Islander Commercial Development Corporation (ATSICDC). ATSICDC agreed to progressively transfer its interests to local Aboriginal people. By 1995, four local Aboriginal communities held 25 per cent equity in the barge-loading facility at the Bing Bong port, 120 km from McArthur River. Other Aboriginal interests owned an additional 25 per cent through ATSICDC. Burns Philp owns the balance of the barge-loading facility.[200]

The then Prime Minister, the Hon Paul Keating, and the Northern Territory Chief Minister, the Hon Shane Stone, opened the mine on 6 September 1995. They praised the co-operation between MIM, local Aboriginal land owners, State and Territory governments, Japanese investors and environmental interests. One of the elders, Harvey Musso, described the arrangements in these words: 'We had a bit of trouble with our people, a bit of trouble with the Europeans…but ultimately this is good not only for me but for my grandchildren.'[201]

In October 1995 the Northern Land Council noted that Bauhinia Downs pastoral property was handed back to the traditional owners. But this was through the initiative of the Federal Government, at no cost to either MIM or to the McArthur River mine. The Northern Land Council also noted that a request for a 50 sq km excision of the McArthur River station covering traditional burial grounds near the old homestead was declined.[202]

The MIM 1997 annual report notes that production began slowly, as low-yielding stockpiled development material was processed first. The zinc–lead–silver mine incurred a loss in the first year of operation, and MIM is considering a range of efficiencies in mining and processing operations. Its annual report states that its commitment to the environment has been maintained through the construction phase and into operations. MIM owns 70 per cent of the McArthur River mine, which is producing a substantial amount of silver, with marginal profitability at the present time.[203]

TANAMI AND ACACIA RESOURCES AND OTTER EXPLORATION LTD, 1995 (NORTHERN TERRITORY)

Aboriginal people have been involved in the Tanami goldmines since early this century, but it is only since the advent of the Aboriginal Land Rights (Northern Territory) Act that we have been able to participate on an equitable basis in the development of mining on our own land.

Tracker Tilmouth, Chair, CLC[204]

The Tanami goldmines are in the central Northern Territory, 100 km from the Western Australia border. Aboriginal people have been involved in these mines for many years. On 22 September 1995 they made an agreement which they considered would provide some equitable basis for their own participation. This agreement was between the Central Land Council and Aboriginal traditional owners on the one hand, and the Central Desert Joint

Summary of mining company and Aboriginal community relations	
Location of mine	Tanami goldmine
Mining town	Fly in–fly out to Alice Springs or Darwin
Name of company	Acacia Resources Ltd and Otter Gold NL
Current parent company	-
Signatories	Central Land Council, Acacia Resources and Otter
Date of agreement	1995
Type of project	Tanami goldmine, Central Australia
Description	Open cut and underground goldmine
Royalties: statutory	Approximately 18% of profits paid to ABR
negotiated	1.5%
(to area affected)	1.5%
Royalty association	Central Desert Land Trust
Scope of agreement	Royalty payments, environmental safeguards, protection of sacred sites and compensation.
Outcomes	Tanami Aboriginal Training and Employment Strategy. 38 Aboriginal people employed in workforce of 190.
Evaluation/studies	-
Statutory land council	Central Land Council.

Venturer on the other. The Central Desert Joint Venturer consists of Mineral Resources (NZ) Ltd, through its subsidiary Otter Exploration (60 per cent), and Acacia Resources Ltd. The Central Desert Joint Venturer undertook to restart goldmining in the Tanami Desert and develop a new mine at Redback Rise, which is some 50 km north of the Dead Bullock Soak mine which is operated by Normandy North Flinders Ltd (see Map 5.3).

It was expected that 100,000 ounces of gold a year would be processed from a million tonnes mined from six pits at Redback Rise, which would commence mining in 1996, and continue for two and a half years. In fact 235,000 ounces of gold were mined in the first two years. The agreement involves royalty payments and also covers environmental safeguards, compensation and the protection of culturally significant sites. The Director of the Central Land Council announced that the agreement would allow Aboriginal people to gain benefits of training and long-term employment, including long-haul trucking operations.[205] The Central Desert Joint Venturer was committed to employing Aboriginal people at all levels of skill. It would also give preference to sub-contractors who make provision for Aboriginal training and employment. It was envisaged that in the long term Aboriginal organisations would have the experience and skilled workforce to compete for contracts in catering, road and vehicle maintenance, haulage, air services and mining-related activities.[206]

An innovative feature of the 1995 agreement was the Tanami Aboriginal Training and Employment Strategy, negotiated to provide Aboriginal people with employment at the mine and the mine contractors. Approximately 25 per cent of the workforce on the Tanami Mine in 1995 were Central Australian Aboriginal people working in various positions, including milling, surveying, exploration, administration, trades, trade work, geology and catering. A cross-cultural course for mine employees was conducted in 1996. The Central Land Council believes that this project is one of the best examples of maximising employment and financial advantages in the Northern Territory.[207] In 1996, the Tanami Mine Joint Venturer workforce numbered 174, and about 35 employees (20 per cent) were Aboriginal. In 1997, 38 of the workforce of 190 were Aboriginal.[208] The Tanami Aboriginal Training and Employment Strategy is supported by the Commonwealth Department of Employment, Education, Training and Youth Assistance (DEETYA). DEETYA's assistance, administered from State and Territory capital cities, has proved useful for mentoring and pre-vocational course subsidies, which include thirteen-week courses organised by the Central Land Council covering such areas as occupational health and safety, literacy and numeracy.

THE NORMANDY MINING GROUP AT WOODCUTTERS AND TENNANT CREEK, 1995 (NORTHERN TERRITORY)

I congratulate Normandy Mining for its positive attitude.

Galarrwuy Yunupingu, Chair, NLC[209]

The Normandy Mining Group, which was founded in 1985 and produces 1.5m ounces of gold a year, is the largest producer of gold in Australia and is ranked fourth in the world outside South Africa by production. The Executive Chair is Robert J. Champion de Crespigny, who is a member of the Council for Aboriginal Reconciliation.[210]

The Normandy Group is also Australia's largest producer of industrial minerals and an active explorer. Normandy Mining owns 80 per cent of North Flinders Mines, which as noted in Chapter 5, focuses on the Northern Territory.[211] In addition, Normandy Mining has a 100 per cent interest in Woodcutters mine in the Northern Territory, which produces zinc and lead products.

Woodcutters zinc and lead mine is located 85 km from Darwin on land held by the Warai and Kungarakan people. It is situated partly on Finniss River Land Trust land granted in 1993. Because the mine predated the

Summary of mining company and Aboriginal community relations	
Location of mine	Woodcutters mine
Mining town	Commute to Darwin, 100 km north
Name of company	Normandy Mining Ltd
Current parent company	Normandy Mining Ltd
Signatories	Normandy Mining Ltd and Northern Land Council
Date of agreement	1995
Type of project	Normandy lead and zinc mine at Woodcutters.
Description	Long-established mine on Aboriginal land.
Royalties: statutory	Approximately 18% of profits to Northern Territory Government
negotiated	1.5%
(to area affected)	-
Royalty association	-
Scope of agreement	Financial compensation, environmental protection, training and employment.
Outcomes	2 to 5 Aboriginal people employed in workforce of 180
Evaluation/studies	-
Statutory land council	Northern Land Council.

restoration of title to the land, there was no legal requirement on behalf of Normandy Mining to make payments to the current land owners. The company, however, approached the Northern Land Council and proposed a 'good neighbour' agreement, which includes compensation, environmental protection, employment and training.

NORMANDY MINING LTD AT WOODCUTTERS AND TENNANT CREEK

Normandy Mining negotiated an arrangement to provide compensation, environmental protection and employment and training opportunities at Woodcutters. The Woodcutters mine is located on vacant Crown land but is surrounded by land owned by Aboriginal land-holders. Normandy has agreed to return the mine leases to the traditional owners at the conclusion of operations.

The final agreement was concluded in July 1995 between the Finniss River Land Trust, the Northern Land Council and Normandy Mining. The agreement included an ongoing quarterly financial payment based on production and the price of base metal concentrates, environmental protection, and employment and training opportunities. In return, the traditional owners agreed to withhold making a native title claim over the mining site. The agreement also referred to the transfer of mining fixtures, such as buildings on site, the establishment of a liaison committee, a dispute resolution mechanism, protection of sacred sites and communication. In 1997 and 1998, there have been two to five local Aboriginal people employed in the mine's workforce of 180 people.[212]

Normandy's approach at Woodcutters of encouraging developments acceptable to Aboriginal people is part of a consistent company policy. The company's approach is to gain the trust and co-operation of Aboriginal communities and make a contribution to Aboriginal development that is durable and beneficial. To this end a program of cross-cultural awareness training was established in 1996.[213]

TENNANT CREEK

Normandy has implemented Indigenous affairs policies in its Tennant Creek project. Peko Ltd originally operated the Tennant Creek goldmine. The Normandy Mining Group has operated the mine through its subsidiary PosGold Ltd for some years in a post-Mabo environment, and has successfully increased positive Aboriginal involvement in the mining project.

It has provided some support to the Julalikari Resource Centre, worked with the Central Land Council as representatives of the Warramungu land owners, and developed a pre-vocational and employment strategy. The company has offered contracts for clean-up and rehabilitation work, and

---

Summary of mining company and Aboriginal community relations

Location of mine	Near Tennant Creek, central Northern Territory
Town	Tennant Creek
Name of company	PosGold Ltd
Current parent company	Normandy Mining Ltd
Description	Long-established goldmine on Aboriginal land.
Royalties: statutory	Approximately 18% of profits to Northern Territory Government
negotiated	1.5%
(to area affected)	-
Scope of arrangement	Environmental protection, training and employment.
Outcomes	34 Aboriginal people employed in workforce of 340.
Evaluation/studies	-
Statutory land council	Central Land Council.

sponsored some business development. It has conducted mine site tours for community members. It has been successful in increasing the number of Aboriginal people employed at the mine site from seven in 1992, to nine in 1995 (2 per cent of workforce) to between 31 and 34 people (10 per cent of workforce) in 1997 and 1998. The site was aiming for high (30 per cent) Indigenous employment by 1999, but this target may be difficult to achieve in the context of a depressed gold price.[214]

ST VIDGEON AND RIO TINTO LTD, 1995 (NORTHERN TERRITORY)

Ngukurr (Roper River) flows into the Gulf of Carpentaria, 180 km north-west of the McArthur River (see Map 4.1). The Wandarang, Marra, Alawa and Ngalakan people of St Vidgeon station near Ngukurr lodged their native title application in September 1994, and it was accepted by the National Native Title Tribunal in December 1994. The claim was over land and waters extending inland from the mouth of the Roper River in the Gulf of Carpentaria.

THE ST VIDGEON AGREEMENT

The native title claimants and CRA Ltd, which has now merged with its parent Rio Tinto Ltd, concluded an agreement with various benefits. The negotiations were undertaken outside the framework of the *Native Title Act* because the native title holders of the land have not yet been established within the processes of the *Native Title Act 1993*. CRA suggested that the *Native Title Act* should be amended to improve the procedures whereby such agreements are later validated, and to protect a mining company that has reasonable grounds for believing that it has negotiated with all native title holders.[215]

CRA Exploration Ltd has exploration licences in the area and negotiated a land access agreement regardless of any subsequent determination on native title status. An innovative feature of the agreement was its special undertakings and indemnity. CRA agreed not to take any action detrimental to the claimants' case with regard to the native title application. In return, the claimants agreed not to challenge the validity of any future grant of exploration licences to Rio Tinto under the *Northern Territory Mining Act*, for the duration of the agreement. The validity of the agreement was not

Summary of mining company and Aboriginal community relations	
Location of mine	St Vidgeon's pastoral property
Mining town	Fly to Darwin
Name of company	Rio Tinto Ltd
Current parent company	-
Signatories	Rio Tinto Ltd and Northern Land Council
Date of agreement	1995
Type of project	Rio Tinto Ltd exploration base metals
Description	Potential lead/ zinc/ copper mine
Royalties: statutory	Approximately 18% of profits to Northern Territory Government
negotiated	-
(to area affected)	-
Scope of agreement	Rio Tinto Ltd to pay 5% of exploration costs to community development.
Outcomes	-
Evaluation/studies	-
Statutory land council	Northern Land Council.

dependent on any future finding regarding the existence of native title or otherwise. The claimants agreed to indemnify Rio Tinto against any loss, expense, damage, or other cost arising from any action by the claimants which was inconsistent with the provisions of the deed that formalised the agreement.

The agreement comprised the following major elements: community benefits, the establishment of a liaison committee, protection of the environment and sacred sites, compensation, training in exploration, and reimbursement of representative body expenses. Employment opportunities were included, and training for two community members over a five-year period. Rio Tinto agreed to pay 5 per cent of exploration costs to the people at Ngukurr for the purpose of community development. Community 'Mine Agreement' negotiation costs are met by CRA Exploration Ltd in advance, and will be deducted from future benefits, if a working mine is established.[216]

Both Rio Tinto's Chief Executive, Leon Davis, and the Northern Land Council, welcomed the exploration agreement, which they described as a 'land-mark'.[217] Normandy Mining Ltd's Indigenous Affairs officer, Noel Bridge, has used the Woodcutters and St Vidgeon agreements to provide a schematic list of issues for mineral exploration, which is summarised in Chapter 8.

ANANGU PITJANTJATJARA AND NAYLOR INGRAM LTD, 1996 (SOUTH AUSTRALIA)

Anangu Pitjantjatjara is the body corporate which vests Pitjantjatjara people with 103,000 sq km of land in the north-west of South Australia (see Map 1.2). Although only an exploration agreement, the 1996 agreement provides a model which might be followed elsewhere in Australia. In February 1996, it was announced that Naylor Ingram Ltd of South Australia had agreed to pay 1.5 to 2.5 per cent *ad valorem* (based on production) of all exploration costs to the Anangu Pitjantjatjara people. In addition, a negotiated royalty on a sliding scale of between 1 and 3 per cent has also been agreed upon for petroleum exploration and production. Naylor Ingram would also provide a buy-in option of 10 per cent of a production joint venture on pro-rata payment of exploration expenditure.[218]

In addition to the negotiated royalty, the South Australian legislation provides that one-third of State Government royalties on Anangu Pitjantjatjara and Maralinga Tjarutja lands are paid to those two statutory Aboriginal organisations. A further one-third of State Government royalties are paid to the Minister for State for Aboriginal Affairs, to be spent on Aboriginal purposes in that State.[219]

Anangu Pitjantjatjara have also successfully concluded exploration agreements with Delta Gold and UAL Ltd since 1996. Generally a number of Aboriginal men and women are employed in clearance work and ensure that sacred sites are protected. Both parties have signed conjunctive agreements, which cover both exploration and mining. The mining companies purchase supplies from community stores.[220]

CAREY MINING AND ACACIA RESOURCES LTD, 1996 (WESTERN AUSTRALIA)

Acacia Resources owns 40 per cent of the Tanami Mine Joint Venturer. As discussed in Chapter 5, the Tanami Mine Joint Venturer is successfully training and employing Aboriginal people in the centre of the Northern Territory. Acacia is also the sole owner of the Sunrise Dam Goldmine, which commenced operation in 1997. Sunrise Dam is 55 km south of Laverton, about 250 km north-east of Kalgoorlie in the Goldfields area of Western Australia (see Map 1.2). The Goldfields Land Council is the Native Title Representative Body for the area around Kalgoorlie, Western Australia. Agreements brokered by Goldfields Land Council areas are discussed in Chapter 7.

Summary of mining company and Aboriginal community relations

Location of mine	Goldfields
Mining town	Laverton
Name of company	Acacia Resources Ltd
Signatories	Acacia Resources Ltd and Carey Mining Ltd
Date of agreement	1996
Type of project	Open cut goldmine
Description	3m ounces of gold available
Royalties: statutory	-
negotiated	-
(to area affected)	Various benefits negotiated with the company.
Royalty association	Nguludharra-Waljen Foundation.
Scope of agreement	Contract work for local Aboriginal businesses. Jobs targeted to local communities.
Outcomes	Cross-cultural training provided. Training for Aboriginal people developed at Laverton. 5 Aboriginal people employed in workforce of 170, and 50 other Aboriginal people employed in associated businesses.
Evaluation/studies	-
Native Title Representative Body	Goldfields Land Council.

The Sunrise Dam Goldmine was one of the first new mines developed under *Native Title Act* processes. The Tucker family, as the Nguludharra-Waljen, and two other claimant groups lodged native title claims over mining leases, and Acacia Resources entered into an agreement with them. The agreement provided payment for each of the three groups to establish administrative services. It provided opportunities for Aboriginal groups to provide contract services such as rehabilitation and earthworks. A rental fee was also paid to each claimant group. All site employees would also undertake a cultural awareness program.[221]

The Aboriginal-owned company, Carey Mining Ltd, has secured a 25 per cent interest in a joint venture which will have a total capital cost of $50m. Carey Mining is composed of the Tucker family, whose Nguludharra-Waljen native title claim was accepted by the National Native Title Tribunal in October 1996. Carey Mining negotiated with Acacia Resources Ltd, and agreed that Acacia Resources could proceed to mine the area. Carey Mining Ltd is a minority partner with AWP contractors, which are a subsidiary of CSR Ltd. It was planned that the joint venture would employ 70 people, and ten of these would be Aboriginal. AWP contractors manage the Acacia goldmining venture. Total employees increased from 150 to 170 in 1997 and 1998, and Aboriginal staff decreased from ten to five persons. The

Aboriginal businesses Carey Mining, Burrna Yurral Aboriginal Corporation and Amos Incorporated employed an estimated 50 Aboriginal people in February 1998.[222]

Acacia has 1200 sq km of exploration licences in the Laverton area. The commitments made to local Aboriginal people and native title claimants were honoured, opportunities for contract work created, cross-cultural education arranged and a co-operative educational and training school was started.[223] It was hoped that the Acacia mine would produce 100,000 ounces of gold a year by 1997, with cash costs below $300 an ounce.[224] In fact, Acacia produced 54,000 ounces of gold between July and December 1997, at costs of $137 an ounce, compared to the industry average of $350 an ounce.[225]

MURRIN MURRIN AND ANACONDA NICKEL LTD, 1996 (WESTERN AUSTRALIA)

Summary of mining company and Aboriginal community relations

Location of mine	Goldfields
Mining town	Kalgoorlie
Name of company	Anaconda Nickel Ltd
Signatories	Anaconda Nickel Ltd and Glencore International Ltd
Date of agreement	November 1996 (16 parties), 3 April 1997 (2 parties)
Type of project	Murrin Murrin and Anaconda nickel/cobalt project.
Description	Large nickel/cobalt project of $900m over 30 years.
Royalties: statutory	-
negotiated	-
(to area affected)	Various benefits negotiated with the company.
Royalty association	North East Goldfields Wongutha Bunna Foundation.
Scope of agreement	$1m to a trust for Aboriginal businesses. 20 per cent of jobs targeted to local communities. Contracts were allocated to Aboriginal construction firms. Anaconda Nickel awarded commercial contract work to local Aborigines.
Outcomes	56 Aboriginal people employed in workforce of 800.
Evaluation/studies	-
Native Title Representative Body	Goldfields Land Council.

The Murrin Murrin project shows how a regional agreement with all Aboriginal native title claimants can be successfully established after negotiation. It involves a $900m nickel and cobalt mine in the Goldfields area of Western Australia.

Agreement was reached with the relevant native title claimants, although obtaining agreement from all groups involved did take some time, and various provisional arrangements were considered then dropped. Consultations commenced in 1995, and on 4 July 1996, Leo Thomas of the Waljen people of Kalgoorlie, and Andrew Forrest of Anaconda Nickel, announced that native title claims had been traded for future mining revenues. Anaconda announced that it would proceed with a $900m nickel and cobalt project between Leonora and Laverton, and would fund a foundation for local Aboriginal people. Construction of a plant would take eighteen months to complete, and employ a permanent workforce of 400 people. Mining companies operating in the region would each pay between $100 and $150,000 a year. Anaconda would make an initial contribution of $50,000 and pay the Chair of the Murrin Murrin Foundation $60,000 a year.[226] The following day it was announced that although four groups of native title claimants wished to agree with the terms offered by Anaconda, there were another four parties of native title claimants that did not waive their native title rights on those terms.[227]

In this instance, a regional agreement with all Aboriginal native title claimants was found to be essential. In November 1996 it was announced that Anaconda planned not to proceed with the funding of a Murrin Foundation, and instead would pursue a regional agreement with a larger number of Aboriginal groups. Under a draft agreement, applications for native title would be referred to working groups set up for an area that would have the power to authorise applications and guarantee that no new claims would emerge. The working group would forfeit its right to compensation if new native title claims were lodged before a tenement was granted.[228]

The United North Eastern Goldfields claimant group finally approved the development on 3 April 1997. Part of the agreement involves Anaconda making an annual contribution of $1m to a trust, formed to enable young Aboriginal people to establish businesses. Three Aboriginal companies have been awarded infrastructure contracts for pre-construction earthworks, bulk earthworks and water installations. Anaconda has also undertaken to employ at least 20 per cent of its workforce from Aboriginal communities.[229]

The Murrin Murrin Nickel/Cobalt Project is being undertaken by Anaconda Nickel Ltd and Glencore International AG. Murrin Murrin is now under construction. Commissioning has been planned for the third quarter of 1998. The plant includes a nickel and cobalt refinery. It will produce 100m pounds per annum of high purity nickel and 6.5m pounds per annum of cobalt metal, with a mine life exceeding 30 years. The Murrin Murrin project is the first large project in the Kalgoorlie area where agreement has been reached with all native title claimants. Agreement was reached outside the *Native Title Act* process.[230]

In much of Australia, the processes for deciding who the native title holders are for a given area of land will take some time to establish and the native title holders will change over time. Many mining and exploration companies have therefore decided to negotiate with native title claimants. In some cases there may be a risk that an additional claimant will emerge after an agreement has been signed. However, if a Native Title Representative Body has worked with the claimants to establish a broadly based agreement with local Aboriginal groups, there is less risk of a late claimant emerging. The benefits of positively involving local Aboriginal communities with mining are obvious to almost everyone.

7 Post-Mabo mining agreements 1997–1998

Five years after the *Mabo (2)* High Court judgment and four years after the *Native Title Act 1993* many more exploration and mining agreements were made over land subject to native title claim in every mainland Australian State. Native Title Representative Bodies gained further expertise in negotiating and making agreements that will provide some benefits to Aboriginal people from mining. The Napranum and Alcan agreement on western Cape York Peninsula, Queensland, attempts to replicate the positive features of the Hopevale and Cape Flattery Silica Mines agreement made in eastern Cape York Peninsula in 1992. As mentioned in Chapter 5, training and employment have been particularly successful at Hopevale, where 46 of the 104 employees, including management, are from the local Aboriginal community, and the mine is considered to be part of that community. It is too early to say whether that success will be replicated in other parts of Australia.

As discussed below, Hamersley Iron in the Pilbara region of Western Australia signed an important agreement with the Gumala Corporation in 1997, which will provide $60m in benefits over twenty years. Hamersley Iron now directly employs some 55 Aboriginal people, who comprise 2 per cent of its total workforce. The company also contracts with seven small businesses and two Community Development Employment Projects, which employ 250 Aboriginal people on a part-time basis. Increasingly such expenditures should be regarded as investments, which will benefit both the company and the local Aboriginal communities.

GOLDFIELDS AGREEMENTS IN WESTERN AUSTRALIA, 1997–1998

The Goldfields area can be divided into traditional-oriented peoples living around the town of Leonora in the north, and more business-oriented peoples living in the north-east, around the Laverton area (see Map 1.1). One of the largest projects to date, the Murrin Murrin and Anaconda Nickel project, was signed by sixteen parties in November 1996, and is discussed in the previous chapter. Two additional parties signed on to the project on 3 April 1997. The Anaconda Nickel project lies between Leonora and Laverton.

Partly because of the previous government policies of dispersing Aboriginal groups, overlapping claims have featured in the Goldfields area. WMC Resources Ltd gained general land access permission from the Wanmulla and Wutha people in 1996. Since that time, steps to encourage Aboriginal claimants to work in cultural rather than family groups have been encouraged.

The press reported that an exploration agreement was signed in early March 1997 by Tjupan Ngalia claimants in the Goldfields area when the claimants agreed to assist Austquip, Hawkslade and Fangio Investments in future grants if they have regard to Aboriginal culture, employment, training and business enterprise opportunities. The agreement was initiated outside the processes of the *Native Title Act*. Should parties appear at a later date claiming to be native title holders for that area, the company which has negotiated the agreement would have to bear the consequential commercial and legal risk of further negotiations.[231]

Since March 1997, the Tjupan Ngalia have been encouraged to work with five other claimant groups as part of the one cultural block. Mediation between families is sometimes required. Native title claimants with no overlapping claims have the right to negotiate with the Western Australian Government. The priorities for the north-west peoples, such as the Tjupan Ngalia, are protecting traditions and sacred sites. Concerns about employment, social, environmental and cultural conditions are important supplementary concerns.[232]

One of Australia's largest clearance agreements was announced on 8 February 1998, when the Goldfields Land Council assisted the Aboriginal North East Independent Body, chaired by Aubrey Lynch, to enter into an agreement with a mining company forum of thirteen miners. The agreement would last initially for three months, and cover an area of 22,000 sq km. A two-stage process will initially identify 'no-go' sites in areas which are likely to contain minerals. Detailed ethnographic studies will allow more intensive drilling and mining programs.[233] The Goldfields Land Council and the mining company forum are encouraging all north-east claimants and all mining and exploration companies operating in the area to join in the arrangement. It is also planned to develop a broader regional agreement in the future, developed from the February 1998 agreement.[234]

MARALINGA TJARUTJA AND RESOLUTE/DOMINION LTD, 1997 (SOUTH AUSTRALIA)

Pitjantjatjara Aboriginal people own 76,000 sq km of former Maralinga lands (a site used by the British for atomic testing in the 1950s, in the west of South Australia) (see Map 1.2).

An exploration agreement covering part of the Maralinga lands was announced on 9 March 1997 when Resolute and Dominion Mining secured an agreement with Maralinga Tjarutja, which is the Native Title Representative Body for that area of South Australia. The agreement covers an area of 5000 sq km. Under the agreement, the Maralinga Tjarutja have secured a 10 per cent interest in the joint venture, at no cost, and Resolute and Dominion Mining each have a 45 per cent interest. The Aboriginal land owners' 10 per cent share of development costs would be paid from gold production, if a decision to mine was made. Dr Archie Barton, the Administrator of Maralinga Tjarutja, said that the agreement with Resolute and Dominion also protected traditional rights and provided for a full works clearance program before the companies entered Maralinga Tjarutja land.[235]

NAPRANUM (WEIPA SOUTH) AND ALCAN LTD, 1997 (QUEENSLAND)

In Cape York, Aboriginal people see training, jobs and future businesses as critical for native title agreements. On 10 March 1997, it was announced that the Cape York Land Council, negotiating on behalf of the Weipa (Napranum) Aboriginal people of North Queensland, had reached in-principle agreement with the aluminium company Alcan for bauxite mining and aluminium production (see Map 4.1).

Alcan South Pacific (Alspac) is a wholly owned subsidiary of Montreal-based Alcan Aluminium Ltd, which has annual revenues of $US 9 billion. The company is developing the Ely Bauxite project 25 km north of Weipa. Alcan acquired the lease in 1965 under a franchise agreement under Queensland legislation. The new project includes a mine, processing plant and a sealed road that is 30 km long. The port and some of the operations

---

Summary of mining company and Aboriginal community relations

Location of mine	25 km north of Weipa
Mining town	Fly in–fly out to Cairns
Name of company	Alcan Ltd
Signatories	Alcan and the Napranum community
Date of agreement	1997
Type of project	Bauxite mining and aluminium production
Description	Large bauxite mine of $200m
Royalties: statutory	Nil
negotiated	More than $0.5m per annum
(to area affected)	-
Royalty association	Napranum Aboriginal Corporation
Scope of agreement	More than $10m in royalty benefits over 20 years. Assist Aboriginal people to participate in training. Assist Aboriginal employment at the mine. Payments to business, education and training trusts.
Outcomes	Agreement to maximise Aboriginal employment and to protect cultural heritage sites.
Evaluation/studies	-
Native Title Representative Body	Cape York Land Council.

---

are on Aboriginal land. The Aboriginal community has agreed to provide Alspac and the Queensland Ports Corporation with a long-term lease for the port and the *Alcan Act 1965 (Qld)* will be amended for this purpose. The mine will produce 2.5m tonnes of washed bauxite per year. The operation will operate on a fly in–fly out basis from Cairns, however most of the workforce will stay on site. It is estimated that there will be little additional demand on the mining town of Weipa.

In 1996, Alspac made approaches to the Aboriginal communities of Cape York, and in August 1996 the Cape York Land Council was appointed to represent them. On 10 September 1996 a memorandum of understanding was signed between all parties. Alspac agreed to fund:

• an anthropological study to identify traditional owners;
• an economic and social impact study to identify issues of concern;
• legal representation and advice on negotiations; and
• meeting costs for Aboriginal communities.

Cape York Land Council agreed to:

• organise and complete the studies by certain deadlines;
• establish a steering committee of traditional owners and community members; and
• inform the community of progress and act on instructions.

Various studies were completed in December 1996. An in-principle agreement was signed at Napranum on 10 March 1997. There was a commitment to maximise Aboriginal employment in the construction and operation of the project, to provide training opportunities for young Aboriginal people, and to provide educational bursaries. Community elders from Old Mapoon see training, jobs and future businesses as important, as is the protection of sacred sites and the environment.[236] Cultural heritage sites would be protected, and Alspac would collaborate with the Aboriginal community in the management of sites. Alspac would work closely with the Aboriginal community in the environmental management of the project and there would be support for an Aboriginal rangers program. It was also agreed that traditional rights would be protected, that there would be a works clearance program and an Aboriginal consultation and reference committee, and that Aboriginal business ventures should be developed through contracting. A negotiated royalty of annual payments exceeding $0.5m per annum, and a $200m mining venture were agreed upon. The Queensland Government would be approached to facilitate agreed arrangements for land tenure and port facility leases.

The final agreement was signed on 3 September 1997. It was initiated outside the processes of the *Native Title Act* and Noel Pearson played a pivotal role in the agreement. He said that agreements in most States are more easily realised if State governments are not involved in the initial stages.[237]

GUMALA AND HAMERSLEY IRON LTD, 1997 (WESTERN AUSTRALIA)

Aboriginal communities of the Pilbara, on the north-west coast of Western Australia, have reached agreement for a $500m iron ore mine at Yandicoogina to proceed about 150 km east of Tom Price. The agreement was made with the Gumala Aboriginal Corporation, which represents the Bunjima, Niapaili and Innawonga communities (see Maps 1.2 and 7.1).

Hamersley Iron Ltd is a wholly owned subsidiary of Rio Tinto Ltd. The company mines, processes and exports iron ore from its Pilbara mines through the company port at Dampier. Hamersley is one of the world's largest iron ore producers, and has operated for 30 years.

THE GUMALA HAMERSLEY AGREEMENT

As a result of negotiations Hamersley has agreed to make contributions over the life of the Yandicoogina mine to establish local business development,

---

Summary of mining company and Aboriginal community relations

Location of mine	Pilbara
Mining town	Port Hedland
Name of company	Hamersley Iron
Current parent company	Rio Tinto Ltd
Signatories	Hamersley Iron and Gumala Aboriginal Corporation
Date of agreement	1997
Type of project	New Hamersley Iron ore mine (in production in 1999)
Description	Large iron ore mine of $500m potential over 30 years
Royalties: statutory	-
negotiated	A package of benefits negotiated with the company
(to area affected)	-
Royalty association	Gumala Aboriginal Corporation
Scope of agreement	Up to $60m in benefits over 20 years. Assist Aboriginal people participate in pastoral operations. Assist Aboriginal employment at the mine. Payments to business, education and training trusts and for community infrastructure.
Outcomes	55 Aboriginal people currently employed, 20 being trained. Up to $3m per annum in training, employment and business benefits.
Evaluation/studies	Senior 1998.
Native Title Representative Body	Nanga-Ngoona Moora-Joorga Land Council.

Aboriginal education, training, community development and protection of culture and welfare in three local Aboriginal communities represented by Gumala Aboriginal Corporation. Gumala was invited to take a shareholding and Board representation in a training organisation.

In 1997 Hamersley employed some 60 Aboriginal people were employed by and another twenty underwent training. During 1998, between 40 and 70 Aboriginal people worked on Hamersley operations.[238] Hamersley's mobile equipment training program has a 95 per cent success rate in achieving full-time employment for Aboriginal people. Hamersley has assisted Aboriginal communities to participate in pastoral station operations, invest funds for the future, preserve Aboriginal access to non-operation areas of some 26,000 sq km of mining leases, and assist Aboriginal employment at the mine. The agreement provides for Aboriginal communities to receive up to $60m of assistance over twenty years, depending on the success of the Yandicoogina mine.

In return, Aboriginal people will support the development of the Yandicoogina mine, to commence mining in 1999. It has a mine life of more than 30 years, and is expected to produce 15m tonnes a year by 2003, with total estimated sales of $500m.

Map 7.1   Hamersley's operations in the Pilbara

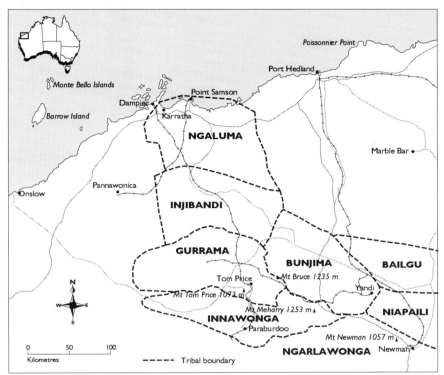

Source: Hamersley Iron

Hamersley commenced consultations in March 1996. A Memorandum of Understanding was signed by Hamersley and Gumala on 20 November 1996, which was endorsed by local communities. The final agreement was ratified by a large community meeting held at Tom Price on 1 March 1997, of 100 people from three communities, and signed on 26 March 1997.[239]

Hamersley Iron won a Council for Aboriginal Reconciliation award in 1997 for benefits to Aboriginal people, improving relationships between Indigenous people and the wider community, and recognition by Aboriginal elders and the general community. The company presented a detailed report on its progress and future commitments.[240] The Ieramugadu Group has employed an Aboriginal labour pool on a contractual basis with Hamersley Iron since 1980. The labour pool has led to training projects in such areas as office administration, pastoral training and community workshops in communication and self-esteem. Aboriginal camps have been cleared for health and hygiene, and surveys have been conducted so that Aboriginal heritage sites are not damaged. Hamersley has also assisted by training health workers and supported a camp for an alcohol and substance abuse program.

Hamersley established an Aboriginal Training and Liaison Department in 1992. Its three program goals are to:

- develop personnel with skills which would be of value to the company or in the wider mining community;
- support education initiatives which will continue to improve educational qualifications for young Aboriginal people at all levels; and
- support commercial initiatives in projects and businesses which would be viable and useful to Hamersley or the communities in which Hamersley operates.

HAMERSLEY'S APPROACH TO TRAINING AND EMPLOYMENT

Hamersley established an Aboriginal training and liaison unit in 1992, with a $3m grant for capital equipment, and an operating budget that now exceeds $3m a year. Professionals then asked people what they wanted, by interviewing 250 Aboriginal adults in person and conducting telephone interviews of 500 people. Action programs were developed in 1995, which have had the following outcomes.

Training modules were developed in four-wheel drive and heavy equipment. Eight modules are taught, each requiring 250 operating hours. Some 21 Aboriginal people have graduated so far, in a multi-skilled operators course for heavy earthmoving equipment, and fifteen of these graduates gained employment with Hamersley.

Commercial trainees undergo training in secretarial and clerical skills. The program incorporates accredited training through Karratha College near Roebourne. Hamersley has offered training in computer and book-keeping skills. One person has completed an apprenticeship, and six are in progress. Some secondary students are sponsored in a five-year program. Six scholarships were awarded between 1994 and 1997, for Aboriginal people to undertake various university degrees and courses.

The company, through its Aboriginal training and liaison team, assists Aboriginal people to establish businesses that are economically viable. Local Indigenous people have set up the following businesses around Roebourne:

- Wani seed-gathering;
- Weymal contractors provide plugs to cap drill holes, and undertake fencing, trough and windmill construction;

- Warba Ngarda group provides a gardening and landscaping service; and
- support has been provided for a new venture which provides traditional bush medicines through the Aboriginal Medical Service. It is exploring commercial applications.

In addition to the 40 to 70 Aboriginal people directly employed by Hamersley in 1998, the company offered varying levels of support to six Aboriginal businesses and two Community Development Employment Projects, which together employ 250 people.

'GOOD NEIGHBOUR' POLICIES

Near the Tom Price mine at Marandoo, Hamersley's newest mine, 4 per cent of the 1994 workforce were Aboriginal people. Since that time Hamersley has developed a 'good neighbour' policy. The programs include cross-cultural training to employees, often taught by Aboriginal elders. Some 40 courses have been conducted with a total of 900 people attending. A further aim is to assist small Aboriginal-owned companies to sell their product to other Pilbara-based businesses. Some Aboriginal people, for example, work on pasture regeneration. Hamersley has assisted communities in the area around Tom Price to establish living areas. It has funded an information resource on local culture, by working closely with Aboriginal elders. The unit also encourages sporting contacts between the company and Aboriginal communities. Sporting clinics have been sponsored, and football players from the West Coast Eagles team in Perth have visited local schools.

HAMERSLEY YANDICOOGINA LAND USE AGREEMENT

The Yandicoogina Land Use agreement is a bipartite regional agreement between the Aboriginal parties and Hamersley Iron. The parties to the agreement are the thirteen registered native title claimants, key traditional owners from the Bunjima, Niapaili and Innawonga communities of the Pilbara, the Gumala Aboriginal Corporation representing the three language groups concerned, and Hamersley Iron Ltd.

The parties have formed a Monitoring and Liaison Committee. The Aboriginal parties have agreed to:

- support current and future project requirements, including the grant of all requisite titles and approvals;
- the grant of exploration titles and regional site clearance procedures; and

- benefits satisfying any compensation entitlements with respect to the Yandicoogina project.

Hamersley commitments include:

- payments to independent Public Benevolent Trusts for enhancing business development; education and training; community development and infrastructure needs; protection of culture; and the long-term welfare of Bunjima, Niapaili and Innawonga communities. Some of the funds must be invested for future generations;
- assisting Gumala to participate in pastoral station operations, and implementing pastoral and operator training;
- preserving Aboriginal access to non-operation areas of the mining lease;
- promoting employment for local people and assisting contracting opportunities;
- environmental protection measures;
- in-kind assistance for community development; and
- protecting Aboriginal heritage, including site clearance procedures for mineral exploration.

The agreement was initiated outside the processes of the *Native Title Act*. However, the final agreement was registered using s. 34 of the *Native Title Act*. Hamersley approached the government to issue a s. 29 notice for the project which ratified the leases, and waited two months for them to be approved. No further native title claim eventuated during this period.[241]

The agreement was made prior to the Federal Government's proposal to amend the *Native Title Act 1993*. It demonstrates that mutually beneficial agreements can be successfully negotiated between Aboriginal people and a major international mining company.

WAANYI (LAWN HILL) AND CZL LTD, 1997 (QUEENSLAND)

Rich lead–zinc mines run along the southern part of the Gulf of Carpentaria. In the Northern Territory, an agreement to explore was made with Aboriginal land owners at Ngukurr in 1994 (St Vidgeon and Rio Tinto); and agreement to mine has been made with Aboriginal land owners at Borroloola in 1994 (Gurdandji and MIM Ltd).

THE CENTURY MINE

Perhaps the richest of all the zinc mines along the Gulf of Carpentaria discovered to date is the Century mine of Lawn Hill, which when completed will produce 8 per cent of the western world's zinc. Following extensive national publicity, the traditional owners agreed to mining developments on their lands on 7 May 1997. Lawn Hill lies some 50 km east of Queensland's border with the Northern Territory, midway between Mt Isa and Burketown (see Map 4.1). There are soaring red cliffs, emerald pools and Aboriginal paintings and artefacts at Lawn Hill which are an estimated 35,000 years old. In 1985 Lawn Hill was proclaimed a national park covering an area of 12,200 ha.[242]

Century Zinc Ltd (CZL) was a subsidiary of CRA (Conzinc Riotinto of Australia), which merged in 1997 with its parent company RTZ (Rio-Tinto Zinc), to become Rio Tinto).[243] CZL holds mineral leases over parts of Lawn Hill pastoral lease, and the company proposed to mine lead and zinc in the area. CZL purchased the Lawn Hill station and transferred part of the station to the Queensland Government. They incorporated it into Lawn Hill National Park. Part of the area transferred was initially designated a 'resource reserve'. Exploration and other commercial activity is permitted in resource reserves until they are declared to be national park.

Summary of mining company and Aboriginal community relations	
Location of mine	Lawn Hill
Mining town	Commute to surrounding towns, such as Mt Isa
Name of company	Century Zinc Ltd (CZL)
Current parent company	Pasminco (formerly CRA)
Signatories	Gulf Regional Aboriginal Corporation and CZL
Date of agreement	1997
Type of project	Century zinc and lead mine at Lawn Hill
Description	Large lead, zinc mine and pipeline to Gulf of Carpentaria.
Royalties: statutory	-
negotiated	A package of benefits negotiated with the company
(to area affected)	-
Royalty association	Gulf Regional Aboriginal Corporation
Scope of agreement	GRAC will receive pastoral properties and other employment and community benefits. $60m in benefits from CZL for 3,700 people over 20 years. $30m infrastructure from the State.
Outcomes	Referred to arbitration in February 1997. Agreement reached 7 May 1997. CZL sold to Pasminco.
Evaluation/studies	Altman and Smith 1998.
Native Title Representative Body	Carpentaria Land Council.

Map 7.2   Lawn Hill, Gulf Region, and proposed pipeline

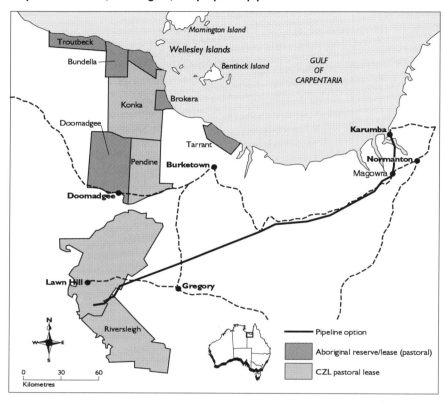

Source: Pasminco Ltd

An April 1995 study proved that there are significant zinc–lead–silver deposits at Century, and found that it was capable of producing 780,000 tonnes of zinc concentrate and 84,000 tonnes of lead concentrate a year, potentially one of the world's largest zinc mines. Rio Tinto developed the plan to pump zinc concentrates, in slurry form, to Karumba in the Gulf of Carpentaria, where it would be dewatered for shipment to markets (see Map 7.2).[244] It is now estimated that the mine will produce 500,000 tonnes of zinc a year, beginning late in 1999, and continuing for twenty years.[245]

The native title claimants saw their application over the coastal corridor through which Rio Tinto wanted access as a means of gaining a share of ownership of the project, similar to the Central Land Council strategy of facilitating site clearance for the Alice Springs to Darwin gas pipeline.

Approval for the Century mine was protracted, in part because of the newness of the procedure, and also because the High Court's *Wik* case had not yet been decided. The Waanyi people in the Gulf of Carpentaria lodged a claim to 247 ha at the Century mine site. The claim was lodged with the National Native Title Tribunal on 27 June 1994, and rejected by the President, Justice French on 14 February 1995.

In his ruling, Justice French accepted that the Waanyi had displaced former Aboriginal inhabitants at the end of last century according to Aboriginal tradition. This ruling follows over twenty years of findings flowing from the *Aboriginal Land Rights (Northern Territory) Act* and may be significant. It is usually difficult to prove that a group of Aboriginal people who occupy land now are descended from the same group who occupied that land in 1788. Justice French ruled that occupation of the land need not be by the same Aboriginal group who occupied that land in 1788.

In 1995, the High Court's *Wik* judgment on the co-existence of native title and pastoral leases had not been handed down. Justice French ruled that the native title of the Waanyi people was extinguished because of a pastoral lease over the land. A water and camping reserve had been established over part of the land in question, and Aboriginal people always had access to it.

Century was granted two mining leases over the Century ore body including the camping and water reserve after a majority of the full Federal Court upheld French's decision. The granted leases remained 'valid' after the Waanyi case. The Queensland Government started the 'right to negotiate process' at the request of Century even though it had not granted leases.

The Carpentaria Land Council believed that native title should be recognised in such an instance. It appealed the decision, and was successful. The High Court in 1996 disallowed Justice French's ruling and the Federal Court's decision not to accept the Waanyi's application.

THE OFFER FOR AGREEMENT

CRA's income in 1994 (before merging with RTZ) was $6536m, its profits after tax were $538m. Royalties paid by the company to various governments amounted to $178m. On 29 August 1995, it was announced that the subsidiary, Century Zinc Ltd (CZL), had offered a consortium of local Aboriginal groups (including the Carpentaria Land Council) a $60m package over twenty years. This was to compensate for the development of one of the world's biggest zinc mines, then estimated to have a value of $750m. The compensation offered included shares in pastoral leases, financial help with business ventures, and untied grants for community development programs. It would extend over the twenty-year life of the mine. The

Carpentaria Land Council had demanded equity in the mining venture, and this was not offered. However, health, education and cultural programs for the 3700 Aboriginal people potentially affected were reportedly part of the offer. The press described the offer as 'an important move for CRA, Australia's largest resource company, which has a reputation in some circles for abysmal dealings with Indigenous people'.[246] The offer by CRA through its chief executive, Leon Davis, signified a new approach to Aboriginal land interests.

An impact assessment study outlined the CZL offer. The study states that possible outcomes would include 'the transfer of land held by CZL under pastoral lease...and the related issue of outstation development and funding'. The offer included untied annual community development grants and annual contributions to infrastructure development, as well as health programs and sport and recreation programs, assistance for Aboriginal people to join the workforce, and a surety to 'promote cultural awareness within its own workforce and encourage it throughout the worksite'.[247]

Since 1995 CRA has merged with its parent company, Rio Tinto Ltd. Paul Wand is now the Vice-President of Aboriginal Relations at Rio Tinto. He made the point that the company welcomes the central tenant of the *Native Title Act*, in that 'it wishes at all times to seek mutually beneficial arrangements with Aboriginal people...it wishes to avoid litigation'.[248]

Rio Tinto identified listening to Aboriginal people as a vital prerequisite to negotiation: 'we do not want to be wandering around offering things that people do not want, or have no say in.'[249] Their offer is a response to the requirements of the people in the Gulf. Rio Tinto's intention was to assist a move from welfare dependency towards self-sufficiency. Negotiations were undertaken with a body formed following the appointment of Hal Wootten as a negotiator under the *Aboriginal and Torres Strait Islander Heritage Protection Act*, and after he had held extensive talks with Gulf people. The body was the United Gulf Regional Aboriginal Negotiating Team, (UGRANT), which would become GRAC after incorporation. The benefits were planned to extend beyond the twenty-year life of the mine, and cover four key areas.

Access to pastoral leases

Provided that CZL can overcome problems associated with the Queensland Government, Konka and Pendine pastoral stations would be immediately available to Aboriginal people with the proviso that the company continues to prospect on those lands, and if successful, mine on them. Aboriginal people would be offered a 25 per cent interest in Lawn Hill and Riversleigh pastoral stations, and have the opportunity to acquire the rest of the property after mining had ceased (see Map 7.2). These last two properties are able to carry stock and are currently sublet to a pastoral group that runs cattle on them for live cattle export. CZL and the owner of the leases would co-operate to establish a training centre for Aboriginal people who wish to be trained in pastoral industries. The Aboriginal-owned cattle enterprise at Delta Downs is seen as a model for this type of enterprise.

Annual grant for community use

The offer includes an untied annual grant of $0.5m.

Expenditure to facilitate employment

The offer includes an initial grant of $3m a year, and then grants of $1m per year for the lifetime of the mine. Rio Tinto's intention was to create jobs for 200 Aboriginal people by the year 2000, including twenty positions for Aboriginal people in technical or administrative roles.

Expenditure to facilitate business development

An initial grant of $1m a year was aimed at expenditure to facilitate business developments such as mining, canteen, trucking or barging contracts, as has been done at Borroloola. Tourist facilities for the Lawn Hill National Park and the large fossil area also present possible business opportunities.[250]

In January 1997, Rio Tinto announced that it would sell CZL and its assets, including the lead–zinc mine, to Pasminco Ltd, subject to completion of a native title agreement and the Queensland Government issuing valid leases. Pasminco agreed to pay $345m for Century and the nearby Dugald River zinc deposit, in order to supply its Budel zinc smelting operations in Holland. When completed, Century will be the world's largest zinc producer, satisfying 8 per cent of world demand and earning $430m in export income.[251]

Pasminco is Australia's only primary producer of zinc and lead metals and is now the world's largest zinc producer. The sale of CZL was conditional on a satisfactory agreement being concluded with Gulf Aboriginal people. CZL imposed a 13 February 1997 deadline for gaining Aboriginal agreement for the mine to proceed. By that time, six of the twelve native title claimants had signed an agreement, but the others had not. In February 1997, CZL therefore applied to the National Native Title Tribunal to arbitrate the dispute.[252]

Agreement was reached on 7 May 1997. Gulf Aboriginal communities will receive $60m from Century Zinc over twenty years. CZL has provided further details on the components of this aggregated future grant. It will comprise:

- employment and training ($23m paid over twenty years), including the cost of developing accredited courses, employing site mentors and community liaison officers, and requiring contractors to employ Aboriginal labour;
- environmental measures, including a $50,000 fund for five years for independent financial advice, and a $250,000 environmental bond, and an environmental officer;
- business opportunities ($16.5m paid over twenty years);
- community development trust ($10.75m paid over twenty years), to provide cultural, sporting and social purposes; and
- regional organisation ($2m paid over twenty years).[253]

The Queensland Government also undertook to provide a $30m infrastructure package for the benefit of those communities. It is not clear whether significant parts of the $30m are additional to normal expenditure on Aboriginal community facilities in the area.[254]

NYOONGAR AND AMITY OIL LTD, 1997 (WESTERN AUSTRALIA)

On 16 May 1997, the Nyoongar community of Busselton, in the south-west corner of Western Australia, signed a deal allowing Amity Oil to explore one of Australia's largest onshore gas deposits in return for undisclosed compensation. Agreement also involved consultation with Amity and site protection (see Map 1.2). The agreement was reached within the processes of the *Native Title Act*.[255]

BUNDJALUNG AND ROSS MINING LTD, 1997 (NEW SOUTH WALES)

This agreement was achieved by the Bundjalung people of Tabulam, at Timbarra in the Tenterfield area of north-eastern New South Wales, who had a native title claim over the mine site. On 18 July 1997 they agreed to allow Ross Mining Ltd to mine gold. The agreement was reached under the 'right to negotiate' processes of the *Native Title Act* and covered future development within the company's 750 sq km surrounding tenement. Ross Mining Ltd was hopeful of commencing construction of its $17m Timbarra gold project in August 1997. It is planned to produce 50,000 ounces a year for five years, in a heap-leach operation that would generate 60 jobs.[256]

The company is an active gold producer, and mined some 80,000 ounces of gold in 1996/97. The company also operates a mine in the Solomon Islands.[257]

On Australia's east coast, it is now recognised that native title agreements should provide education, training, employment and community works, in order to provide long-term benefits to Indigenous communities. This agreement also provided a protocol for resolving Aboriginal heritage issues.

SOUTH AUSTRALIAN ACCESS CLEARANCES, 1997 (SOUTH AUSTRALIA)

On 15 August 1997, five groups from south-western South Australia signed access agreements with fourteen companies for exploration in the Gawler–Craton area of the south-west of the State, with Goldstream Mining. These agreements provide for two years of exploration covering 44,000 sq km of territory in South Australia's far-west, over an area the size of Tasmania. A new body, the Far West Coast Working Group, has been formed to establish Aboriginal sites of significance. A sixth native title claimant, Ted Roberts, did not sign the agreement in August 1997, but negotiated at a later date.

Consultations commenced in April 1997. Aboriginal parties and the miners met in Ceduna over two days to discuss co-operation. It is possible that current overlapping native title claims may be merged at a later stage. The South Australian group signed a formal document 44 days after negotiations commenced.

It was agreed that a survey would be conducted with key traditional owners and specialist anthropologists, to determine areas of Aboriginal significance, and to streamline exploration processes. Exploration would proceed subject to protection and avoidance of culturally significant sites. It was expected that the survey would take two months, and that specific companies would then negotiate specific commercial agreements after that date. The agreement was initiated outside the processes of the *Native Title Act*. It was to run from August 1997 to August 1998, which is the duration of many of the mining tenements involved. If minerals are discovered, native title claims will still have to go through mediation and 'right to negotiate' provisions.[258]

Bradley Selway QC, Solicitor General for South Australia, has described the approach of the South Australian Government to native title agreements. He believes that the real issues about native title are policy issues, not legal issues, and that they can only be negotiated by native title agreements. He points out that Canada took twenty years of litigation until regional agreements with Aboriginal groups became an accepted way of life. The South Australian Government is keen to negotiate both generally and in detail.[259]

KIMBERLEY AGREEMENTS IN WESTERN AUSTRALIA

In 1995, the Kimberley Land Council of Western Australia negotiated separate exploration agreements with Tanami gold explorers and Glengarry Resources, and with BHP Pty Ltd. Other exploration agreements negotiated by the Kimberley Land Council in the eastern Kimberleys include the agreement, in 1996, with Geograph Resources and Otter Exploration exploring for gold over the Durabalan claim, and the Stockdale clearance agreement, in 1997, exploring for diamonds over Moola Boola station.

The exploration and mining agreement between Striker Resources and the Balangarra people is one of the major mining exploration agreements negotiated by the Kimberley Land Council. Striker Resources NL is a Western Australian-based diamond company. The significance of the agreement is that it shows that smaller companies also see benefits in negotiation. Balangarra lodged two native title claims over their land in the Forrest River Aboriginal Reserve and land north-west of Wyndham in the eastern Kimberleys, north of the Argyle diamond mine, in July 1995 and November 1995. On 20 August 1997 they reached agreement with Striker Resources. They will receive compensation for disruption and impact on their land, and hope to gain jobs, training, some business opportunities, compensation payments and community infrastructure. The Balangarra native title claim covers more than 27,000 sq km, and Striker has mining tenements over 6500 sq km of this land. The agreement covers both exploration and the eventuality of future mining.

Traditional owners receive a fee based on a percentage of ground exploration costs each year. If Striker establishes a mining operation in the region, an additional payment of 1.5 per cent of the capital costs involved in building a plant will be payable. When a mine is operating, the claimants will get part of the quarterly sales proceeds. Annual land rents will be calculated on the area disturbed. Striker will also maintain major roads in the remote area and develop an environmental management plan. At present the Kimberley Land Council holds moneys received for the Balangarra on trust, and assets will be transferred to a Prescribed Body Corporate. The agreement was initiated outside the processes of the *Native Title Act*.[260]

NGAANYATJARRA AGREEMENTS IN WESTERN AUSTRALIA

The Ngaanyatjarra Council is the legal lessee of the Western Desert lands of the Pintubi. According to Aboriginal law the Pintubi own an area of 250,000 sq km extending along the Northern Territory and South Australian border in Western Australia (see Map 1.2). Around 1800 Aboriginal people live here. Some of them first met non-Aboriginal people in 1984. Warburton, with 600 people is the largest community.

About 80,000 sq km is Aboriginal reserve land secured by a 99-year lease, granted by the Western Australian Government in 1988. A further 80,000 sq km is held by a 50-year lease also granted in 1988, but with a weaker mining access regime which is less favourable to Aboriginal people.

The stronger 1988 lease provides that an exploration licence cannot be granted until an access agreement is negotiated with the Ngaanyatjarra Council. If the Ngaanyatjarra Council refuses, or proposes unacceptable conditions, the matter is referred to an arbitrator, whose recommendations are ultimately subject to Ministerial power.[261]

The Ngaanyatjarra Council had lodged ten native title claims on behalf of traditional owners by 1997. The northern-most Kiwirrkura claim was designed as a model for other claims. Ten major mining exploration agreements were signed between 1988 and 1998 with CRA, WMC Resources Ltd, and BHP, and with Aurora Gold in September 1997. The Ngaanyatjarra Council consented to exploration by Aurora Gold within days of the exploration licence being granted by the Western Australian Minister for Mines. Since then Aurora Gold has drilled between Kiwirrkura and Kintore.

WMC Resources Ltd has explored around Mantamaru and Nyinnga. Payments for exploration licences have been made to traditional owners, apart from the Cosmo Newberry area, 80 km from the Laverton goldfields near Kalgoorlie, where payments of about $50,000 per annum over a number of years have been made for community facilities such as buildings and a basketball court. Exploration licence payments have amounted to between $200,000 and $300,000 between 1992 and 1996. A common practice is for the mining company to pay 1 to 5 per cent of exploration costs.[262]

The mining industry's evidence to the Joint Parliamentary Committee on Native Title in reference to negotiations on the Ngaanyatjarra lands said: 'We find the ease of dealing with areas such as Warburton to be an absolute relief. There is certainty of who you are talking to. The expertise is there. It is just a question of the gate money. How much it is going to cost you to get in.'[263]

GAS PIPELINE AGREEMENTS, 1997 (VICTORIA, NEW SOUTH WALES, QUEENSLAND)

Four gas pipeline agreements were signed in 1997 between Native Title Representative Bodies and major gas companies. The parties involved concluded that the agreements are an example of co-existence at work.

EASTERN GAS PIPELINE AGREEMENT IN GIPPSLAND (VICTORIA)

This pipeline crosses country traditionally owned by the Gunai-Kurnai, the Bidawal, and the Monero-Ngarigo peoples of eastern Victoria. Mirimbiak Nations Aboriginal Corporation, which is the Native Title Representative Body for Victoria, and the New South Wales Aboriginal Land Council negotiated with BHP Petroleum and Westcoast Energy Australia. The agreement was signed on 28 August 1997. It covers New South Wales and Victoria, and is a large resource industry settlement under the *Native Title Act*. It provides guarantees in regard to three key Aboriginal concerns:

1. the protection of sites of both archaeological and cultural significance;
2. employment and training; and
3. compensation for the acquisition of native title rights and interests.

CARISBROOK TO ARARAT–STAWELL–HORSHAM GAS PIPELINE AGREEMENT (VICTORIA)

This pipeline crosses country traditionally owned by the Gournditch Mara, Wotjobaluk and Dja Dja Wurung peoples of western Victoria. Mirimbiak Nations Aboriginal Corporation commenced negotiations with Gascor (Victoria's Gas and Fuel Corporation) and the Victorian Government on 7 April 1997. The agreement was signed on 3 September 1997. Cultural heritage protection and employment opportunities will be provided under the agreement.[264]

WODONGA GAS PIPELINE AGREEMENT (VICTORIA)

An application was lodged in response to a s. 29 notice on 10 April 1997 over parcels of Crown land crossed by the Barnawartha to Wagga Wagga pipeline. The pipeline crosses country traditionally owned by the Wiradjuri and Dhudhuroa. Mirimbiak Nations Aboriginal Corporation negotiated with GTC (Gas Transmissions Corporation), with the Victorian Government as observer. The agreement was signed on 23 September 1997.

MARSDEN TO DUBBO GAS PIPELINE AGREEMENT (NEW SOUTH WALES)

Wiradjuri and Wongaibon elders from Peak Hill in central New South Wales reached agreement with AGL on 9 December 1997. A $55m gas pipeline will proceed over 255 km.[265] The agreement provides for the protection of Aboriginal cultural heritage during construction, employment opportunities and the establishment of trust funds for community development purposes, including scholarships and cultural education. The agreement would particularly benefit young people in communities.[266]

If one estimates the cash value of the amount paid for compensation and for funding cultural and business projects among Aboriginal communities, the amount has varied from $3000 per km for remote areas to $40,000 for a critical 0.5 km in an urban area. Parties have stressed the importance of the protection of cultural sites as well as a package of measures that will assist the economic, educational and social development of depressed communities. Well-targeted assistance can have an effect far greater than its financial value.

The following agreements were under negotiation during 1997 with Mirimbiak Nations Aboriginal Corporation for three pipelines in northern Victoria, with the Victorian Government as observer. They were the Drouin to Bunyip gas pipeline, the Wollert to Tallarook gas pipeline, and the Euroa to Baddaginnie gas pipeline in western, northern and eastern Victoria.[267]

CAPE YORK TO SOUTHERN QUEENSLAND GAS PIPELINE

Cape York, North Queensland, Central Queensland and the Gurang Land Councils negotiated with Chevron South Pacific in January 1998 for a major gas pipeline, extending over 3000 km, from Papua New Guinea to the Port of Gladstone, which is 400 km north of Brisbane. Many of the traditional owners involved have assented to the terms of the proposed agreement.[268]

8 Conclusions

> The commercial reality for mining companies now is that they must adopt a co-operative approach.
>
> Mick Dodson,[269] as Aboriginal and Torres Strait Islander
> Social Justice Commissioner

> Indigenous Australians should no longer be regarded as obstacles to development nor even as spectators or occasional beneficiaries of development. Aboriginal and Torres Strait Islander people are, by virtue of the Mabo decision and the *Native Title Act*, key stakeholders in Australia's future.
>
> Murray Chapman,[270] as Assistant General Manager
> (Land Heritage and Culture), ATSIC

The well-being of Australia's Aboriginal community is of particular importance as we enter the twenty-first century. Australian Aboriginal people are increasingly looking to the situation of Indigenous people in other countries. This need not be threatening. It might eventually reflect well on Australia. There are many successful enterprises involving Indigenous people overseas, from which Australia can learn. And some of the developments have achieved good results for Indigenous people in specific areas.

One of the great ideas of the twentieth century was that individuals had rights. The key English, European and American political philosophers, thinkers and writers of last century, and the founding fathers who drafted the Australian Constitution, wrote at a time of revolutionary changes in Europe which affected the rest of the globe. And if their works have a common thread it is perhaps that human beings are on their own. If they cannot create heaven on earth, at least it is within their grasp to behave reasonably towards other citizens.

At the end of the twentieth century, Indigenous peoples of the Fourth World somehow tenaciously reasserted their right to continue to exist as separate communities, adopting what they choose from First World societies, but retaining and developing their own cultures at their own pace.

The Pintubi of Western Australia are one of these groups. They first met white people in 1964, and left some of their families in the Western Desert when they were brought into Central Australian settlements of Papunya and Haasts Bluff, 200 km west of Alice Springs. There they suffered serious consequences of disease, alcoholism and social dislocation. In 1984, the Pintubi families left in the desert, and unknown to all non-Pintubi people, also came into what is called modern Australian civilisation. At that time a national Labor government promised, but did not deliver, national land rights for all Aboriginal people, particularly for those in Western Australia and Queensland, where State Governments had not recognised native title or the rights of traditional owners to own their own lands.

Progressive policies at the end of the twentieth century must recognise group rights, such as the right of Indigenous peoples to own their own lands, and consequential customary rights, such as the right to grow and develop with the freedom to speak one's own language. The United Nations passed relevant international covenants in 1966. Australia ratified these covenants between 1975 and 1980. They speak of the right of all peoples to 'freely pursue their economic, social and cultural development',[271] and the right of minorities 'to enjoy their own culture, to profess and practise their own religion, or to use their own languages'.[272]

To retain the uniqueness of one's traditional culture, and secure an economic livelihood in a radically different world is difficult for many Indigenous people. But these rights have proven reasonable and possible, at least in much of Canada, the United States and New Zealand. Maori people, for instance, have achieved much over recent years in the context of a shrinking government sector and tight economic conditions. They have retained and developed their culture as a distinct group. Their rights as a group have been recognised, and such recognition has resulted in a fairer outcome for them. Maori people have revived their language, won some fourteen seats in a National Parliament of 120 members, educated 300 lawyers and 180 medical practitioners, created broad-ranging Maori language and Maori studies departments in major universities, established flourishing businesses, and had their sporting and creative achievements recognised.[273]

Map 8.1   Contemporary land tenure

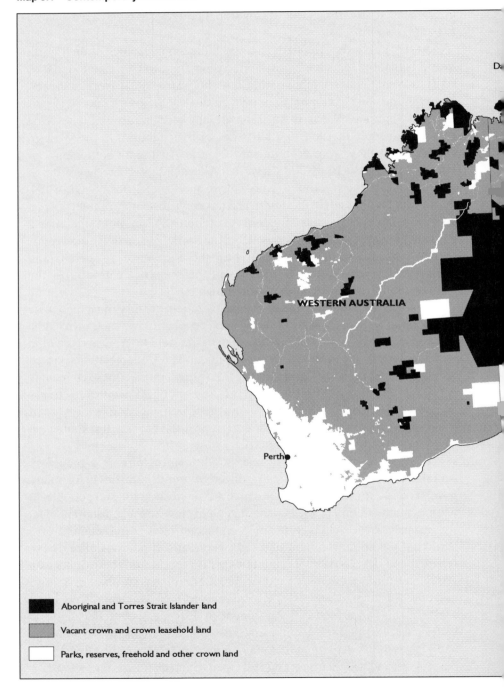

Source: LANDINFO Pty Ltd

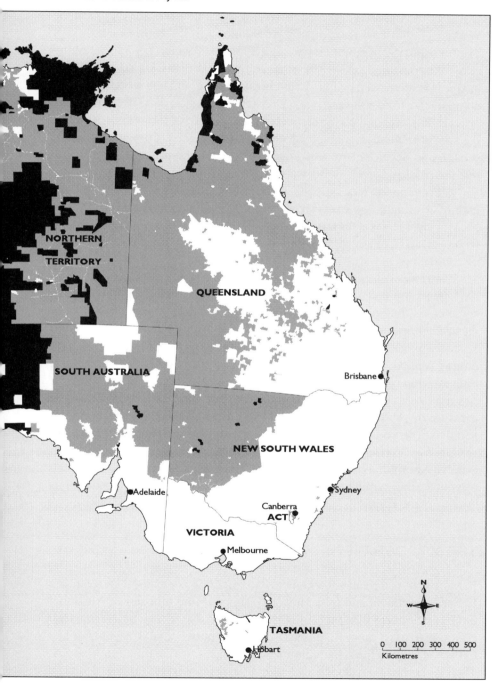

They have also entered into major resource agreements with the National Government, including the Sealord fishing agreement worth $150m and the Waikato-Tainui coal agreement near Hamilton in the North Island worth $170m. Agreement monies have funded some 500 Maori people, including seventeen postgraduates with scholarships, and many successful Maori businesses have been established. Other Maori graduates work in claims, computer technology, fisheries, governance structures and accounting, in order to implement their agreements for the benefit of the community. The Pakeha (non-Maori) community does not feel threatened or resentful of Maori growth and development. It is educated and enlightened enough to know that the whole nation benefits when Maoris prosper.

In Farmington, New Mexico, in the United States, 800 of the 1000 mine employees, including executives, are Native American Indians. At Fort McMurray in Saskatchewan, Canada, 330 Aboriginal people are directly employed at the mine, and an additional 250 Aboriginal people are employed as contractors.

Mining developments in northern Australia during the past 30 years have generally had a less beneficial effect on Aboriginal land owners. In some cases, Indigenous people have been left outcasts in their own land. Australia does not yet have places where Aboriginal people can proudly show the world what they have achieved in the face of rapid change in a mining context. Projects such as the Pilbara and Hopevale mines could over time develop like the best North American and New Zealand examples.

Improvements for the next 30 years will come about by persistent political pressure by Aboriginal people, and by some enlightened non-Aboriginal people, on farms and mines, in universities and schools, in parliaments and in churches working positively with Aboriginal people and helping them achieve Aboriginal objectives. When that comes about, Australia will catch up with the more enlightened policies and practices of other developed nations bordering the Pacific.

THE WIK DEBATE

In March 1996, the Liberal–National Party Coalition defeated Paul Keating's Labor government and John Howard became Prime Minister of Australia. On 23 December 1996, the High Court found in *Wik* [274] that native title may continue to exist on pastoral leases. The extent of vacant Crown land and Crown leasehold land, including pastoral leases, is illustrated in Map 8.1. The Government developed a 10 Point Plan in response to the *Wik* decision, which was released in May 1997. The House of Representatives passed Howard's Native Title Amendment Bill, which implemented the plan, on 29 October 1997. It attempts to shift the pendulum away from the group rights of Aboriginal and Torres Strait Islander people, towards the rights of others. All Australian Indigenous peoples, the Australian Labor Party Opposition and minor parties and Independents, believe it is an unacceptable shift.

The Senate did make significant amendments to John Howard's ten-point plan. The House of Representatives indicated that it did not accept some of those amendments. The Government re-introduced the Native Title Amendment Bill to the House of Representatives and then the Senate in March 1998. The House of Representatives again found the amendments of the Senate unacceptable, and while accepting some amendments has laid the Bill aside. The Government has threatened to call a double dissolution sometime in 1998.[275] The Aboriginal and Torres Strait Islander Commission, the National Indigenous Working Party, and former Liberal–National Party Ministers, such as Ian Viner QC have published objections to the ten-point plan.[276] The ten points are as follows.

POINT 1 VALIDATE LEASES ISSUED BETWEEN 1994 AND 1996

The Native Title Amendment Bill would validate leases granted between 1 January 1994 and 23 December 1996, the date of the *Wik* decision. This is particularly useful for the Queensland Government as it ignored the processes of the *Native Title Act* and issued a whole variety of land titles, particularly mining leases over pastoral lease land, without going through the processes of the Act. Instead of allowing these titles to be validated after negotiation with Aboriginal people, John Howard would validate all these titles, and leave Aboriginal and Torres Strait Islander people with the task of obtaining compensation through the courts, if they can. The Senate passed this provision with the support of Independent Senators.[277]

POINT 2 EXTINGUISHMENT OF NATIVE TITLE ON EXCLUSIVE TENURES

The Native Title Amendment Bill would confirm the extinguishment of native title on exclusive tenures, permanently. This issue is not left to courts. Ian Viner identified constitutional problems with John Howard's plan, specifically:[278]

(i)   Is this provision an act of racial discrimination under the *Racial Discrimination Act 1975*?

(ii)   Is such a law detrimental to Aboriginal people, rather than beneficial, and thus not permitted by the 'race' power in the Constitution?

The Government proposed amendments to the Bill that would enable a native title claim to proceed notwithstanding past extinguishment where the claimants are in occupation of the land and there are no current third party interests and no current government reservations. To some extent this may overcome the effect of 'historic' but no longer existing tenures.

POINT 3 GOVERNMENT SERVICES

Under the Native Title Amendment Bill, facilities for services to the public can be provided, notwithstanding native title. Native title holders will only retain access to their land. Aboriginal and other informed Australians are concerned that State and Territory Governments will use this provision to interfere with native title rights. The Bill will allow governments in good faith to implement past reservations of land for a particular purpose. If that reservation was for a public work, the building of the work will extinguish native title. If the Native Title Amendment Bill is passed, governments will not have to compulsorily acquire native title rights before repairing or constructing any new facility for services to the public.[279]

POINT 4   NATIVE TITLE AND PASTORAL LEASES

The Bill specifically prevents State and Territory Governments from upgrading any pastoral lease, from, for example, grazing cattle, to an exclusive tenure except by agreement with the native title holders or by a non-discretionary compulsory acquisition. Lesser developments are allowed, but for many of these the native title holders must be notified and consulted. A pastoral lessee could be allowed to conduct incidental or other primary production activities, for example, farmstay tourism, provided this does not involve Aboriginal culture.

POINT 5 STATUTORY ACCESS RIGHTS

Statutory access rights to pastoral leases are provided to Indigenous people who can prove they had current physical access at the time of the *Wik* decision.

Further, in order for a claimant to be registered and therefore obtain the right to negotiate, one member of the group must have had a traditional physical connection. Indigenous people who want to take advantage of an interim statutory access will have to be registered native title claimants. They will have to have had physical access with that land and their access will be limited to the scope of their access as at 23 December 1996, the date the *Wik* decision was declared.[280]

Many Aboriginal groups have been forcibly removed from their land, locked out of pastoral properties, and Aboriginal children have been taken from their mothers and families.[281] The Bill would compound these injustices. The Senate did pass an amendment that said that a 'regular physical access' test would not apply if access to an area before 1996 was denied by the pastoralist or because of an act of government.

POINT 6 FUTURE MINING ACTIVITY

Under the Native Title Amendment Bill, there will be a once-only opportunity for Indigenous people to negotiate at the prospecting stage where they specifically agree to this. Exploration can be removed from the full right to negotiate where the State or Territory puts in place an alternative regime. The regime will only require consultation between native title claimants and miners for the protection of sites and access issues.

The right to negotiate for mining will not apply to some gold and tin mining, opal mining, and mining in towns and cities. Most importantly, the States and Territories will be able to put in place their own regimes for mining on current and historical pastoral lease or reserved lands, provided only that certain minimal requirements are met.

Again, this would appear to lessen the rights which Indigenous people enjoy under the current *Native Title Act.*

POINT 7 FUTURE GOVERNMENT ACTS AND COMMERCIAL DEVELOPMENT

The Bill will also limit the existing right to negotiate for compulsory acquisition for third parties. The right to negotiate will not be required where the acquisition is for an infrastructure facility, which is very broadly defined.

In removing the right of native title holders to negotiate in many instances, Australia generally is out of step with the modern world. In countries such as Canada and New Zealand, the approach is to provide Aboriginal peoples with the right to negotiate an economic base, so that Indigenous communities can gain self-sufficiency by means of scholarships and training, business support and economic ventures. It is not to pay off the loss of Indigenous people's rights with a compensation payment.

POINT 8 WATER RESOURCES, AIR SPACE AND RESERVED LANDS

According to Aboriginal traditions, customary rights could cover water and sea. The Bill allows native title to exist in waters, but confirms that Governments can manage and regulate water. Native title can be extinguished by agreement with the title holders or by non-discriminatory compulsory acquisition.

The grant of licences in relation to waters must be notified to native title holders and they must be given an opportunity to object. The Chair of the Northern Land Council, Galarrwuy Yunupingu, described the amendment which suppresses native title in offshore waters as 'a blatant attempt at pre-emptive extinguishment of native title'.[282]

Ian Viner also is concerned that huge areas of land could be dammed by a State Government, and native title rights impaired.[283]

POINT 9 MANAGEMENT OF CLAIMS

Aboriginal people, and Ian Viner, have criticised the Bill for ignoring a spiritual link with the land, which is the basis of Aboriginal culture. They note that the Bill provides a different test of native title from *Mabo (2)*. The High Court's test is that: 'Where a clan or group has continued to acknowledge the laws whereby their traditional connection with land has been substantially maintained, the traditional community title of that clan or group can be said to remain in existence.'[284]

Furthermore, after six years, Aboriginal and Torres Strait Islander people would be denied a right to make further native title claims under the *Native Title Act*. Common law claims could still be lodged.

POINT 10 NATIVE TITLE AGREEMENTS

Native title agreements would continue to be permitted, instead of legal confrontation. Aboriginal representatives and their supporters argue that, with native title extinguished and impaired in so many areas, and the right to negotiation removed from non-exclusive tenures, there would appear to be little that Aboriginal and Torres Strait Islander people could make agreements about. Jenny Clarke's published study of the Native Title Amendment Bill concludes that: 'its main impact on native title in pastoral areas will be one of extensive and permanent suppression by expanded pastoral land uses, at significant public expense.'[285]

THE SENATE'S AMENDMENTS

The Liberal–National Party Government does not have a majority in the Senate. The Australian Labor Party and an Independent, Brian Harradine,[286] passed the Native Title Amendment Bill with the following key amendments:

- the sunset clause for claims was rejected;
- it was agreed that there should be a higher registration test before claimants obtained the right to negotiate, but the Coalition's proposed physical connection test was rejected;
- the Native Title Amendment Bill was to be subject to the *Racial Discrimination Act*;
- native title rights which conflict with pastoral rights were to be suppressed rather than extinguished;
- native title could be claimed on vacant Crown land and Aboriginal reserves regardless of tenure history;
- the proposal to remove the right to negotiate for pastoral leases and national parks was rejected;
- ministerial intervention in the right to negotiate was rejected.[287]

JOHN HOWARD'S POSITION

The Senate passed the Native Title Amendment Bill with amendments on two occasions, on 5 December 1997 and 7 April 1998. The Government rejected key Senate amendments to the Native Title Amendment Bill. There are four key issues on which the Senate and House of Representatives could, on both occasions, not agree. The Government's Bill allows the States and Territories to replace the 'right to negotiate' concerning such matters as mining on pastoral leases with their own regimes. It introduces a sunset clause for Aboriginal native title rights under the *Native Title Act*. It raises the threshold test for registering a native title claim. It does not require that the native title amendments be consistent with the *Racial Discrimination Act*.[288] The Government's Bill can be passed at a joint sitting of both Houses of Parliament, if both Houses of Parliament are dissolved and a Federal election is held later in 1998. This of course assumes that the Liberal–National Party gains office and has a sufficient majority when both Houses sit jointly. Such an outcome is by no means assured.

The Deputy Prime Minister and leader of the National Party, Tim Fischer, has said that the 29 October 1997 amendments to the *Native Title Act* provide 'bucketloads of extinguishment'.[289] The Government's response to the 1996 *Wik* High Court judgment is not a generous settlement with Australia's Indigenous people. It has left Aboriginal and Torres Strait Islander people, and many other Australians, confused, bitter and alienated. The Governor-General, Sir William Deane, in his 26 January 1998 Australia Day message to all Australians, has said that reconciliation between Indigenous and other Australians is of the highest priority.[290] Reconciliation is much less likely if the Native Title Amendment Bill, as passed by the House of Representatives, becomes law.

Why is John Howard doing this? Geoffrey Barker, senior journalist with the *Australian Financial Review*, has questioned the Prime Minister's motives in his article, 'Dr Jekyll and Mr Howard'.

According to Barker's argument, John Howard is reasonable and respectable on economics, but almost monstrous on any social policy that cannot be grasped by his monocultural background (Methodist family, converted to Anglican), which makes him feel comfortable in the Sydney petty bourgeoisie society of the 1950s. From his Methodist background he draws his tenacity, and his appearance of a fundamental sort of decency when dealing with other white Anglo-Saxon Protestants, or people sharing that culture. This strength is also a weakness when dealing with people and groups radically different from his own.[291]

John Howard would appear to lack a natural sympathy for Aboriginal people as a group. A former Liberal Party press secretary, David Barnett, together with Prue Goward, wrote John Howard's officially sanctioned biography. It includes the judgment that the Fraser government's Northern Territory land rights legislation was 'an act of well-intentioned naivety, handing more than 50 per cent of the Territory and 80 per cent of its coastline to a handful of people, merely because they had asked for it'.[292]

Modern Australian Prime Ministers would be outraged when accused of racism. Perhaps Australian Prime Ministers in the past had an easier life. They could mix with English-speaking Anglo-Celtic Australians who enjoyed football and cricket and shared white-Australian values. They chose not to understand peoples of radically different cultures, such as those Aboriginal Australians whose third or fourth language is English, who first met whites in 1964 in some cases, and whose values, beliefs and priorities belong to somewhat different worlds.

The fact of prior Aboriginal ownership of traditional lands can only be questioned if one refuses to recognise the rights of an Indigenous people as a group. One would think that John Howard might be out of step with modern Australia on this issue, and if he risked going to a double dissolution on his Wik Bill, he would lose disastrously. This is not necessarily the case, partly because of broad social and economic changes in Australia, and their uneven regional impact.

Both major parties collect polling information on major issues by types of electorate. Aboriginal and Torres Strait Islander people comprise 2 per cent of the national population and do not vote as a unified group. Polling suggests that two other broad groupings of the Australian nation have emerged. The first is cosmopolitan Australia, which is concentrated in the south-eastern corner of the continent and represented in Perth and Brisbane. The second group lives in the rest of the continent, in remote, rural and regional Australia. Along the Sydney–Melbourne axis in the south-east of Australia, 51.4 per cent of electors voted for the Keating Labor government in the March 1996 election. A majority voted for his emphasis on major national issues, including a republic, Aboriginal reconciliation, native title, engagement with Asia, multiculturalism and economic restructuring. Outside the Sydney–Melbourne axis, Labor gained only 43.1 per cent of the two-party preferred vote, and eighteen out of 94 Federal seats.[293]

The House of Representatives has 148 Members: 94 are held by the Liberal–National Party Coalition. The former Liberal, and now First Nation Party leader, Pauline Hanson holds one seat, and 49 seats are held by the Labor Party. Away from urban south-eastern Australia, the Liberal–National Party Coalition holds sway, and holds 71 of the 94 seats. The Coalition holds 40 of the 43 'rural and regional' seats.[294] Regional Australia voted massively against Keating's Labor government in 1996. They had been hit hard by economic restructuring and did not accept the Labor government's policies on a republic, Aboriginal reconciliation, native title, immigration and multiculturalism. In regional Australia 57 per cent voted against the Keating Labor government, and were attracted by John Howard's statement that he wanted all Australians to be 'relaxed and comfortable'.[295] It is likely that the Liberal–National Party polling has shown that most urban Australians, in the end, will not change their vote because of the Native Title Amendment Bill. It is also likely that most rural Australians will not vote for the party, in this case the Labor Party, which is softer on Aboriginal rights, particularly the relatively new rights of native title.

In summary, Aboriginal and Torres Strait Islander people have slightly more rights in Australia since the 1992 *Mabo (2)* High Court judgment. Many are potential native title holders or native title claimants and they may be able to prove native title to large areas of Australia's land mass, the 'marginal' lands to which grazing licences and pastoral leases, and no other tenure, have been issued during the past 210 years. Many people in regional Australia do not agree with such recognition of native title rights.

In Canada during the 1970s and early 1980s there was a great deal of confrontation and litigation between Indigenous groups and other Canadians. In Canada and New Zealand in the 1990s governments, businesses and local communities made regional agreements with Indigenous groups. At the beginning of the third millennium will Australia choose confrontation and litigation with Indigenous people, or choose to make agreements and work for reconciliation? It is in everyone's interests if Aboriginal peoples, particularly in remote areas, have economic opportunities. Justice and common sense demand it. Unquestionably if we persist with 1970s Indigenous policies of ignoring Indigenous rights and forcing litigation, Australia will be judged harshly in the eyes of the world.

THE ECONOMIC IMPACT OF ROYALTIES AND EMPLOYMENT ON ABORIGINAL PEOPLE

There is now an appreciation by enlightened mining companies and the general community that acceptable mining agreements should guarantee educational assistance, training, and employment of local Indigenous people. It is vital that there are appropriate structures in place. The work of previous years is beginning to return dividends, and the press regularly reports major mining agreements with Aboriginal peoples. It is still too early to report on the monitoring and outcomes of these recent agreements.

In Chapter 5, the amount of royalty-equivalent payments per community member for some of the major agreements made under the *Aboriginal Land Rights (Northern Territory) Act* were identified. The usual pattern is that the amount of money provided per individual is quite modest. However, one needs to examine the poverty of most Aboriginal communities to understand that even modest per capita payments can have a dramatic effect. It is particularly important that the structure of compensation payments is effective and well managed, so that this effect is positive.

Studies have found that only 66,600 Aboriginal and Torres Strait Islander people throughout Australia are employed, or 36 per cent of the total Indigenous population, and 17,167, or 25 per cent, of them are engaged under Community Development Employment Programs. Income is consequently low for a majority of Aboriginal and Torres Strait Islander people.[296] Australia's total unemployment rate is 8.1 per cent, and Aboriginal and Torres Strait Islander people's 1997 unemployment rate is 40 per cent. This figure excludes (counting as 'employed') those Aboriginals and Torres Strait Islanders engaged in the Community Development Employment Program, which is a government-funded scheme whereby one works for unemployment benefits.

The rural Indigenous median family income is $5256. This amount is 70 per cent of the non-Indigenous rural family median income, or 61 per cent when the different household size is taken into account, as the average Aboriginal household has 4.5 people, compared to 3.1 persons for other households. If, therefore, in a typical case, mining royalties in the Northern Territory amount to $700 per person each year, for the duration of a mine, they provide $3150 each year to the average Aboriginal household, or a 60 per cent increase in wealth.[297] If some of this money is used for investment, training, education and securing future jobs, it can have a powerful positive effect.

Against this possible cash benefit, Indigenous leaders must weigh the cost of even temporary loss of hunting and gathering lands, and the negative aspects of a major mine near a small community, when most of the workforce has a radically different culture and background. Of particular importance, therefore, are the non-royalty aspects of a negotiated mining agreement. Good outcomes are likely if a mining agreement guarantees suitable provision for educational assistance, training and employment of local Indigenous people. It is vital that there are appropriate structures in place to manage these influences and that there are training and jobs for local people. Aboriginal and Torres Strait Islander people have emphasised the need for cultural education for miners and other visitors. They are increasingly seeking opportunities for Indigenous business ventures to be associated with approval for a major mining development.

Senior Aboriginal spokespeople have emphasised that they are seeking a co-operative approach with mining companies. They also point out that, by virtue of the *Mabo* decision and the *Native Title Act*, Indigenous Australians are key stakeholders in Australia's future. The economic impact of the changed legal situation can potentially benefit both Aboriginal and Torres Strait Islander peoples and mining companies, if both parties work intelligently together. Contemporary Australia now has potential multiple land tenure over unalienated Crown lands and pastoral leases (see Map 8.1). Indigenous people and miners will have to work out the practical implications of the modern era when both Federal legislation and common law guarantees Indigenous people some negotiating rights over much of the continent.

Table 8.1 summarises key results of a survey undertaken in February 1998 of Australia's major operating mines whose owners have made agreements with Aboriginal and Torres Strait Islander people. Information was collected on Aboriginal and Torres Strait Islander employees of the

Table 8.1   Employment and royalties at operating mines

MINE	ATSI employed	% 1997	ATSI employed	% 1998	Non-mine employed	Royalties $	People
Anaconda	28	7	56	7	0	0	?
Argyle	36	4	33	4	60	0	1,500
CFSM	49	45	46	44	0	600	1,000
GEMCO	25	6	36	9	19	5,600	1,200
Gove	30	3	30	3	50	3,700	1,200
Granites	16	8	8	4	0	1,700	1,200
Hamersley	55	2	55	2	250	0	?
McArthur	20	9	25	10	8	0	?
Magellan	0	0	1	9	0	3,130	1,500
Ranger	18	8	19	8	45	12,000	330
Sunrise	10	7	5	3	50	0	?
Tanami	38	20	37	20	0	2,000	1,200
Tennant	31	9	34	10	5	0	?
Weipa	30	6	30	6	10	0	200

Key:
- 'ATSI employed' is the number of Aboriginal and Torres Strait Islander people employed by the company, as estimated by that company, in June 1997 and February 1998.
- '% 1997' refers to the number of Indigenous employees as a percentage of total company employees in 1997.
- 'Non-mine employed' refers to all Indigenous people employed in 1998 by Aboriginal organisations supported or contracted by the local mining company.
- 'Royalties' refers to annual dollar royalty-equivalent monies paid locally, both statutory and negotiated, divided by the number of adult members of the royalty association.
- 'People' refers to the number of adult members of royalty associations.
- CFSM is the Cape Flattery Silica Mines near Hopevale, North Queensland.
- 'Granites' includes the Granites and Dead Bullock Soak mines in the Tanami Desert operated by Normandy North Flinders.
- 'Magellan' is all of Magellan Petroleum's oil and gas operations in the Northern Territory, including Mereenie and Palm Valley, which are operated jointly with Santos.
- Olympic Dam, owned by WMC Resources Ltd, in South Australia, employed no Aboriginal people in 1997 and 1 Aboriginal person of 792 employees in 1998. It provided unspecified training and employment opportunities to Aboriginal businesses. No royalty-equivalents are payable to Aboriginal organisations.
- 'Sunrise' is the Sunrise Dam Goldmine in the Kalgoorlie region of Western Australia, owned by Acacia Resources Ltd.
- 'Tanami' is the Tanami Mine Joint Venture, owned by Acacia Resources Ltd and Otter Gold Ltd.

mining companies in 1997 and 1998, the total number of all employees at the mining operations. The number of Aboriginal and Torres Strait Islander employees in associated businesses in 1998 which have been used or supported by the mining company that operates the site have also been surveyed. The total local annual royalties received by a local royalty association and the estimated total number of people in that royalty association are included in the table, using publicly available information.

It was made clear that 'Aboriginal and Torres Strait Islander person' included Aboriginal people and Torres Strait Islanders irrespective of what part of Australia they come from, and 'employed' was defined as 'working in paid employment for five hours or more per week'.

Generally the numbers of Indigenous people in direct employment at major mines ranges from 19 to 56 employees, which is 2 to 10 per cent of the workforce. The two exceptions are Cape Flattery Silica Mines north of Hopevale, which employs 46 local Aboriginal people in full-time employment, and they comprise 44 per cent of the workforce, and the Central Desert Joint Venture in the Tanami Desert, where 37 Aboriginal people comprise 20 per cent of the workforce.

My national survey of Indigenous employment on key mine sites was confirmed in general terms by Michael Coughlan, Manager, Indigenous Affairs at Normandy Mining and Chair of the Aboriginal Mining Enterprise Taskforce. He reported that throughout the Northern Territory in December 1997, 290 Aboriginal people were employed in the mining industry. They comprised only 7 per cent of the workforce, even though Aboriginal people comprise 25 per cent of the population in the Northern Territory. He also reported that only 145 Aboriginal people were employed in mining in 1993. He believes that low literacy and numeracy skills hinder Aboriginal employment. Twelve-week pre-vocational courses have assisted, but a three-year pre-vocational program is required.[298] On the other hand, there is an impressive Indigenous employment record at Hopevale, North Queensland and a strong base at Anaconda, Argyle and Hamersley, particularly if one includes Indigenous people employed in enterprises supported by mining companies. This base should be extended by scholarships, effective training and by supporting success.

Notional per capita annual royalty-equivalent payments for Aboriginal people are only significant at four places in Australia. They are the ERA mine at Ranger ($12,000 notional per capita trust payment), the GEMCO mine at Groote Eylandt ($5600), the Nabalco mine at Gove ($3700), and Magellan Petroleum oil and gas operations west of Alice Springs ($3130). Lesser per capita royalties are also paid at the Granites goldmines and the Tanami Desert Joint Venture north-west of Alice Springs. By themselves royalty-equivalent payments will not free people from poverty. Only the development of their skills and a package of support will achieve that.

MAJOR ELEMENTS OF SUCCESSFUL AGREEMENTS

Some principles for good mining practice have emerged from this review. Care for the country, care for the land, for both the sacred sites and the land's capacity for regeneration, are paramount. Land councils in Australia, and Indigenous peoples in North America and the Pacific, have emphasised the importance of caring for the environment as a major requirement in agreeing to a mining project going ahead.

There are several other elements of a successful mining agreement. A reciprocal relationship between the mining company and the community is important. Teaching of Aboriginal culture to mining employees, and training and employment of Aboriginal people are priorities. Planning for the payments of royalty-equivalents should ensure that some funds are available for such purposes as transport to outstations and other parts of traditional lands.

A MODEL OF BEST AUSTRALIAN PRACTICE

ITEM	EXAMPLES
Environmental protection and regeneration	Nabarlek NT
Demonstrated effective training	Hamersley WA
Significant Aboriginal employment	Hopevale Qld
	Anaconda,
	Hamersley WA
Further work from sub-contracting	Argyle, Hamersley WA
Business investments	McArthur River NT
Royalty-equivalent funding, based on production	Aboriginal land, NT
Significant amount of royalties over time	Ranger, Groote
	Eylandt NT
Investment of half of area-affected monies	Ngurratjuta NT
Profitable, safe investments	Groote Eylandt,
	Ngurratjuta NT
Aboriginal ownership of high-profile local assets	Ranger NT
Cross-cultural training	Tanami NT
Good rapport with miners and community	Normandy North
	Flinders NT

Item by item, there are examples of good practice in Australia. The challenge is to combine more than six key elements in as many locations as possible, so that communities have the best chance of success and positive outcomes from mining.

A MODEL FOR MODERN MINING AGREEMENTS

Enlightened companies operating in Australia are becoming more aware of a philosophy of promoting Indigenous issues. For instance, Normandy Mining Ltd has emphasised long-term relationships with Aboriginal people, based on mutual respect and trust. It has recognised the Indigenous parties' attachment to the land and the importance of cultural heritage, and agreed to ensure that areas of special significance are identified and protected, through its majority holding in Normandy North Flinders (Chapter 5) and directly at Woodcutters (Chapter 6).

ISSUES IN MINING AGREEMENTS

Issues in mining agreements which have been identified by Normandy Mining Ltd are as follows:

1. Parties

Who is exploring
who is affected
representative ability, authority to speak, process for identifying the relevant traditional owners.

2. Means of notification of intent to explore

Statutory requirements.

3. Area to be explored

And nature of exploration process.

4. How the company behaves

How many employees and where situated
policies towards alcohol, firearms etc

where will the workers be situated
what other activities will then be carried on in the area.

5. Site protocols

Identification and protection of sacred sites.

6. Tenure of the land

7. Involvement of community in the exploration process

8. Environmental rehabilitation

9. Compensation for disturbance

Whether cash payments
extent of compensation at exploration stage.

10. Joint venture issues

11. Resources for Aboriginal negotiators

12. Legislative and statutory framework

Including environmental impact statements.

13. Development issues

Including education, training, employment, housing, health and infrastructure.

14. Communication issues

Liaison committee.

15. Conflict resolution

16. Minimum standards for negotiation

A standard across the industry.

17. Enforcement issues

Including certainty.

18. Flexibility

Should there be a process to allow change.

19. Media

Communication with the media about the project.[299]

Underlying these agreements is Normandy Mining's philosophy of promoting Indigenous issues. One should:

- only enter an Aboriginal region if one has received an invitation or permission;
- set up operations only after they have been explained to the community;
- listen to the concerns and acknowledge the heritage of a community.

These goals have been implemented by Normandy Mining at its mining and exploration sites, where there are joint ventures for employing and educating Indigenous groups. Normandy Mining's 5000 employees also receive cross-cultural awareness training to implement these philosophies.[300]

The Aboriginal Mining Enterprise Task Force, an informal group of predominantly miners and Aboriginal people, has developed this approach since 1996. The Chair of the group, Michael Coughlan, who is employed by Normandy Mining, has said that companies with community support have identified the following strategies for effective Indigenous involvement:

- increasing of Aboriginal students' awareness of opportunities in mining;
- group Indigenous peoples' policies;
- numeracy and literacy programs;
- informing the workforce in regard to programs;
- men's and women's pre-vocational or access training courses;
- twelve-month traineeships;
- tertiary study sponsorship programs;
- flexible work agreements or arrangements;
- setting appropriate communication channels;
- employment of skilled Aboriginal people in senior positions;
- tours of mining projects;
- assessing and where necessary changing management styles; and
- cross-cultural awareness programs.[301]

At the best situations for Aboriginal employment in mining—at the Cape Flattery Silica Mines at Hopevale, North Queensland, and Hamersley in the Pilbara—these strategies are part of a long-established culture, and there are successful role models for Aboriginal adolescents to follow into mine employment.

EMERGING PRINCIPLES

The key principle for mining companies and other individuals and companies operating in Australia is to build long-term relationships with Indigenous people. Aboriginal people have created land councils to negotiate mining and other provisions with non-Aboriginal parties. These land councils cover the Australian continent (see Map 1.2). Land councils would encourage all mining companies to conform to best practice and to involve land councils and local Aboriginal people in partnerships, to work for the mutual benefit of themselves and other Australians. In some cases, non-Australian companies have been more ready to negotiate with Indigenous people than have Australia's largest and oldest companies. Good relations have also been established between some of the older smaller companies that have a long record of dealing with Aboriginal people on reasonable terms.

The Northern Land Council has outlined a policy position towards mining negotiations:

> The Northern Land Council resolves that position 1 (below) is the most desirable way to negotiate exploration agreements but where an applicant does not agree, position 2 (below) is the only reasonable alternative to protect interests of traditional Aboriginal owners as required by the *Aboriginal Land Rights (Northern Territory) Act.*

> 1. The traditional owners, the Land Council and the mining company can agree that if something worth mining is found, the company will need the further permission of the traditional owners and the Land Council before they start mining. If that permission is not given, there will be no mining. So there should be two consents—firstly to explore and later to mine. The legal arrangements for this are not as simple as they were before the 1987 Amendments [to the *Aboriginal Land Rights (Northern Territory) Act*] ...
>   OR

> 2. The traditional owners, the Land Council and the mining company can agree that if something worth mining is found, a mine can go ahead, but only if there is Agreement before

exploration begins about things that are most important to traditional owners including:

(a)   consent to only one mining project;

(b)   protection of sacred sites;

(c)   protection of the environment including no release of contaminated water;

(d)   when the mine is finished, rehabilitation of the land occur to a level satisfactory to traditional owners;

(e)   no new town on Aboriginal land;

(f)   employment for Aboriginal people;

(g)   how much the company is prepared to pay for mining on Aboriginal land. This may be all agreed up front, or a minimum to be further negotiated when more is known about the mine.[302]

MODELS FOR INCORPORATION

The legal structure of land council organisations is an important issue. For instance, the Cape York Land Council was incorporated in November 1993. The organisation found it helpful to obtain status as a public benevolent institution (PBI). However, to qualify for PBI status the objectives must be exclusively charitable. Cape York Land Council's original objectives included profit-making activities, which were later changed with some difficulty.[303] Marra Worra Worra, a resource organisation in Fitzroy Crossing in the Kimberleys in Western Australia, also gained PBI status after extensive negotiations. PBIs must have a non-profit clause in the objects of association. Such organisations have added the following preambles: 'To provide direct relief from poverty, sickness, suffering, destitution, misfortune, distress and helplessness to all Aboriginals in the district of/or in the State of ...without discrimination.' If wound up, property or money must be transferred or paid to another association having similar objectives.[304]

The Waringarri Aboriginal Corporation in Kununurra, in the east Kimberleys, undertakes most of its functions through one incorporated organisation. Waringarri's solicitors recommended a unit trust structure with a corporate trustee, with each enterprise arm having a separate structure. They have recommended separately incorporating each enterprise under a structure consisting of a unit trust with a corporate trustee (Pty Ltd company). In this way the assets of each enterprise are not put at risk should any of the other enterprises become insolvent or go into liquidation.[305]

These legal models have been adopted by many other Indigenous organisations in other parts of Australia.

KEY CONSIDERATIONS

Because native title is an innovation in Australian law, and covers land outside the Northern Territory, the formulation of how native title will work in practice is still being developed. In Australia, there has always been a range of other interests capable of co-existing over the same land. For instance, restrictive covenants may limit the height, composition or size of buildings, or preserve natural features. There may be easements for water or sewerage, and a land owner may have rights of access to adjacent land. Similarly, mining tenements allow the holder of a licence to enter land and extract minerals. In Western Australia, the Northern Territory and South Australia, pastoral leases have included reservations in favour of Aboriginal people using land for hunting and gathering, ceremonies or erecting traditional dwellings. However, native title will vary from place to place, and is derived from the customs and traditions of native title holders. Co-existence of interests in land is a dominant feature of the common law, and will also apply to native title.[306]

Aboriginal and Torres Strait Islander peoples and mining companies in many cases have co-existing rights. Modern Australia's multiple land tenure, particularly in marginal lands and pastoral leases is a legal fact (see Map 8.1). Recognising this fact is the first step to assisting Aboriginal and Torres Strait Islander people towards regaining the self-sufficiency they enjoyed before European settlement of Australia.

A key task in establishing viable and useful long-term agreements is to maximise benefits and minimise conflict. Negotiations are complex, not open-ended, and a community is stuck with the results of a negotiation for ten years or more. Processes, strategic objectives and outcomes are all important. At Cape Flattery Silica Mines the community found that when negotiating, it is wise to put oneself in the shoes of the other party.

Representative bodies established under the *Native Title Act* have a crucial role to play in such negotiations. They must have a significant scale and expertise, be Aboriginal controlled, employ quality professional expertise, which is available to multinational companies such as Rio Tinto and MIM, and also assist community advisers in their developmental and monitoring roles. The organisations must control the lawyers and make their own decisions.

In the Northern Territory, there are long-established procedures known to both Indigenous communities and mining companies under the *Aboriginal Land Rights (Northern Territory) Act* for the exploration and mining of Aboriginal land. By 1998, exploration and mining covered 68,000 sq km in central Northern Territory. Proportionately as much Aboriginal land as non-Aboriginal land was under exploration.[307]

The agreements provide that landowners are compensated for exploration on their land, and they may also have a joint ownership option if mining subsequently occurs. There are strong provisions for protection of sacred sites, social and environmental protection and guarantees of rehabilitation of bushland. In central Australia, exploration-licence agreements provide for protection of sacred sites, training and employment programs and provisions for Aboriginal people if the exploration is successful.[308]

The President of the Minerals Council of Australia, Jerry Ellis, released a statement of principles of consultation and possible agreements between Aboriginal groups and mining companies.[309] The Minerals Council of Australia statement of principles for land access and mineral development on Indigenous land identified as key considerations:[310]

> Access for land for exploration and development is an essential requirement for the minerals industry.
>
> Australia's Indigenous peoples have native title recognised under the common law of Australia. Native title exists in accordance with the laws and customs of Indigenous people subject to certain conditions.
>
> Where native title rights are unresolved, unrecognised or pending under the Statutes, the minerals industry will consult with Indigenous people that have maintained a traditional use or occupancy of, and affinity for, the land on which mineral development is desired.
>
> Australia's Indigenous peoples are entitled to opportunities to participate in mineral development projects including by direct employment and related economic or business opportunities.
>
> The minerals industry will seek to develop relationships with Indigenous peoples in which there is a better awareness of respective issues, needs and concerns, and a higher level of mutual understanding.

In evaluating mining agreements it is important to consider the extent to which an agreement:

- reflects an effective mobilisation of the bargaining power which Aboriginal and Torres Strait Islander people had available to them;
- meets community aspirations;

- establishes precedents which influence a broader negotiating environment;[311] and
- the scope for investing half of the areas' affected monies, so that there is something left for the future.[312]

The *Mabo (2)* and *Wik* High Court judgments and the *Native Title Act 1993* have provided a radically different context for mining over unalienated Crown land and pastoral leases throughout Australia. It is likely that Aboriginal communities will move towards forming comprehensive agreements with mining companies, and will look to mutual benefit, training and employment of Indigenous people, and protection of the environment, as principles guiding future mineral development in those areas. Successful programs will build good relationships between company staff and Aboriginal employees and communities.

If, however, the unamended Native Title Amendment Bill 1997 were to become law, it is likely that Aboriginal and Torres Strait Islander people would proceed to challenge its provisions in the High Court. They will look to developments in North America and New Zealand, where Indigenous peoples have been assisted towards self-sufficiency through forming regional agreements to control or share in the management of natural resources. A key focus of such agreements is training and employment, helping people to establish their own businesses, and gaining national government recognition of their rights as Indigenous peoples. Outside Australia, it has long been the case that Aboriginal rights are understood through constitutional recognition of Aboriginal cultures. For 'Aboriginal cultures are the water through which Aboriginal rights swim'.[313]

Afterword 1
Thinking With the Land

Patrick Dodson

First Chair, Council for Aboriginal Reconciliation[314]

Many Australians don't know how to think themselves into the country, the land. They find it hard to think with the land. We Aboriginal people find it hard to think without the land. My grandfather taught me how to think about relationships by showing me places. He showed me where the creeks and rivers swirl into the sea, the fresh water meets the salt, the different worlds of ocean and river are mixing together.

He showed me the foam and the turbulence, pointed to the eddies and swirling mud, the colours intermingling. And he showed me where it was always good to put a line into the water and wait for a feed.

The river is the river and the sea is the sea. Salt water and fresh, two separate domains. Each has its own complex patterns, origins, stories. Even though they come together they will always exist in their own right.

My hopes for reconciliation are like that. Reconciliation can mean many different things. It might be as simple as a handshake with your Aboriginal neighbour or, more broadly, better relations between Indigenous communities and other Australians in all places we share across this land.

Above all it must mean some form of agreement that deals with the legacies of our history, provides justice for all and takes us forward as a nation. The tides of national political debate ebb and flow.

The latest tide has brought with it a pressing concern for infrastructure, auditing and accountability. Fair enough, some may say. But we should also ask: what might have gone out on the last tide? By all means let us have accountability. But let us not also lose sight of Justice and rights for Indigenous people, and of the need to redress the wrongs of history.

Some commentators and politicians say that today's non-Indigenous Australians should not feel guilty for the sins of the past. True.

But should today's Indigenous Australians continue to suffer the legacies of the past because the nation has not yet found the ways to overcome them? Let's avoid guilt trips but let's also dump victim blaming.

The track behind us is littered with the relics of policies, programs and projects that failed, that wasted taxpayers' money and failed to deliver real outcomes to those crying out for them. They failed mainly because they did not include Indigenous people in making the decisions.

Let's remember that politicians and bureaucrats set the agendas and made the decisions for decades before the Aboriginal and Torres Strait Islander Commission and other Indigenous organisations were established. It is universally agreed that they singularly failed to lift the health standards, to improve the housing, to provide education and jobs.

For years before ATSIC was established, it was widely acknowledged that the bureaucracy in the Aboriginal Affairs Department had failed to get the funds down to the grass roots communities, and to get good value for them.

This historical fact does not excuse any Indigenous organisation for waste or mismanagement, nor any individual for fraud or corruption.

Go to any remote settlement and see the burnt-out twisted shells of buildings constructed for the benefit of some forgotten government program, dreamed up in an urban office by some forgotten public servant.

To impose policies, to impose programs without participation, without involvement, without concern for self-determination or empowerment, is to return to the bitter mistakes of our past.

Underlying all past and current problems is the dispossession of our people from the lands they owned and cared for, the lands to which their traditions bound them, the lands so central to their spiritual and cultural beliefs.

Mabo put Indigenous people back into the picture that for too long we were painted out of. Today there is no need to repeat the original mistake.

Seeking to prematurely foreclose on that tiny portion of land left open to native title claim after the High Court's decision without any regard for, or appreciation of, the umbilical link of Aboriginal people to the land, would be nothing but national madness and tantamount to sanctifying greed.

If we sever that link, we will generate more of the social dislocation we are trying to mend. We would be opening up a new sore before the old one scarcely had a chance to heal.

The current push to seek a ruling that pastoral leases extinguish native title merely continues the incremental process of dispossession; it extends the continuum and implicates us all in a tragedy we do not need.

Afterword 2
Success in Business With Aborigines

Aden Ridgeway

Executive Director, New South Wales Aboriginal
Land Council[315]

In my dealings with bankers and others in the financial community, I can feel an unexpressed question: 'Can we or should we do business with Aboriginal communities?'

The answer is an emphatic 'yes'. But, like any customers, Aboriginal communities have certain expectations and conditions. In terms of cultural awareness, they are no different from business with any substantial client.

The first 'condition' is recognition that business with an Aboriginal community must take account of the pivotal role of land. Indigenous people feel a sacred obligation to exercise immense responsibilities for land, sea and other resources, to use them with care and diligence for the benefit of future generations.

To state as much is not to quote from a green political tract but an article of historical fact. Business with Aboriginal communities cannot be divorced from issues which the non-Aboriginal community terms 'green'.

Aboriginal communities have not been given sufficient credit for the relatively pristine condition in which Europeans found this continent.

Those seeking to deal with us need to recognise the links between the land and the people, the culture, and the moral, political, and perhaps legal imperatives to deliver social justice.

Again, this is not an ephemeral issue to be divorced from business affairs. Our communities will only respond to those who recognise the need for proper consultation for access to land, and the competition for land among the various interest groups.

Land, sea and other resources are fundamental components arising from the *Mabo* decision. Only through these processes will hunting, fishing and gathering continue to be important traditional and economic activities and provide the foundation for new opportunities.

The tension that may exist between Aboriginal people, the mining, agricultural and environmental groups, arises over questions of jurisdiction and ownership of land, sea and other resources—this is the point at which the tension arises and where uncertainty occurs.

It is not uncommon for individuals and other bodies to express concern about title to their property—businesses are concerned about the future of their endeavours, new investment is discouraged, and Aboriginal people, through no fault of their own, see traditional lands being dramatically altered without their consent.

Each of us is trying to achieve certainty. Certainty will create levels of confidence and understanding to facilitate sustainable growth. However, it is highly unlikely that this level of certainty will be achieved through blanket extinguishment of native title. A further prerequisite is to understand the hurt and injustice that Aboriginal people feel at their past treatment and their continuing lack of opportunities. Again, the conventional response is that this is a political position merely echoing the past, with no place in business. But our sense of injury cannot be dismissed by money, and it cannot be ignored by those seeking to do business with us. There will always be carpetbaggers, and those in Aboriginal communities who look to short-term gain or listen to the blandishments of snake-oil salesmen, but those genuinely seeking a long-term relationship must seek goals and purposes which may differ from a purely material outcome. The first priority is that a project should have social benefits for the community—for example, employment, infrastructure, housing and health. CAAMA radio services in the Northern Territory, Gumbayyngirr Housing Corporation and Weinteriga Sheep Station in New South Wales and Tandanya Cultural Centre in South Australia are good examples. The second priority is the need to create a wealth base for sustainable activities for future generations. Examples are Burnie Kmart Shopping Centre and Furneaux Island Group Oysters in Tasmania, Sunwood Timber, Victoria, Kings Canyon and Mirambeen resorts and the P Kittle Toyota–Mitsubishi dealership in the Northern Territory, and the Western White Linen Service in New South Wales.

Do not be fooled by headlines or stereotypes. Misappropriation and mismanagement are not more prevalent in Aboriginal organisations than in the community at large. In general, expect the same kinds of demands for planning, budget and accountability as one would for any other client. For example, the NSW Aboriginal Land Council investment fund has increased its asset base from around $280 million to $370 million over the last two years [between 1994 and 1996] a performance made possible through constant attention to fiscal monitoring and accountability. Do not expect to work exclusively with central authorities. The final decision in any business venture must be made at the local level. Consider what you can do to earn the respect and co-operation of Aboriginal communities—there is a tremendous need for training, employment, and education. Can bankers do business with Aboriginal communities? Yes. Should they? Yes. Opportunities will increase with time. For example, the NSW Aboriginal Land Council recently announced the establishment of a new credit union and mortgage fund, as well as initiatives in housing, training, land acquisition and sport. The only proviso is this: that business cannot be placed neatly in a little box marked 'business' and divorced from other issues. The relationship with the land, sea and other resources is too strong, the background too recent, and the sense of hurt and injustice too personal to permit such isolation.

Appendix A

Payment of mining royalties in the Northern Territory

The basis of determining most royalty arrangements is the *Mineral Royalty Act 1982* (Northern Territory). However, royalties for prescribed substances, such as uranium, are subject to Commonwealth regulation. Parties may negotiate a royalty arrangement which differs from the rates prescribed in the *Mineral Royalty Act 1982*. Royalty agreements in place are as follows.

Energy Resources of Australia at Ranger

A royalty of 5.5 per cent *ad valorem* for uranium mining is paid to the Commonwealth. This percentage is applied to the gross sales value of production less certain costs. Of the 5.5 per cent, 4.25 per cent is credited to the Aboriginals Benefit Reserve and 1.25 per cent is passed on to the Northern Territory Government by the Commonwealth.

GEMCO, Groote Eylandt, North Flinders Mines Ltd and Zapopan at Mt Todd

Royalties are paid in accordance with the *Northern Territory Mineral Royalty Act 1982*. The basic formula applied under s. 10 has been summarised as follows:

$$\text{Royalty} = GR - (OC + CRD + EEE) \times 18\% - 9000$$

GR: gross realisation from the production unit for the royalty year
CRD: capital recognition deduction
EEE: any eligible exploration expenditure
Where the net value of a mineral commodity is equal to or less than $50,000 the net royalty is nil.

Nabalco Joint Venturers at Gove

A new royalty regime was negotiated to operate from 1 January 1993. Under the regime, royalties are calculated as the maximum of the following three elements:

- minimum of $1.50 per tonne of bauxite exported and $0.75 per tonne of bauxite domestic;
- 10 per cent of sales of bauxite at market rates;
- 10 per cent of rolling average of sales at market rates for the previous five years.

Mereenie Joint Venturers and Palm Valley Joint Venturers

Royalties are levied under the *Petroleum (Prospecting and Mining) Act 1978* and are levied at the rate of 10 per cent of the well head value of gas and oil.[316]

Appendix B

Aboriginal statutory and non-statutory land councils*

New South Wales

NSW Aboriginal Land Council*
PO Box 1125
Parramatta 2124
ph (02) 9689 4444 fax (02) 9687 1234

Victoria

Mirimbiak Nations Aboriginal Corporation
PO Box 11
Abbotsford 3067
ph (03) 9486 9166 fax (03) 9486 9105

Queensland

Cape York Land Council
PO Box 2496
Cairns 4870
ph (070) 519 077 fax (070) 510 097

Carpentaria Land Council
PO Box 71
Burketown 4830
ph (077) 455 132 fax (074) 745 5204

Central Queensland Land Council
PO Box 3331
North Mackay 4740
ph (079) 511 899 fax (079) 513 629

Faira Aboriginal Corporation
PO Box 8402
Woolloongabba 4102
ph (07) 3391 4677 fax (07) 3391 4551

Goolburri Land Council
PO Box 2562
Toowoomba 4350
ph (076) 394 766 fax (074) 639 4926

Gurang Land Council
PO Box 1551
Bundaberg 4670
ph (071) 533 800 fax (071) 529 661

North Queensland Land Council Aboriginal Corporation
PO Box 679N
Smithfield 4878
ph (070) 314 779 fax (070) 317 414

Torres Strait Regional Authority
PO Box 388
Thursday Island 4875
ph (070) 692 581 fax (070) 692 582

South Australia

Aboriginal Legal Rights Movement Inc
321–325 King William Street
Adelaide 5000
ph (08) 8211 8824 fax (08) 8211 7424

Anangu Pitjantjatjara*
PMB Umuwa
via Alice Springs 0872
ph (08) 8950 1501 fax (08) 8950 1511

Maralinga Tjarutja*
PO Box 435
Ceduna 5690
ph (0886) 252 946 fax (0886) 253 076

Western Australia

Aboriginal Legal Service of Western Australia
PO Box 8194

Perth 6849
ph (08) 9265 6666 fax (08) 9221 1767

Goldfields Land Council
PO Box 10006
Kalgoorlie 6433
ph (0890) 911 661 fax (0890) 911 662

Kimberley Land Council
PO Box 377
Derby 6728
ph (0891) 931 118 fax (0891) 931 163

Nanga-Ngoona Moora-Joorga West Pilbara Land Council
PO Box 230
Roebourne 6718
ph (0891) 821 081 fax (0891) 821 387

Ngaanyatjarra Council
PO Box 644
Alice Springs 0871
ph (08) 8950 1711 fax (08) 8953 1892

Noongar Land Council
PO Box 8432
Perth 6000
ph (089) 2254 1111 fax (089) 2254 133

Pilbara Land Council
PO Box 764
Port Hedland 6721
ph (089) 173 3003 fax (089) 173 3006

Western Desert Puntukurnuparna
PO Box 2358
South Hedland 6722
ph (089) 172 3299 fax (089) 172 3202

Yamatji Barna Baba Maaja Aboriginal Corporation
PO Box 2119

Geraldton 6530
ph (089) 964 5645 fax (089) 964 5646

Northern Territory

Northern Land Council*
PO Box 42921
Casuarina 0811
ph (08) 8920 5100 fax (08) 8945 2633

Central Land Council*
PO Box 3321
Alice Springs 0871
ph (08) 8951 6211 fax (08) 8953 4343

Tiwi Land Council*
PO Box 38545
Winnellie 0821
ph (08) 8981 4898 fax (08) 8981 4282

References

BOOKS, ARTICLES AND REPORTS

Aboriginal and Torres Strait Islander Commission (ATSIC), 1997a. *Annual Report 1997.* Aboriginal and Torres Strait Islander Commission, Canberra.

—— 1997b. *ATSIC Reporter 1997.* Aboriginal and Torres Strait Islander Commission, Canberra.

Aboriginal Land Commissioner (Justice Michael Maurice) 1990. *Report on Mataranka Area Land Claim (Report No 31).* Australian GovernmentPublishing Service, Canberra.

ACIL Economics, Policy and Strategy Consultants, 1993. *The Contribution of the Ranger Uranium Mine to the Northern Territory and Australian Economies: The report of a study for Energy Resources of Australia Ltd,* unpublished report, Canberra.

Altman, J.C. 1983. *Aborigines and Mining Royalties in the Northern Territory.* Australian Institute of Aboriginal Studies, Canberra.

—— 1984. *Report on the Review of the Aboriginals Benefit Reserve (and Related Financial Matters) in the Northern Territory Land Rights Legislation.* ANUTECH Pty Ltd, Canberra.

—— 1985. *Aborigines, Tourism and Development: the Northern Territory Experience.* Australian National University, North Australia Research Unit, Darwin.

—— 1991. 'The Economic Impact of Australian Aboriginal Land Rights' in *Society and Culture: Economic Perspectives. Proceedings of the Sesquicentennial Conference of New Zealand Association of Economists, 20–22 August, 1990,* Auckland.

—— 1994. *Implementing Native Title: economic lessons from the Northern Territory.* Centre for Aboriginal Economic Policy Research (CAEPR) Discussion paper no. 64, Australian National University, Canberra.

—— 1995. *Native Title Act: implementation issues for resource developers.* Centre for Aboriginal Economic Policy Research (CAEPR), Discussion paper no. 88, Australian National University, Canberra.

—— 1996. 'Review of the Gagudju Association (Stage 2): structure, statutory, economic and political considerations.' Centre for Aboriginal

Economic Policy Research, Australian National University, unpublished report.

—— 1998. 'Compensation for native title: land rights lessons on how to get effective and fair regimes.' Unpublished compensation workshop paper, Australian National University, 19–20 February 1998.

Altman, J.C. and Dillon, M.C. 1988. 'Aboriginal Land Rights, Land Councils and the Development of the Northern Territory' in Deborah Wade-Marshall and Peter Loveday *Contemporary Issues in Development.* Australian National University. North Australia Research Unit, Darwin.

Altman, J.C., Ginn, A. and Smith, D.E. 1993. *Existing and Potential Mechanisms for Indigenous Involvement in Coastal Zone Resource Management Consultancy Report,* Centre for Aboriginal Economic Policy Research (CAEPR) Discussion paper, Australian National University, Canberra.

Altman, J.C. and Smith, D.E. 1994. *The economic impact of mining moneys: the Nabarlek case, Western Arnhem Land,* Centre for Aboriginal Economic Policy Research (CAEPR), Discussion paper no. 63, Australian National University, Canberra.

Aminco and Associates. 1975. *The background to Nabarlek: a summary report on uranium in Australia prepared for the Northern Land Council,* unpublished report, Canberra.

Attwood, B. 1993. *In the Age of Mabo: History, Aborigines and Australia.* Allen & Unwin, Sydney.

Australian Bureau of Agricultural and Resource Economics (ABARE) 1997. *Australian Commodities December 1996,* vol. 27, Canberra.

Bachelard, M. 1997. *The Great Land Grab.* Hyland House, South Melbourne.

Barker, G. 1997. 'Dr Jekyll and Mr Howard', *Australian Rationalist,* no. 44: 15–18.

Barnett, D. and Goward, P. 1997. *John Howard, Prime Minister.* Viking, Melbourne.

Bartlett, R.H. 1993. 'Legislative Regulation in Western Australia' in *Laws of Australia,* Law Book Company, Sydney.

Blackshield, S. 1997. 'Crescent Head Native Title Agreement', *Aboriginal Law Bulletin,* vol. 3, no. 88, January: 9–11.

Blainey, G. 'The Gold Rushes: the Year of Decision', *Historical Studies, Australia and New Zealand,* vol. 10, no. 38, Melbourne University.

Bonner, N. 1996. *Report of the Review of the Aboriginal Lands Trust,* The Aboriginal Lands Trust Review Team. Aboriginal Affairs Department, Perth.

Bridge, N. 1996. 'The Framework for Mineral Exploration to Proceed without triggering the Native Title Act procedure'. Unpublished paper. *Doing Business with Aboriginal Communities Conference*, Darwin.

—— 1998. *An Overview of Contemporary Projects involving Aboriginal Communities and Mining Company agreements.* Unpublished paper. *Doing Business with Aboriginal Communities Conference*, Alice Springs.

Broome, R. 1994. *Aboriginal Australians: Black Responses to White Dominance 1788–1994.* Allen & Unwin, Sydney.

Burke, P. 1998. 'The Native Title Amendment Bill: what happened in the Senate' *Indigenous Law Bulletin,* February 1998, vol. 4, issue 9.

Central Land Council 1998. Submission to the Review of the *Aboriginal Land Rights (Northern Territory) Act 1976.*

Christensen, W. 1980. *Aborigines and the Argyle Diamond Project,* Working Paper no. 3, East Kimberley Impact Assessment Project, Centre for Resource and Environmental Studies, Australian National University, Canberra.

Clark, I. and Cook, B. 1992. *Introduction to Australia's Minerals: Uranium.* ERA WMC Resources Ltd, Adelaide.

Clarke, J. 1997. *'The Native Title Amendment Bill 1997: a different order of uncertainty'*, Centre for Aboriginal Economic Policy Research (CAEPR), Discussion paper no. 144. Australian National University, Canberra.

Coghlan, M. 1998. 'An outline of the Aboriginal Mining Enterprise Task Force', *Doing Business with Aboriginal Communities Conference,* 24–27 February. Unpublished paper, Alice Springs.

Commonwealth of Australia, Joint House Department of Parliament House, 1993. *Expressing Australia, Art in Parliament House.* Joint House Department of Parliament House, Canberra.

Connell, J. and Howitt, R. 1991. *Mining and Indigenous Peoples in Australia.* Sydney University Press, Sydney.

Cooper, V. (Chair). 1997. *Report of Social Impact Study.* Report of the Aboriginal Project Committee. Supervising Scientist, Canberra.

Cousins, D. and Nieuwenhuysen, J. 1984. *Aboriginals and the Mining Industry: Case studies of the Australian Experience.* Allen & Unwin, Sydney.

Cowlishaw, G. 1995. 'Did the Earth Move for You', *Australian Journal of Anthropology,* vol. 6: 1 & 2: 43–63.

Cribben, J. 1984. *The Killing Times: the Coniston massacre 1928.* Fontana/ Collins, Sydney.

Dillon, M. 1991. 'Aborigines and Diamond Mining' in Connell and Howitt. *Mining and Indigenous Peoples in Australia.* Sydney University Press, Sydney.

Dixon, R.A. and Dillon, M.C. 1990. *Aborigines and Diamond Mining: the Politics of Resource Development in the East Kimberley Western Australia.* University of Western Australia Press, Nedlands, Western Australia.

Djerrkura, G. 1998. *ATSIC Submission to the Review of the Aboriginal Land Rights (Northern Territory) Act 1976.* Aboriginal and Torres Strait Islander Commission, Canberra.

Dodson, M. 1995a. 'The Mining Industry and Indigenous Land Owners: a post *Native Title Act* analysis'. *Outlook:* 371–387.

—— 1995b. *Native Title Report: Report of the Aboriginal and Torres Strait Islander Social Justice Commission.* Aboriginal and Torres Strait Islander Social Justice Commission, Sydney.

Dodson, P. (Chair) 1997. *Kakadu Region Social Impact Study: Community action plan.* Report of Social Study Advisory Group. Supervising Scientist, Canberra.

Dunn, J. 1995. 'Legacy of the golden fleece', *Age,* 2 October 1995.

Fingleton, J. 1996. *Review of the Aboriginal Councils and Associations Act 1976.* Australian Institute of Aboriginal and Torres Strait Islander Studies. Canberra. Volume 1 Report. Volume 2 Case studies.

Fingleton, J., Edmunds, M. and McRandle, P. (eds) 1995. *Proof and Management of Native Title: summary of proceedings of a workshop.* Australian Institute of Aboriginal and Torres Strait Islander Studies, Canberra.

Fingleton, J. and Finlayson, J. (eds) 1995. *Anthropology in the Native Title Era: Proceedings of a workshop.* Australian Institute of Aboriginal and Torres Strait Islander Studies, Canberra.

Fitzgerald, J. 1995. *Proving Native Title: a critical guide. Aboriginal Law Bulletin,* vol. 3, no. 74, June.

Flannery, T. 1994. *The Future Eaters: An ecological history of the Australasian Lands and People.* Reed, Port Melbourne.

Flood, J. 1995. *Archaeology of the Dreamtime: The story of prehistoric Australia and its people.* Angus & Robertson, Sydney.

Forbes, J.R. 1995. 'Radical Changes to the NNTT? The French Memorandum', *Native Title News,* vol. 1, no. 6: 81–83.

Fox, R.W. 1977. *Ranger Uranium Environmental Inquiry,* second report, Australian Government Publishing Service, Canberra.

Goot, M. and Rowse, T. 1994. *Make a Better Offer: the politics of Mabo.* Pluto Press, Sydney.

Gorman, S. 1998 (forthcoming). *Native Title agreements: reference document for Industry.* Unpublished Neville Stanley studentship for Faculty of Law, University of Western Australia.

Gray, W. J. 1980. 'The Ranger and Nabarlek Mining Agreement', in Harris, S. (ed) 1980. *Social and Environmental Choice: the impact of uranium mining in the Northern Territory.* Centre for Resource and Environmental Studies, Australian National University, Canberra.

Hall, R., Rawson, P.F. and others 1975. *The Illustrated Encyclopedia of the Earth's Resources.* Marshall Cavendish, London.

Hamersley Iron Pty Ltd 1997. *Aboriginal Training and Liaison: Australian Reconciliation Award Category: Cultural/Land and Business/Industry.* unpublished report. Dampier, Western Australia.

Harris, M. 1972. *The Rise of Anthropological Theory.* Routledge and Kegan Paul, London.

Havnen, O. 1997. 'Black Holes, Fiscal Policy and Human Rights' in Fletcher, C. (ed) *Federalism in the Northern Territory: Options for Fiscal Maturity.* Australian National University, North Australia Research Unit, Darwin.

Horton, D. H. (ed) 1994. *Encyclopaedia of Aboriginal Australia,* Australian Institute of Aboriginal and Torres Strait Islander Studies Press, Canberra.

Howitt, R. 1991. 'Aborigines and Gold Mining in Central Australia' in Connell, J. and Howitt, R., *Mining and Indigenous Peoples in Australia.* Sydney University Press, Sydney.

Hunter, B. and Taylor, J. 1996. 'Indigenous labour force status to the year 2000: estimated impacts of recent Budget cuts'. Centre for Aboriginal Economic Policy Research (CAEPR) Discussion paper no. 119. Australian National University, Canberra.

Industry Commission. 1991. *Mining and Mineral Processing in Australia.* Report no.7. Australian Government Publishing Service, Canberra.

Ireland, T. 1996. 'Exploring for Gold on Aboriginal Land in the Northern Territory'. Unpublished paper delivered to the Third International and Twenty-First Annual Mineral Council of Australia, Newcastle, 14–18 October 1996.

Jull, P., Mulrennan, M., Sullivan, M., Crough, G. and Lea, D. (eds) 1994. *Surviving Columbus: Indigenous Peoples, Political Reform and Environmental Management in North Australia.* The Australian National University, North Australia Research Unit, Darwin.

Kauffman, P. 1979. 'The new Aborigines: the politics of tradition in the Groote Eylandt Area of Arnhem Land'. Master of Arts thesis. Australian National University, Canberra.

—— 1997a. *First Nations: Australia's Native Title Representative Bodies Report on North America.* Australian Centre for Regional and Local Government Studies. University of Canberra, Canberra.

—— 1997b. *Deals and Agreements: mining on Aboriginal land in Australia.* Australian Centre for Regional and Local Government Studies, University of Canberra, Canberra.

—— 1998. *Sharing Land and Sea: Report on New Zealand.* Australian Centre for Regional and Local Government Studies. University of Canberra, Canberra.

Kauffman, P. and Elu, J. 1994. *National Aboriginal Health Strategy Evaluation Report on North Queensland.* Unpublished report. Aboriginal and Torres Strait Islander Commission, Canberra.

Kauffman, P. and Springford, T. 1997. *Pathways to Agreement: Mirimbiak Nations Aboriginal Corporation and Native Title in Victoria.* Mirimbiak Nations Aboriginal Corporation. Unpublished report, Melbourne.

Keen, I. 1980. 'The Alligator Rivers Aborigines: retrospect and prospect', in Jones, R. (ed), *North Australia: options and implications.* Research School of Pacific Studies. Australian National University, Canberra.

Keon-Cohen, B.A. 1982. 'Land Rights News', *Aboriginal Law Bulletin,* vol. 4: 12-13.

—— 1993. 'Some Problems of Proof: the Admissibility of Traditional Evidence', in Stephenson, M.A. and Ratnapala, S. *Mabo: a judicial revolution: the Aboriginal Land Rights Decision and its impact on Australian Law.* University of Queensland Press, Brisbane.

Kulchyski, P. 1994. *Unjust Relations: Aboriginal Rights in Canadian Courts.* Oxford University Press, Toronto.

Levitus, R. 1991. 'The Boundaries of Gagudju Association Membership: Anthropology, Law and Public Policy', in Connell, J. and Howitt, R. (eds), *Mining and Indigenous Peoples in Australia,* Sydney University Press, Sydney: 153–168.

Lewis, M. 1996. 'A Review of Gagudju Association's Commercial Enterprises commissioned by the Northern Land Council'. Unpublished report, Darwin.

Love, M. 1997. 'Lighting the Wik of Change'. *Land, Rights, Laws: Issues of Native Title.* Native Titles Research Unit. Issues paper no. 14, February.

McIntyre, G. 1994. 'Proving Native Title' in Bartlett, R.H. and Meyers, G.D. *Native Title Legislation in Australia.* Centre for Commercial and Resources Law. The University of Western Australia and Murdoch University, Perth: 121–157.

McNeil, K. 1997. 'Co-existence of Indigenous and non-Indigenous land rights: Australia and Canada compared in light of the *Wik* decision', *Indigenous Law Bulletin*, vol. 4, issue 5. University of New South Wales, Sydney.

Maddock, K. 1983. '"Owners" and "Managers" and the choice of statutory traditional owners by anthropologists and lawyers' in Peterson, N. and Langton, M. (eds), *Aboriginal Land and Land Rights*. Australian Institute of Aboriginal Studies, Canberra.

Marshall, C. 1994. 'The impact of royalty payments on Aboriginal communities in the Northern Territory', in Jull, P. and others. *Surviving Columbus: Indigenous Peoples, Political Reform and Environmental Management in North Australia,* North Australia Research Unit, Darwin.

Martin, D. 1995. *Report to the Hon. Robert Tickner regarding the Proposal to establish the North East Arnhem Ringgitj Land Council.* Unpublished report, Canberra.

—— 1996. 'Report on Napranum', in Fingleton, J. 1996. *Review of the Aboriginal Councils and Associations Act 1976.* Australian Institute of Aboriginal and Torres Strait Islander Studies, Canberra. Volume 2 Case studies.

Melleuish, G. 1998. *The Packaging of Australia: Politics and Culture Wars.* University of New South Wales Press, Sydney.

Merlan, F. 1995. 'The regimentation of Customary Practice: from Northern Territory Land Claims to Mabo'. *Australian Journal of Anthropology,* vol. 6: 1 & 2: 64–82.

Meyers, G.D., Piper, C.M. and Rumley, H.E. 1997. 'Asking the Minerals Question: Rights in Minerals as an Incident of Native Title'. *Australian Indigenous Law Reporter,* vol. 2, no. 2: 202–250. Indigenous Law Centre, University of New South Wales.

Minerals Council of Australia, 1996a. *Annual Report 1996.* Canberra.

—— 1996b. *Positioning for the Future: Fact sheets.* Canberra.

National Native Title Tribunal, 1997. *Proforma agreements,* short proforma agreements for mining and future acts can be found on the internet. See www.nntt.gov.au.

Neate, G. 1989. *Aboriginal Land Rights Law in the Northern Territory*, vol. 1. Alternative Publishing Co-operative, Sydney.

—— 1995. 'Determining Native Title Claims: Learning from experience in Queensland and the Northern Territory', *The Australian Law Journal,* vol. 69, no. 7, July.

—— 1998. 'Compensation for native title: some legal issues' Unpublished compensation workshop paper, Australian National University, 19–20 February.

O'Faircheallaigh, C. 1988. 'Uranium royalties and Aboriginal economic development', in Wade-Marshall, D. and Loveday, P. (eds). *Northern Australia Progress and Prospects, Volume 1 Contemporary Issues in Development,* North Australia Research Unit, Darwin.

—— 1994. *Negotiations between mining companies and Aboriginal communities: process and structure.* Centre for Aboriginal Economic Policy Research (CAEPR) Discussion paper no. 64, Australian National University, Canberra.

—— 1995. *Mineral development agreements negotiated by Aboriginal communities in the 1990s,* Centre for Aboriginal Economic Policy Research (CAEPR) Discussion paper no. 85, Australian National University, Canberra.

O'Faircheallaigh, C. and Holden, A. 1995. *Economic and Social Impact of Silica Mining at Cape Flattery,* Centre for Australian Public Sector Management Research Monograph no. 1. Griffith University, Brisbane.

Parker, G. (Chairman) 1995. *Review of Native Title Representative Bodies.* Aboriginal and Torres Strait Islander Commission, Canberra.

Peterson, N. and Lampert, R.J. 1985. 'A Central Australian ochre mine'. *Records of the Australian Museum,* vol. 37(1): 1–9.

Peterson, N. and Langton, M. 1983. *Aborigines, Land and Land Rights.* Australian Institute of Aboriginal Studies Press, Canberra.

Pritchard, B. and Gibson, C. 1996. *The Black Economy: Regional Development Strategies in the Northern Territory.* Australian National University, North Australia Research Unit, Darwin.

Roberts, J. 1978. *From Massacres to Mining,* War on Want and CIMRA. London.

Rowley, C.D. 1972. *The Remote Aborigines,* Penguin, Ringwood.

Senior, C. 1998. 'The Yandicoogina Process: A Model for Negotiating Land Use Agreements', 'Land, Rights, Laws', *Issues of Native Title Regional Agreements paper no. 6,* Australian Institute of Aboriginal and Torres Strait Islander Studies, Canberra.

Selway, B. 1998. 'Negotiating agreements on Pastoral Lands: the South Australian Approach', Doing Business with Aboriginal Communities Conference, 24–27 February. Unpublished paper.

Sexton, S. 1996. 'Aboriginal Land Rights, the Law, and Empowerment: the failure of Economic Theory as a critique of land rights'. The Australian National University North Australia Research Unit. Discussion paper no. 3, 1996. Darwin.

Smith, D. and Daley, A.E. 1996. *The economic status of Indigenous Australian households: a statistical and ethnographic analysis*, Centre for Aboriginal Economic Policy Research (CAEPR). Discussion paper no. 109. Australian National University, Canberra.

Stephenson, M.A. and Ratnapala, S. 1993. *Mabo: a judicial revolution, The Aboriginal Land Rights Decision and Its Impact on Australian Law.* University of Queensland Press, Brisbane.

Tehan, M. 1997. 'Land, Rights, Laws', *Native Title issues paper no. 12.* Australian Institute of Aboriginal and Torres Strait Islander Studies, Canberra.

Toohey, J. 1984. *Seven Years On: report by Mr Justice Toohey to the Minister for Aboriginal Affairs on the Aboriginal Land Rights (Northern Territory) Act 1976 and Related Matters.* Australian Government Publishing Service, Canberra.

Viner, I. 1997. 'The *Wik* 10 point plan', *Australian Rationalist*, no. 45: 63–70.

Walter and Turnbull, 1993. *Aboriginals Benefit Trust Account: Strategy for the Management of the Net Assets/ Accumulated Funds of the Trust Account.* Unpublished report, Canberra.

Warren, P. 1989.'The Argyle Story: the search for Australia's diamonds' in *Mining and the return of the living environment,* vol. 2. Australian Mining Industry Council, Canberra.

Wilson, R. 1997. *Bringing Them Home: Report of the National Inquiry into the Separation of Aboriginal and Torres Strait Islander Children from Their Families.* Human Rights and Equal Opportunity Commission, Sydney.

Winwood-Smith, A. 1997. 'Yuendumu Mining Company N.L.: Hiring of rural Aborigines for the Mineral Exploration Industry'. *Down to Earth: Journal of the Northern Territory Minerals Council,* March, Darwin.

Woodward, A.E. 1973. *Aboriginal Land Rights Commission: First Report, July 1973.* Australian Government Publishing Service, Canberra.

—— 1974. *Aboriginal Land Rights Commission: Second Report, April 1974.* Australian Government Publishing Service, Canberra.

Wootten, H. 1994. 'Mabo: Issues and Challenges', *The Judicial Review,* vol. 1.

—— 1995. 'Mabo and the lawyers', *Australian Journal of Anthropology,* vol. 6: 1 & 2: 116–132.

Yunupingu, G. (ed) 1997. *Our Land is Our Life: Land Rights—Past, Present and Future.* University of Queensland Press, Brisbane.

ANNUAL REPORTS

All public companies in Australia, including Australian mining and resource companies, must publish an annual report which outlines their recent activities. The reports provide excellent background information for Aboriginal and Torres Strait Islander people wishing to negotiate with a mining company. A copy of the annual report is usually available by telephoning the head office of the company concerned.

Commonwealth Government departments and statutory authorities

Aboriginal and Torres Strait Islander Commission, 1991–97.
Aboriginal and Torres Strait Islander Commercial Development Corporation, 1991–97.
Anindilyakwa Land Council, 1993–97.
Central Land Council, 1977–97.
Northern Land Council 1977–97.

State and Territory departments and statutory authorities

Queensland Department of Family Services and Aboriginal and Islander Affairs, *Annual Reports* 1992–97. Brisbane.
State Aboriginal Affairs Department [South Australia], *Annual Report* 1994–97, South Australian House of Assembly. Adelaide.
Western Australian Aboriginal Affairs Planning Authority and Aboriginal Lands Trust, *Annual Reports* 1992–97. Perth.

Annual reports of public companies, 1993–97, and their contact addresses

Acacia Resources Ltd
Level 11, 60 City Road
South Melbourne Vic 3205
ph (03) 9684 4999 fax (03) 9696 9977

BHP Ltd
600 Bourke Street
Melbourne Vic 3000
ph (03) 9609 3333 fax (03) 9609 3015

Comalco Ltd
55 Collins Street
Melbourne Vic 3000
ph (03) 9283 3000 fax (03) 9283 3707

Magellan Petroleum Australia Ltd
c/- Coopers & Lybrand, 17th Floor Waterfront Place 1 Eagle Street
Brisbane Qld 4000
ph (07) 3877 8888 fax (07) 3877 8000

MIM Holdings Ltd
GPO Box 1433
Brisbane Qld 4001
ph (07) 3833 8000 fax (07) 3832 2426

Newcrest Mining Ltd
Level 9
600 St Kilda Road
Melbourne Vic 3004
ph (03) 9522 5333 fax (03) 9525 2996

North Ltd
North House, Level 6 476 St Kilda Road
Melbourne Vic 3004
ph (03) 9207 5111 fax (03) 9867 4351

Normandy Mining Ltd; and
Normandy North Flinders Mines Ltd
PO Box 7175 Hutt Street
Adelaide SA 5001
ph (08) 8303 1700 fax (08) 8303 1900

Pasminco Ltd
Level 15
380 St Kilda Road
Melbourne Vic 3000
ph (03) 9288 0333 fax (03) 9288 0406

Rio Tinto Ltd
55 Collins Street
Melbourne Vic 3000
ph (03) 9283 3333 fax (03) 9283 3707

Santos Ltd
39 Grenfell Street

Adelaide SA 5000
ph (08) 8218 5111 fax (08) 8218 5274

WMC Resources Ltd
GPO Box 860K
Melbourne Vic 3001
ph (03) 9685 6000 fax (03) 9685 6115

AUSTRALIAN GOVERNMENTS' LEGISLATION RELEVANT TO ABORIGINAL MINING RIGHTS

Commonwealth Government

Aboriginal Land Grant (Jervis Bay Territory) Act 1986
Aboriginal Land Rights (Northern Territory) Act 1976
Aboriginal and Torres Strait Islander Heritage Protection Act 1984
Evidence Act 1995
Native Title Act 1993
Native Title Amendment Bill 1997
Racial Discrimination Act 1975

New South Wales

Aboriginal Land Rights Act 1983

Victoria

Aboriginal Lands Act 1970
Aboriginal Land (Lake Condah and Framlingham Forest) Act 1987 (Cth)

Queensland

Aboriginal and Torres Strait Islander (Land Holding) Act 1985
Aboriginal Land Act 1991
Alcan Act 1965
Mineral Resources Act 1989
Torres Strait Land Act 1991

South Australia

Maralinga-Tjarutja Land Rights Act 1984
Pitjantjatjara Land Rights Act 1981

Western Australia

Aboriginal Affairs Planning Authority Act 1972

Northern Territory

Granites Exploration Agreement Ratification Act 1994
Mineral Royalty Act 1982

KEY COURT JUDGMENTS

Northern Territory Supreme Court
Stockdale, J. (1992) *Northern Territory v Northern Land Council* ALR 81 NTR 1.
Martin, C.J. (1996) *Flynn, J. v Mamarika,* unreported, no. 132 of 1995.

Federal Court

Blackburn, J. (1971) *Milirrpum v Nabalco and the Commonwealth of Australia* (1991) 17 FLR 141.
Pareroultja v Tickner (1993) 42 FCR 32, 117 ALR 206.

High Court

Mabo v The State of Queensland (No 2) (1992) 175 CLR 1.
Wik and others v The State of Queensland (1996) 187 CLR 1.

MAPS

Copyright to maps is held by the following organisations: 'Native Title Representative Bodies' by the Aboriginal and Torres Strait Islander Commission; 'Aboriginal land in the Northern Territory' by the Northern Territory Department of Lands, Planning and Environment; 'Uranium deposits in Australia' by the Bureau of Resource Sciences; 'Kakadu National Park, Ranger and Jawoyn land' by ERA Ltd; 'Mining sites around the Gulf of Carpentaria' by the Australian Institute of Aboriginal and Torres Strait islander Studies; 'Mining on Groote Eylandt' by the Anindilyakwa Land Council; 'Hamersley's operations in the Pilbara' by Hamersley Iron Pty Ltd; 'Lawn Hill, Gulf Region, Qld' by Pasminco Ltd and 'Contemporary land tenure' by Landinfo Pty Ltd. Their permission to reproduce these maps is gratefully acknowledged.

Notes

1   Introduction

1. Fox 1977.
2. Balance of the NSWALC Statutory Fund, 31 January 1998, personal communication, Mr Talat Shanawani, 18 February 1998. Government income to the Fund ceases on 31 December 1998.
3. Minerals Council of Australia 1996a: 13.
4. *Australian* 1 October 1995.
5. ABARE *Australian Commodities* 1997, Table 26.
6. Minerals Council of Australia 1996b.
7. *Mabo v the State of Queensland (No 2)* (1992) 175 CLR at 15 *Mabo (2)*.
8. *Mabo (No 2)* (1992) 174–175 CLR.
9. *Milirrpum v Nabalco* 17 FLR 141.
10. Brennan J. *Mabo (2)* (1992) 175 CLR 1 at 57, 58 and 70.
11. Deane J and Gaudron J. *Mabo No 2* (1992) 175 CLR at 15.
12. Stephenson and Ratnapala, 1993.
13. Justice O'Loughlin of the Federal Court found that native title was permanently extinguished, with respect to the Larrakia land claim around Darwin, by freehold land grants made in 1882 (*Canberra Times* 28 February 1998: 5).
14. *Mabo v The State of Queensland (No 2)* (1992) 107 ALR *Mabo (2)*.
15. *Wik and others v The State of Queensland* (1996) 121 ALR 129.
16. *Pareroultja v Tickner* (1993) 117 ALR 206, 209–210.
17. Parliamentary Joint Committee on Native Title, *Proceedings,* 27 October 1995: 1490.
18. *Native Title Act,* s. 35.
19. *Native Title Act,* s. 36.
20. Brennan J *Mabo (2)* (1992) 107 ALR 1, especially at 42–45 and 51–52.
21. Toohey J *Mabo (2)* at 188.
22. *Coe v Commonwealth* Mason CJ (1993) 38 ALJR 110. See National Native Title Tribunal members' criticisms of this view, quoted in Fitzgerald J. 1995: 5.

23. *Mabo (2)* 175 CLR 1 at 58–63 and 70 per Brennan J, 88–90, 99–100 and 109–110 per Deane and Gaudron JJ.
24. Brennan J *Mabo (2)* (1992) 175 CLR 1 at 88, 99, 110.
25. Fitzgerald J 1995: 5.
26. *ATSIC News,* Summer 1997: 11.
27. Blackshield, S. 1997.
28. *Sydney Morning Herald,* 8 April 1997.
29. *Sydney Morning Herald,* 11 October 1996: 15–17; *Australian Financial Review,* 3 February 1997: 8.
30. *Australian,* 9 December 1997.

2   The Aboriginal Land Rights (Northern Territory) Act 1976

31. Woodward J 1975: 28.
32. Commonwealth of Australia, Joint House Department of Parliament House, 1993: 29.
33. Northern Land Council *Annual Report 1994*: 4–5.
34. Altman, J. 1983: 44; Jull, P. 1994.
35. Toohey J 1984.
36. Toohey J 1984: 37 and Maddock, K. 1983: 98.
37. *Aboriginal Land Rights (Northern Territory) Act,* ss 48(1), 68.
38. The *Audit (Transitional and Miscellaneous) Amendment Act 1977,* which commenced on 24 October 1997, changed the ABTA to the ABR.
39. Altman, J. 1995.
40. *Aboriginal Land Rights (Northern Territory) Act,* s. 48(5).
41. *Aboriginal Land Rights (Northern Territory) Act,* s. 64(4).
42. *Aboriginal Land Rights (Northern Territory) Act,* s. 64(5).
43. *Aboriginal Land Rights (Northern Territory) Act,* s. 64(7).
44. Aboriginals Benefit Reserve *Annual Report 1997*: 31.
45. *Aboriginal Land Rights (Northern Territory) Act,* ss 41, 46, 48A; Neate, G. 1989: 382–383.
46. *Northern Territory v Northern Land Council* ALR 81 NTR 1. Sexton, S. 1996.
47. ATSIC *Annual Report 1997:* 83.
48. Pritchard, B. and C. Gibson 1996: 24.
49. ATSIC *Annual Report 1997:* 117–123.
50. Pritchard, B. and C. Gibson 1996: 23.
51. Havnen, O. and Tilmouth, T. in G. Yunupingu 1997.
52. Australian Bureau of Census and Statistics *1996 Census,* special analysis.

53. Pritchard, B. and C. Gibson 1996: 24.
54. *The Concise Oxford Dictionary* 1963. Clarendon Press, Oxford.
55. Tilmouth, T. in G. Yunupingu 1997: 22.
56. Aboriginal Land Commissioner 1990: vi.
57. Havnen, O. in G. Yunupingu 1997: 87.
58. *Age,* 19 March 1997.
59. The Hon Shane Stone QC, 1 December 1997, Ministerial statement to the Northern Territory Legislative Assembly on the Review of the *Aboriginal Land Rights (Northern Territory) Act.* Darwin.
60. Avery, D., letter of 3 March 1998 and Ireland, T. 1996: 311–312.

3   State legislation

61. Kauffman, P. and Springford, T. 1997.
62. *Aboriginal Land (Lake Condah and Framlingham Forest) Act 1987* (Cth), s. 33(4).
63. *Aboriginal Land Act 1991*, s. 7.02 and Aboriginal Land Regulation 1991 (Qld), Queensland, *Government Gazette*, 21 December 1991: 2308.
64. State Aboriginal Affairs Department *Annual Report 1994–95*: 7.
65. *Annual Report of the Aboriginal Affairs Department, 1997,* of the State of Western Australia: 73–92.
66. Bonner, N. 1996.
67. Bartlett, R. 1993.
68. *Hansard: Proceedings of the Joint Committee on Native Title*, 27 October 1995: 1474–8.

4   Mining agreements prior to the Aboriginal Land Rights (Northern Territory) Act 1976

69. Rowley, C.D. 1974..
70. Altman, J. 1983: 27.
71. Kauffman, P. 1997 and 1998.
72. Rowley, C.D. 1972: 137–146, Roberts, J. 1978: 119–123.
73. *Wik v The State of Queensland* (1996) 121 ALR 129.
74. Comalco *1996 Annual Report*: 40.
75. Comalco *1996 Annual Report*: 3.
76. *Age,* 25 February 1997.
77. *Australian,* 24 February 1998: 23.
78. Broome, R. 1994: 141.
79. Kauffman, P. and Elu, J. 1994.

80. Kauffman, P. February 1998 survey of companies operating major mining sites. Information was collected on the last pay fortnight to 30 June 1997, and the first pay fortnight of February 1998. Aboriginal and Torres Strait Islander person was defined as 'any person of Aboriginal and Torres Strait Islander descent who identifies as Aboriginal or Torres Strait Islander, irrespective of what part of Australia they come from'. 'Employed' was defined as 'working in paid employment for five hours or more per week'. Each mining company estimated the number of Indigenous employees.
81. Comalco *1995 Annual Report*: 19.
82. Fingleton, J. 1996, vol. 2: 16.
83. Broome, R. 1994: 141.
84. *Milirrpum v Nabalco and the Commonwealth of Australia* (1971) FLR 141 17.
85. Altman, J. 1983: 102.
86. *Land Rights News,* October 1995: 5.
87. Martin, D. 1995: 65–72, and Kauffman P. February 1998 survey.
88. Kauffman, P. 1979: 45–50.
89. Kauffman, P. February 1998 survey.
90. GEMCO Personnel, personal communications August 1997 and February 1998.
91. Walter and Turnbull. 1993: 36.
92. Altman, J. 1983: 115.
93. *Flynn J v Mamarika* Unreported, NT Supreme Court, No. 132 of 1995, Martin CJ, 20 March 1996.
94. Anindilyakwa Land Council, *Annual Report* 1994: 5.
95. Anindilyakwa Land Council, *Annual Report* 1997: 5, 12–14.

5   Mining agreements during the Aboriginal Land Rights (Northern Territory) Act 1976 era

96. Altman, J. 1995.
97. Clark, I. and Cook, B. 1992. There are also significant reserves in Western Australia, at Yeelirrie (53,000 tonnes) and Kintyre (36,000 tonnes). Over 1700 tonnes of uranium a year is also being mined by Western Mining at their Olympic Dam project in South Australia (*Western Mining Corporation Annual Report* 1997). Olympic Dam annual uranium production will increase to 4600 tonnes by the year 2000 (*Uranium Fact Sheet,* Bureau of Resource Sciences, 1997).
98. Altman, J. 1983: 57, ACIL, 1993: 16–17.
99. Gray, W.J. 1980.

100. NBHP, now known as North Ltd.

101. Over the period 1981–1997, U3O8 annual output ranged from 2908 to 4237 tonnes. Stockpiles are sufficient to maintain production to 1999. ERA's annual profit before income tax has ranged from $45m to $131m. (ERA *Annual Report* 1984; North Ltd *Annual Reports* 1988–97).

102. Pursuant to a s. 44 agreement of the *Aboriginal Land Rights (Northern Territory) Act* during the currency of the agreement.

103. Pursuant to s. 63(5) of the *Aboriginal Land Rights (Northern Territory) Act.*

104. For the purpose of rehabilitating the mine site, when the fund is in deficit. (North's *Annual Report 1996, Financial statements*: 19).

105. North Ltd *Annual Report* 1996: 12–13, 28.

106. Levitus, R. 1991: 157.

107. Altman, J. 1985: 187–188.

108. *Aboriginal Land Rights (Northern Territory) Act,* s. 35(2)(b); Levitus, R. 1991.

109. Lewis, M. 1996.

110. Altman, J. 1996.

111. *Aboriginal Land Rights (Northern Territory) Act,* s. 64(3).

112. Aboriginals Benefit Trust Account *Annual Reports* 1978–97; Annual financial statements of the Gagudju Association; Altman, J. 1996: 55.

113. Altman, J. 1996: 25.

114. Cooper, V. 1997.

115. *Australian,* 18 October 1997: 26.

116. Levitus, R. 1991.

117. *Canberra Times,* 27 April 1997.

118. *Australian,* 18 October 1997.

119. Dodson, P. 1997, Cooper, V. 1997.

120. Dodson, P. 1997. D'Abbs, P. and Jones, T. *Kakadu Alcohol Report,* Menzies School of Health Research, Darwin; *Australian,* 18 October 1997.

121. Kauffman, P. February 1998 survey and Bridge, N. 1998.

122. *Aboriginal Land Rights (Northern Territory) Act,* s. 35(2)(b).

123. Toohey, J. 1984: 108–109.

124. Gray 1980.

125. Aminco and Associates 1975. They suggested that the royalty rate should take account of Queensland Mines' profitability, with an upper limit of 10.8%, if the ratio of taxable income ever equalled the revenue.

126. Aminco and Associates, 1975: 34, 75.

127. Keen, I. 1980; Altman, J. 1983: 65–67.
128. Altman, J. 1983: 59–61, 129; *Land Rights News,* July 1995, vol. 2, no. 36.
129. O'Faircheallaigh, C. 1988.
130. Altman, J. and Smith, D. 1994.
131. *Land Rights News,* July 1995.
132. *Aboriginal Land Rights (Northern Territory) Act,* s. 63.
133. *Aboriginal Land Rights (Northern Territory) Act,* ss 27 and 43.
134. The balance is owned by Santos (18%), Sagasco (18%) and others. Santos owns 65% and Magellan Petroleum Australia owns 35% of the total Mereenie field (Magellan Petroleum Australian Ltd *Annual Report* 1995).
135. Cumulative gas production amounted to 68.9 BCF (Magellan Petroleum Australian Ltd *Annual Report* 1997: 11).
136. Aboriginals Benefit Trust Account *Annual Reports* 1984–97 and *Hansard,* 25 November 1997.
137. Marshall, C. 1994.
138. Floreani, C. personal communication, 25 February 1998.
139. The agreement was concluded under the *Aboriginal Land Rights (Northern Territory) Act,* s. 19(4).
140. *Land Rights News,* July 1995: 4.
141. Cumulative gas production from Palm Valley from commencement to 1997 amounted to 89.3 BCF. (Magellan Petroleum Australian Ltd *Annual Report* 1997: 12).
142. Dixon, R. and Dillon, M. 1990: 83–88.
143. Dillon, M. 1991.
144. Dixon and Dillon 1990: 87–88.
145. Warren, P. 1989.
146. Dixon, R. and Dillon, M. 1990: 53.
147. *Canberra Times,* 31 January 1998.
148. *CRA Annual Report* 1995: 37.
149. *CRA Annual Report* 1995: 37.
150. February 1998 telephone and fax survey.
151. *CRA Report to Shareholders* 1994: 40–41.
152. CRA and Argyle press release, 3 October 1996.
153. Kauffman, P. February 1998 survey and fax from P. Wand, Rio Tinto Ltd, 22 April 1998.
154. Dixon, R. and Dillon, M.: 92.
155. *West Australian,* 28 July 1980; Dixon, R. and Dillon, M.: 65.
156. Dillon, M. 1991: 144.

157. Bridge 1998.

158. Keon-Cohen, B.A. 1982: 12–13.

159. Altman, J. 1983: 64–65.

160. *Courier Mail,* 1 November 1996: 8.

161. *Australian,* 18 October 1997: 26.

162. *Australian Financial Review,* 4 April 1997: 7.

163. *Age,* 10 February 1998: 24. See *Australian Financial Review,* 14 November 1997: 3.

164. *Australian Financial Review,* 17 October 1997: 11.

165. *Australian,* 18 October 1997: 24; see also Dodson, P. 1997.

166. Cribben, J. 1984.

167. Howitt, R. 1991.

168. *North Flinders Mines Shareholders Report 1985:* 13.

169. Howitt, R. 1991: 124, and N. Bridge, Normandy Mining Ltd 10 March 1998 personal communication.

170. Central Land Council *Annual Reports* 1985–1989; Howitt, R. 1991: 124–133.

171. Total North Flinders Mining reserves were 1,319,000 ounces, mainly at Callie and Dead Bullock Soak (*North Flinders Mines Shareholders Report* 1996: 7, 19).

172. *North Flinders Mines Shareholders Report* 1995: 21.

173. *North Flinders Mines Shareholders Report* 1996: 7.

174. Central Land Council's *Annual Report* 1994. In 1994–95, agreements and sacred site clearances were signed at Mt Davidson group, Homestead (west of Dead Bullock Soak) and Wilsons Range (in the far west of their tenement) (*North Flinders Mines Shareholders Report* 1995: 21).

175. *North Flinders Mines Shareholders Report* 1996: 11.

176. *Land Rights News,* February 1998: 10 and David Avery letter of 3 March 1998.

177. Central Land Council 1998. Submission to the Review of the *Aboriginal Land Rights (Northern Territory) Act 1976:* 95–98.

178. *Land Rights News*, September 1996: 3.

179. Winwood-Smith 1997 and personal communication Frank Baarda and Adrian Winwood-Smith, 13 March 1998.

180. Ireland, T. 1996: 311–312.

181. *Normandy Mining Ltd Annual Report* 1996: 6.

182. Central Land Council submission to the Review of the *Aboriginal Land Rights (Northern Territory) Act 1976,* January 1998.

183. Kauffman, P. 1997 and 1998a.

184. O'Faircheallaigh, C. 1995: 11.
185. ABC 'Four Corners' program, on Hopevale native title, August 1995.
186. O'Faircheallaigh and Holden 1995: 33, and personal communication C. O'Faircheallaigh, 12 March 1998.
187. Personal communication Alexander Temperley CFSM, 3 March 1998.

6   Post-Mabo mining agreements 1993–1996

188. I am indebted to Chips Mackinolty of the Jawoyn Association for his assistance on 26 March 1998 in correcting and expanding an earlier draft text and providing further background material.
189. Fingleton, J., Edmunds, M. and McRandle, P. (eds) 1995: 115–118.
190. O'Faircheallaigh, C. 1995: 8, 20.
191. *Northern Territory News,* October 1996: 11.
192. *Australian Financial Review,* 20 January 1993; *Business Review Weekly,* 16 July 1993; *Sydney Morning Herald,* 16 April 1994, 14 March 1995; O'Faircheallaigh, C. 1995: 5–8.
193. *Australian,* 2 October 1995: 24.
194. *Australian,* 25 February 1998: 32.
195. *Northern Territory News,* 18 August 1995: 10; and *Land Rights News,* September 1996: 3.
196. John Ah Kit, speech to the Economic Development for Australia, July 1994.
197. *Northern Territory News,* 12 November 1995: 9.
198. ANT hold the interests of Nippon Mining and Metals Co Ltd (15%), Mitsui and Co Ltd (5%), Mitsubishi Materials Corporation (5%) and Marubeni Corporation (5%).
199. *Age,* 26 June 1993; O'Faircheallaigh, C. 1995: 10; NLC *Annual Report* 1994: 36.
200. *Australian Financial Review,* 10 December 1993.
201. *Australian Financial Review,* 8 September 1995: 12.
202. *Land Rights News,* October 1995.
203. MIM's share of production was 75,600 tonnes of zinc concentrate, 19,000 tonnes of lead concentrate and 643,000 ounces of silver concentrate from the mine in 1997—*MIM Holdings Ltd Annual Report* 1997: 18.
204. *Land Rights News,* October 1995: 2.
205. Zapopan, the previous owners of Tanami, recovered 430,000 ounces of gold. The new owners of Tanami purchased Zapopan's 1.4m tonne

a year gold plant for $9.3m—*Northern Territory News,* 25 September 1995: 30; *Land Rights News,* October 1995; *Australian,* 2 October 1995: 24.

206. *Land Rights News,* vol. 2, no. 37 October 1995: 2.
207. Central Land Council *Annual Report* 1995/96: 48.
208. *Acacia Resources Annual Report* 1996: 18, *Annual Report* 1997: 26.
209. *Land Rights News,* vol. 2, no. 37 October 1995: 5.
210. Mr de Crespigny is one of five members of the Council for Aboriginal Reconciliation to serve for three terms, between 1991 and 2001.
211. Posgold, owned by Normandy Mining, is the principal explorer, with Mount Leyshon Goldmines (76% owned by Normandy Mining), Goldmines of Kalgoorlie, owned by Normandy Mining, focusing on Queensland and Western Australia respectively. *Normandy Mining Ltd Annual Shareholders Report* 1996: 25.
212. Normandy Mining Ltd *Annual Shareholders Report* 1995: 3. Personal communication N. Bridge 10 March 1998.
213. *Normandy Mining Ltd Annual Shareholders Report* 1996: 6.
214. *Normandy Mining Ltd Annual Shareholders Report* 1996: 37. *Australian,* 25 February 1998: 32.
215. Parliamentary Joint Committee on Native Title, *Hansard,* 27 October 1995: 1491.
216. Bridge, N. 1998.
217. *Sydney Morning Herald,* 11 November 1995: 37.
218. *Australian Financial Review,* 28 February 1996.
219. *Pitjantjatjara Land Rights Act 1980* (SA), s. 22(1) & (2); *Maralinga Tjarutja 1984* (SA), s. 20 (1)&(2).
220. Personal communication G. Borchers and Dr G. Stotz AP, 26 February 1998.
221. Bridge, N. 1998.
222. Kauffman, P. February 1998 survey.
223. *Acacia Resources Annual Report* 1996: 20.
224. *The West Australian,* 13 July 1996: 4, per Dr Michael Folie, CEO of Acacia.
225. *Business Review Weekly,* 16 February 1998: 37–38.
226. *The West Australian,* 4 July 1996: 1.
227. *The West Australian,* 5 July 1996: 32.
228. *The West Australian,* 2 November 1996.
229. *Australian Financial Review,* 4 April 1997.
230. *Australian,* 20 October 1997: 58.

7   Post-Mabo mining agreements 1997–1998

231. *Australian,* 20 October 1997: 58.
232. Personal communication, Penny Joyce, Goldfields Land Council, 29 January 1998.
233. *Canberra Times,* 9 February 1998: 2.
234. Goldfields Land Council press release 8 February 1998. Ms Sadie Canning is an elder of Thithee Bieni Bunna Wiya, which is one of sixteen groups that negotiated with Anaconda. The final two groups to sign were Bibila-Lunutjarra, and Goolburthunoo, represented by their elder, Bobby Scott.
235. *West Australian,* 10 March 1997.
236. Cape York Land Council press release 10 March 1997; *Australian,* 11 March 1997; e-mail C. O'Faircheallaigh 14 April 1997. David Clough represented Alspac and John Cockatoo was a key elder from Old Mapoon.
237. *Australian,* 20 October 1997: 58.
238. Kauffman, P. February 1998 survey.
239. The agreement was formally signed on 26 March 1997 by Hamersley's Managing Director of development, Mr Malcolm Richards, and Gumala's Chair Mr Charlie Smith and ten other Gumala negotiators.
240. Hamersley Iron Pty Ltd, 1997. The account relies on this report, confirmed in general terms by Gorman 1998.
241. Hamersley media release. *Australian,* 27 March 1997: 21 and 18 October 1997: 58; *Australian Financial Review,* 27 March 1997: 3.
242. *Australian,* 14 October 1995.
243. In January 1996, CRA merged with its parent RTZ Corp (Rio-Tinto Zinc).
244. *CRA's Annual Report to Shareholders* 1994: 42-44.
245. *Australian,* 26 February 1998: 34. Pasminco will spend $890m developing the mine.
246. *Australian,* 29 August 1995: 3.
247. Kinhill, Cameron and McNamara, quoted in Proceedings of the Joint Parliamentary Committee on Native Title, *Hansard,* 27 October 1995: 1484.
248. Proceedings of the Joint Parliamentary Committee on Native Title, *Hansard,* 27 October 1995: 1484.
249. Proceedings of the Joint Parliamentary Committee on Native Title, *Hansard,* 27 October 1995: 1485.

250. Proceedings of the Joint Parliamentary Committee on Native Title, *Hansard,* 27 October 1995: 1486–7.
251. *Australian Financial Review,* 10 January 1997.
252. *Australian,* 15 February 1997.
253. Bridge 1998.
254. *Australian,* 20 October 1997: 58.
255. *Australian,* 20 October 1997: 58.
256. *Australian,* 28 July 1997: 22; 20 October 1997: 58. Media releases of 25 July 1997 by the New South Wales Aboriginal Land Council, Ross Mining NL and the Hon Bob Martin MP, New South Wales Minister for Mineral Resources.
257. The Hon Paul Tovua, Speaker of the Solomon Islands National Parliament is on the Board of the Solomon operations—Ian Huntley Pty Ltd, 20 August 1997.
258. *Australian,* 18 August 1997: 24. Earlier in August 1997, Grenfell Resources, another Craton explorer, reached agreement with traditional land owners for a two-year exploration clearance on its Tarcoola Ridge, Warburton and Sunshine exploration projects.
259. Selway, B. 1998.
260. *Australian,* 21 August 1997: 2 and 18 October 1997: 58. *West Australian* 21, August 1997: 10. *Australian Journal of Mining,* September 1997: 27. *Kalgoorlie Miner,* 21 August 1997: 4.
261. Aboriginal Land Trust 99 Lease, signed on 29 November 1988, clause 6.5.
262. Joint Committee on Native Title, *Hansard,* 12 September 1997: 686–698. D. O'Dea personal communication 25 February 1998.
263. Joint Committee on Native Title, *Hansard,* 12 September 1997: 744.
264. *Pyrenees Advocate,* 12 September 1997; *Ararat Advertiser,* 4 September 1997.
265. *Sydney Morning Herald,* 15 December 1997.
266. AGL and Wiradjuri and Wongaibon press release, 9 December 1997.
267. Kauffman, P. and Springford, T. 1997.
268. Cape York Land Council November 1997 press release; T. Bonici Gurang Land Council personal communication 30 January 1998.

8 Conclusions

269. Dodson, M. 1995. Report of the Social Justice Commissioner on Native Title.

270. Chapman, in Parker, G. 1995. *Review of Native Title Representative Bodies*, ATSIC, Canberra.
271. United Nations International Covenant on Economic Social and Cultural Rights art: 1.
272. United Nations International Covenant on Civil and Political Rights art: 27.
273. Kauffman, P. 1998.
274. *Wik and others v The State of Queensland* (1996) 121 ALR 129.
275. Bachelard, M. 1997.
276. Viner, I. 1997: 63–70.
277. Burke, P. 1998: 4.
278. Viner, I. 1997: 65–66.
279. Burke, P. 1998: 5.
280. Burke, P. 1998: 6.
281. Wilson, R. 1997.
282. Burke, P. 1998: 5 and *Land Rights News,* February 1998: 6.
283. Viner, I. 1997: 68.
284. *Mabo (2)* 175 CLR 1 at 58–63 and 70 per Brennan J, 88–90, 99–100, in Viner, I. 1997: 69.
285. Clarke, J. 1997.
286. Senator Brian Harradine, a former member of the Labor Party in Tasmania.
287. ATSIC 1997b: 4.
288. Senator Bob Brown of the Greens said that the Bill followed 'the stolen lands, and the stolen children with the stolen rights. This is taking their heart [of Aboriginal people], their dignity'. Senate *Hansard,* 7 April 1998. *Age,* 13 April 1998: 6.
289. Bachelard, M. 1997: 126.
290. Address by the Governor-General, Sir William Deane, 26 January 1998. Office of the Governor-General, Canberra.
291. Barker, G. 1997:15.
292. Barnett, D. and Goward, P. 1997.
293. Melleuish, G. 1997.
294. *Age,* 17 February 1998: 5.
295. John Howard made this statement during a television interview in the March 1996 election campaign, and the sentiment assumed symbolic power. Hedonism and wowserism (its opposite) are two powerful elements in (white) Australian culture. Successful politicians promote both elements (eg. Bob Hawke presented himself as a former alcoholic and former womaniser).

296. Hunter, B. and Taylor, J. 1996: 4.
297. Smith, D. and Daley, A. 1996: 103.
298. The Taskforce was formed in 1996 and has met three times a year. Michael Coughlan also reported that only 7% of Aboriginal people around Katherine are literate. *Australian,* 25 February 1998: 32, and Coughlan 1998.
299. Bridge, N. 1996.
300. *Normandy Mining Annual Report* 1997: 36
301. Coughlan 1998.
302. Northern Land Council *Annual Report* 1990: 11.
303. Fingleton, J. vol. 2: CYLC 3.
304. Fingleton, J. vol. 2: MWWAC 8.
305. Fingleton, J. vol. 2: WAC 50.
306. Tehan, M. 1977.
307. *Land Rights News,* February 1998: 10.
308. Exploration licence agreements were made with Poseidon, North Flinders, Sons of Gwalia, Zapopan and Otter Exploration *Land Rights News,* July 1995.
309. *Australian Financial Review,* 28 September 1995.
310. Paper to the Indigenous Land Use Conference held in Darwin in 1995.
311. O'Faircheallaigh, C. 1995: 21–22.
312. Marshall, C. 1994: 127–128.
313. Kulchyski, P. 1994: 13.

Afterwords and Appendices

314. This is an edited extract of a paper delivered to the National Press Club in 1996.
315. This is an edited version of a paper delivered to the Australian Bankers Association in 1996.
316. Aboriginals Benefit Trust Account, *Annual Reports* 1985–1997; Walter and Turnbull, 1993: 22–33.

Index